margarit (handwritten)

CHOICES FOR '76

A REGIONAL PLAN ASSOCIATION PUBLICATION
FOR THE TOWN MEETING PROJECT

Regional Plan Association is a voluntary citizens' organization supported by individual memberships, corporate subscriptions, foundation and government grants. It is the nation's first metropolitan planning organization, started in 1922 by the Russell Sage Foundation. Its FIRST REGIONAL PLAN (1929–65) influenced the Region's development standards, the expansion of its parks, and the location of its highways. Today the Association researches and advances programs to improve the environmental, economic, and social conditions of the 31-county New Jersey–New York–Connecticut Urban Region, analyzes proposals of state, federal, and interstate agencies, and seeks immediate action on current issues that affect the Region.

Regional Plan Association relies on public participation in planning. In 1963, the Association organized the Region's first TV-citizen response program. It tested public reaction to the prospects for the Region if then-current trends continued. A committee of 125 diverse leaders, evaluated the research and policy proposals for a SECOND REGIONAL PLAN looking to the year 2000. That was the beginning of a participatory process that is now expanded to CHOICES FOR '76.

Regional Plan Association Inc., a New York not-for-profit corporation, is located at 235 East 45th Street, New York, New York 10017.

Other SIGNET Books of Special Interest

HOW TO SAVE URBAN AMERICA

Regional Plan Association
CHOICES FOR '76

Edited and with an introduction by
WILLIAM A. CALDWELL
Sections One and Three by
WILLIAM B. SHORE
Sections Two, Four, and Five by
BORIS S. PUSHKAREV
Economic calculations by
REGINA BELZ ARMSTRONG

MICHAEL J. McMANUS,
Executive Director
CHOICES FOR '76

A SIGNET SPECIAL
NEW AMERICAN LIBRARY
TIMES MIRROR

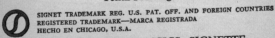

SIGNET, SIGNET CLASSICS, SIGNETTE,
MENTOR and PLUME BOOKS
are published by the New American Library, Inc.
1301 Avenue of the Americas, New York, New York 10019

First Printing, March, 1973

PRINTED IN THE UNITED STATES OF AMERICA

CHOICES FOR '76
CITIZEN ADVISORY COMMITTEE

Chairman:
Francis Keppel

Vice Chairmen:
H. Lee Dennison
Manuel Diaz, Jr.
Alfred E. Driscoll
Betty Furness
Dorothy I. Height
Gustav Heningburg
Theodore W. Kheel
William T. Knowles
T. Vincent Learson
The Right Rev.
 Paul Moore, Jr.
John O. Nicklis
Howard Samuel
Albert Shanker
David Starr
Mrs. Webster Todd
Alvin Toffler
Jose Torres
Rabbi Marc Tanenbaum

Members:
Vincent M. Albanese
Mrs. Dexter Otis Arnold
Rev. William Ayres
Norman R. Baker
Jorge Batista
Monroe Benton
Rabbi Irwin Blank
Mary L. Blassingame
Lois Blume
Richard J. Bornstein
Susan Boyd
Paul T. Brady
Ellen Brathwaite
John Brewer

John Bunzel
Sidney Bykofsky
Eugene Campbell
Thomas Carmichael
Dr. Vernal G. Cave
Martha Coles
Samuel M. Convissor
Paul F. Coyle
Helen Credidio
Richard M. Cummings
Hugh Curran
Linda Davidoff
George Delgado
George Dessart
David Doniger
Joseph Doria, Jr.
James F. Drinane
Anita Epstein
Milton Feitelson
Raymond P. Fitzgerald
Ellis T. Fleming
Mrs. Pauline Flippen
Robert Fried
Mrs. S. Thomas Gagliano
Father Luis R. Gigante
James B. Godbout
Francis Gottfried
Golda Gottlieb
Herbert Green
Lorretta Eve Gressey
J. Frank Griffin
Fred Haas
William Haskins
William E. Havemeyer
Robert J. Helbock

(List continues on following page.)

REGIONAL PLAN ASSOCIATION STAFF

COOPERATING AGENCIES

Connecticut Office of State Planning
Metropolitan Regional Council
New Jersey Department of Community Affairs
New York City Planning Commission
New York State Metropolitan Transportation
   Authority
New York State Office of Planning Services
New York State Urban Development Corporation
The Port Authority of New York and New Jersey
Tri-State Regional Planning Commission

Numerous other public and private groups contributed
to CHOICES FOR '76, for which appreciation is grate-
fully acknowledged. Regional Plan Association, however, is solely responsible for the contents of this book.

FUNDING FOR
CHOICES FOR '76

Financial support has included a major grant from the U.S. Department of Housing and Urban Development and contributions from the following foundations and corporations (as of Dec. 31, 1972).

Foundations:

Vincent Astor Foundation
The Ford Foundation
Fund For The City Of New York
J. M. Kaplan Fund
Charles F. Kettering Foundation
New York Community Trust
New York Foundation
Ralph E. Ogden Foundation
Olin Corporation Charitable Trust
The Prospect Hill Foundation
Rockefeller Brothers Fund
Rockefeller Foundation
The Florence and John Schumann Foundation
Taconic Foundation
Wallace-Eljabar Fund

Corporations:

PRIME SPONSORS
Bell System
Chase Manhattan Bank
Coca-Cola Bottling Company of New York
IBM

INDUSTRIAL CORPORATIONS
Ciba-Geigy Corporation
Continental Can Company
General Electric Company
General Telephone & Electronics Corporation
Pfizer
Schering Corporation
Singer Company

(list continues on following page.)

COMMERCIAL BANKS
Bankers Trust Company
Chemical Bank
Connecticut Bank & Trust Company—Darien
First National City Bank
Irving Trust Company
Manufacturers Hanover Trust Company
Marine Midland Bank—New York
Peoples Trust of New Jersey—Hackensack
Prospect Park National Bank—New Jersey
State National Bank of Connecticut—Bridgeport

SAVINGS BANKS
Bowery Savings Bank
The Bronx Savings Bank
Central Savings Bank
City Savings Bank—Bridgeport
Dime Savings Bank of New York
Dry Dock Savings Bank
Emigrant Savings Bank
Greenwich Federal Savings and Loan Association
New York Bank for Savings
Norwalk Savings Society
People's Savings Bank—Bridgeport
South Norwalk Savings Bank
Stamford Savings Bank

LIFE INSURANCE COMPANIES
Equitable Life Assurance Society
Mutual Life Insurance Co. of New York
Prudential Insurance Co. of America
Teachers Insurance & Annuity Association of America

SECURITIES INDUSTRY
Charles E. Merrill Trust
Paine, Webber, Jackson & Curtis
Shearson, Hammill & Co.

UTILITIES
Bell Laboratories
Consolidated Edison Company of New York
New Jersey Bell Telephone Company
New York Telephone Company
Southern New England Telephone Company
Western Electric

Advertising:
Ogilvy & Mather

CHOICES FOR '76 "addresses two of the nation's most critical needs: improving the way our largest urban areas are developing and improving the democratic process itself . . .

One thing is certain. If it can be done in the New York–New Jersey–Connecticut Urban Region, it can be done anywhere in the country. This project could thus be a major advance for all of urban America."

James L. Buckley
(Conservative-Republican, N.Y.)

Clifford P. Case
(Republican, N.J.)

Jacob K. Javits
(Republican-Liberal, N.Y.)

Abraham Ribicoff
(Democrat, Conn.)

Lowell P. Weicker, Jr.
(Republican, Conn.)

Harrison A. Williams, Jr.
(Democrat, N.J.)

CONTENTS

III. TOWN MEETING ON THE ENVIRONMENT

IV. TOWN MEETING ON POVERTY

Contents xvii

FOREWORD

Urban America is beset by a host of competing wants. Which takes precedence? Production or pollution control, housing or home rule, bridges or open water, highways or open land? And how should the decisions be made?

The political process is the final arbiter. Planning is an aid to that process. Stripped of its technical aspects, planning consists of testing the long-range broad impact of competing interests. The planner attempts to fill a void, to look beyond the immediate effect of public and corporate policies.

How is the planner by virtue of his technical competence endowed more than any other citizen to sense and express the values of all of us? The answer is—he isn't.

So Regional Plan Association has developed over the past decade a method of citizen participation of which this book is an expression. We have set down the issues—the value issues —on which citizens are the experts, separating them as best we are able from the technical questions on which the technicians are the experts. You, the reader, are asked to make the choices for urban America.

This work represents the distillate ideas of literally thousands of people, those who have taken part in committees and participatory meetings over the past decade, and it represents the input of public and private agency personnel far too numerous to list. The policy guidance of the Association's Board of Directors is reflected in it, as is the work of staff and consultants who came and went during that decade. Above all, it is the culmination of the faith of the Association's chairman, Morris D. Crawford, Jr., in citizen participation in planning.

And now what are your choices?

John P. Keith
PRESIDENT
REGIONAL PLAN ASSOCIATION

December 1, 1972

HOW TO SAVE
URBAN AMERICA
Regional Plan Association
CHOICES FOR '76

INTRODUCTION: THE COURAGE
TO IMAGINE THE WORLD WE WANT

> Finding out what we want should become a major object
> of our attention. It is a trite saying that we live in an age
> of very swift change. But there is a vast difference be-
> tween letting changes occur under the impact of techno-
> logical advances and choosing the changes we want to
> bring about by our technological means.
>
> —*Bertrand de Jouvenel*

The subject of this book is the predicament of modern Man—
the 165 million modern men, women, and children living in
the cities and suburbs of North America, and specifically the
20 million living along the Atlantic Seaboard in the Urban
Region of New York, New Jersey, and Connecticut. The question we shall raise in scores of searching forms, some of them
painfully probing, is whether modern Man can contrive to deliver himself from his predicament—and, if so, how.

We come early to the moment of commitment. Either you
believe that people collectively are wise and brave and decent
enough to take command of their destiny and shape it to their
ends, or you shrug and grin and concede that the forces which
apportion to us our enjoyment of life, liberty, and the pursuit
of happiness have passed beyond our control.

> They're getting along in years now, and they live in a
> little assembly-line house in a suburb. "We're trapped,"
> he says. "Property taxes are killing us, but we can't find
> a decent place to live that would cost us less than this."
> "And our kids," she says—"they can't find a decent place
> to live at all. One is paying $300 for a ridiculous garden
> apartment with a superhighway, not a garden, in the back-
> yard. Our other son has a skimpy flat in the city and his
> wife's afraid to go walking by herself."

Let's deal straightforwardly with the possibility that under
our form of government, fragmented in such a way that a
region cannot respond regionally to problems that are bigger
than any town or county or state, we are forever incapable of

making common cause against our troubles. Then let us perceive that nowhere on earth and nowhere in history have men been able to conceive a government that could enforce conformity to a central plan without enforcing abject submission.

That need not detain us long. Not to be pretentious about it, self-transformation, adaptation, is what we're good at. If we want regional governance responsive to our will—reconcilation of diverse interests without oppression—we shall invent it. If we choose to transfer the decision-making power from the internal-combustion engine, the real estate promoters, the highway lobbyists, and other such strange pantheons back to the common lot of mankind—we'll do it.

> "When we got married, we traded up," she said. "Our folks were living in tenements, and we young people found we could buy these whole houses with trees and green grass around them for just about what they were paying in rent. They say the United States is getting richer. Then how come our children are having to trade down for their nasty little apartments?" "And if the richest country in the world is so damned short of houses," he said, "how come people are abandoning them by tens of thousands in the cities? How come?"

In this book and in the television series for which the book serves as a text and continuing reference, we are dealing with the realities in the Urban Region, which are gloomy, and with optional methods of searching for our ideals.

The proposition that people should be asked what kind of future for the Region they want was conceived by Regional Plan Association, or RPA, a private citizen-based research and planning agency, beholden to no other instrumentality in government or out. For half a century it has been influential in the development of the Tri-State Urban Region within roughly 80 miles of Manhattan Island. But today, the Region may be lapsing into crisis of a kind unprecedented in its experience. Not only are matters in such fields as housing, land use, transportation, the environment, poverty, and governance growing worse, and sometimes disastrously worse by the day —not only that, but people in large numbers seem to be resigning themselves to the supposition that the situation is hopeless. The cities would have to die, what else? The countrysides couldn't possibly be saved from the bulldozer and the all-conquering automobile. Taxes would eat us alive, and what could anyone do but vote against school budgets and bond issues for colleges or hospitals? Sullen apathy and a bitter, often violent, isolationism seem to be taking over. In this crisis of the spirit something had to be done.

And this is what RPA is doing. This is CHOICES FOR '76:

In the spring of 1973, a series of five one-hour films is being broadcast by 18 TV stations in the Region. Beginning March 17–19 and every two weeks thereafter, the films are telecast, at different times, on Channels 2, 4, 5, 7, 9, 11, 25, and 31 (New York) as well as 13 and 47 (Newark), 21 (Garden City), 24 (Hartford), 41 (Paterson), 49 (Bridgeport), 52 (Trenton), 53 (Norwich), and 8 and 71 (New Haven). The Region's most pressing problems are taken up one at a time, laid out by screen and script for objective study, but this part of the process does not terminate in routine exposure of the way things have gone wrong.

Rather, each program presents a series of possible solutions. They are offered in the form of eight to ten basic choices on where the Region ought to be headed by 1976, America's 200th anniversary (hence the title CHOICES FOR '76, of course). Each viewer of the television programs, or each reader of this book, is invited to mark a ballot on which CHOICES FOR '76 he or she would make.

The ballots, along with a brief form "about yourself," are made available in advance of the television programs to anyone who writes to CHOICES FOR '76, 110 E. 42nd Street, Room 1112, New York, N.Y. 10017. They are also published by some two dozen of the Region's newspapers, along with stories on the problems and the pros and cons of the options, on the same weekends that the television programs are broadcast.

Finally, Regional Plan Association is striving to organize hundreds of thousands of citizens to meet in small groups to watch the programs, read this book, discuss the issues, mark ballots on their CHOICES FOR '76, and mail them in for computer processing by George Gallup. The results of the vote will be widely publicized. Thus, by harnessing the collective power of the mass media to present the options and by giving people a way to be heard on what *they* think ought to be done, a new kind of town meeting is being created. Our town this time is the Region, with 20 million residents from New Haven to Trenton, from Ocean County to the Catskills to Montauk Point (Fig. 1).

Those who participate in the town meetings will be able to say what they want in a better informed and more accurate way than is possible in a political election. The elector in the booth at the polling place in November is compelled to choose between Candidate A and Candidate B—and much too often

Figure 1

THE URBAN REGION OF NEW YORK, NEW JERSEY AND CONNECTICUT

to guess what they can and will do about the things that baffle and torment us all.

The RPA referendum does not focus on personalities for public office, but on people's preferences with respect to 44 specific issues. What outcome will most closely approach your own innermost ideals? "With the aid of ideals," said Lewis Mumford in the journal *Daedalus*, "a community may select, among a multitude of possibilities, those which are consonant with its own nature or that promise to further human development."

Two great questions are being brought to the court of public opinion:

I. THE SHAPE OF THINGS TO COME. Do we rebuild our cities

—or do we abandon them? Should new offices, colleges, and stores be scattered here and there throughout the Region, or should more of them go into downtowns old and new? And should houses and apartments go on marching, horizon to horizon, across such open space as is left, or should the housing people need be built compactly in and around the existent cities and their suburbs?

II. WHO'S IN CHARGE OF TOMORROW? Should county and state government take a more decisive part in the way the Region is developed? *Can* they assume regional responsibilities? Shall we have to devise a new level of self-government?

Bring it down to details:

—Should the citizen at large take part in deciding what kind of housing is built on open land around and between the old cities and suburbs? Or should people living in each municipality be entitled to decide all by themselves what kind of housing they'll accept?

—In the interests of saving thousands of apartments now being abandoned in the inner cities, should the traditional patterns of real estate ownership be changed so as to empower neighborhood organizations to manage such housing? And should we resort to housing allowances for all those who cannot buy into the Region's housing market, or continue to build special projects for them?

—Do we really want to go on trying to run or back away from people with less money than we have? Do we want to be sure that our society provides every man or woman who wants to work with the opportunity to do so? And more generally, do we want the gap between the rich and the poor to grow wider? Or stay the same? Or shall we make an effort to narrow it?

—There are people who just cannot work and earn; should they be guaranteed, by common consent, income enough to live decently, and should their children be guaranteed a fair chance to do better? And how is that done without weakening the incentive to work?

—As our incomes go up should we spend more on improving public places and services, or shall we get a better buy through acquiring more personal possessions and services for ourselves and our families?

—No one of us is wealthy enough to buy clean air and pure water, but how do we pay the price of getting pollution under control? If we require the polluters to clean up and charge the cost to them until they do it, perhaps the job will be done sooner, better, and more cheaply than if government builds the treatment apparatus or grants polluters tax credits for doing it.

—How important do you judge it is that we save the best of

the open land—now—from the bulldozer? That we open up
the cities by creating more parks within them? If we bought
today the parklands that will be needed over your lifetime and
your children's, we could get them cheaper, even counting
interest on the bonds, than we could if we were to go on acquiring them a piece at a time for cash. We'd be getting what
we want, not what was left over after the developers have their
way. But would such massive outlay on open space be justified
when other immediate problems remain unsolved?

Gertrude and Jenny, widows, huddle close together on the
bench in the little park in the city. The grass is scuffed
threadbare, the trees are sick, many of the once bright
benches have been broken or stolen. "My children have a
whole acre of grass around their house," says Gertrude,
"and they're complaining." "Children do complain," says
Jenny. "What is it this time?" "My son-in-law says, 'We
went away out in the country'—40 miles they went—'to
find a place with farms around it, and we loved it, and
some big developer bought the land and built houses all
up and down new streets, and there aren't any farms
anymore.' A yard as big as this whole park, and he's
complaining!" "And yet if they went 40 miles out in the
country you'd think they might have a little country
around them," says Jenny gently.

—People regionwide, people in road-weary millions, insist
they want fewer miles of new highway and better mass transit.
But transit doesn't work and can't unless more jobs are concentrated in the downtowns and housing is focused in such a
way that the scheduled bus or train can compete in door-to-
door travel time with the auto, and so collect fares enough to
justify its running. What do people really want—superhigh-
ways for themselves, perhaps, and mass transit for other
people?

The state highway engineer sits on the schoolhouse stage
and listens impassively as people jamming the public
hearing call him a vandal, a wrecker, a tool of the
asphalt and concrete lobbies, a destroyer of shrines and
churches, a ghoul. He has heard it all before: "You don't
consider people. All you want is to shatter this town to
pieces so that some damned stranger can drive through it
to his job (the airport) (the football game) (the shore) at
75 miles an hour. Who needs it? Who needs you? Don't

cover our countryside with your filthy pavement. We don't want your highway!"

Then they all stalk out and get in their cars and drive home on the highway he built last year.

—Transit fares have been rising at least three times as fast as the cost of living, and the quality of service has been rotting away. Fares will increase more and more, pricing the mass carrier out of usefulness and existence, unless people who don't ride in steel-wheeled cars or in buses pay more of the cost of what is in effect a social service. Should they? If so, how? And who—motorists, persons who own property whose value is affected by its access to transit lines, the general taxpayer? Through state or through federal taxes?

—The Region is being turned inside out. Factories are moving farther and farther away from their blue-collar workers in cities, and office workers are moving farther and farther away from their downtown office jobs. We allow the offices to follow the white-collar worker in the move to the suburbs, but we don't allow the blue-collar worker to follow his job into the suburbs, doubly depriving the cities of economic opportunity. Cities are declining into warehouses for the poor, slag heaps into which are dumped the losers, to stare and curse their fate and die.

—If we persist in the course we are taking, our cities will turn into Indian reservations walled off from the rest of society, guarded by police, with welfare checks mailed in to keep them from exploding. We still have the opportunity—perhaps unique in history—to create a truly pluralistic, multiracial society in the Urban Region. Are we going to blow it?

—"It was in the city," says thoughtful Lewis Mumford, "that men came together not only to survive military attack or to become wealthy in trade but to live the best life possible." Some chose to live near the city center, to be near their work and their places of recreation. Others elected to endure the long commute from the suburbs so that around their home they could have space and the look of green growing things. Now all that is changed. Shopping centers and colleges and office campuses are wandering out along the highways to remote places that can be reached only by private automobile. Housing is located according to whims or hunches influenced by arbitrary zoning rules and the peculiarities of the real estate market rather than by accessibility to job, transportation, or the civilized amenities. So . . .

—Should or shouldn't we bring things back downtown? The people now left behind in the cities would have more opportunity, better income, adequate services, lower taxes; more people of all the income brackets would want to live in town again; the countryside would be spared further invasion by things and people fleeing from the city.

—Or is it too late to save the city, too much trouble to attempt bringing things together again? Do we really want the sense of community? At some time during these sessions shall we want to say something about such values as home and friends and deep roots and the certainty that one belongs?

> "Why would anyone live in the city now?" said Sue. "Everything we need is out here—my husband's job, good schools, doctors, hospitals, shops, clean air, peace and quiet. Why would anyone live in the city now?" "Some people can't afford to live anywhere else," the RPA leg man said. "What's going to happen to the cities if all the good things move out and only crime and poverty and pollution are left?" "I don't know," said Sue. "That's not my problem."

Or is it? Those are some of the questions, and RPA's planners are aware that other people may have other questions and different priorities or scales of urgency. A diligent effort has been made to identify the main issues; once RPA embarked on a program that would let people at large participate in the $50 million worth of planning research going on in the Region, its staff began drafting background papers for these town meetings.

The papers were subjected to two processes of review and refinement.

First, specialists in more than two dozen agencies, public and private, criticized each of the papers. Dr. George Gallup pretested the questions to be put to the town meetings. Revisions were made.

Second, a 120-member Citizens Advisory Committee, having as chairman former United States Commissioner of Education Francis Keppel and composed of citizen activists chosen to represent demographic constituencies, reviewed the papers —often unsparingly. RPA has dropped some choices, added others, and rewritten 80 percent of the rest to clear them as much as possible of ambiguity or bias, and the results appear in this book.

The process remains imperfect, and RPA knows this. People have been known to fight and die for a fair share in the making of the decisions that affect their lives, but nobody can be compelled to be interested or responsible. It goes without saying that the choices voted in the spring of 1973 will be made by those who vote—the returns will represent the opinions of those who know and care, and it can be argued that these are a politically powerless albeit morally persuasive minority. And, again, it may be that, despite all its precautions, RPA is not raising the right questions in the right form or the right order.

So much being cheerfully conceded, it will have to be insisted cheerfully that we have to start somewhere, somehow, finding out what it is we want. In the Spring 1965 issue of *Daedalus,* Bertrand de Jouvenel wrote:

> The lack of any clear images of the style of life we are building is a cause of anxiety . . . It is time that experts represented the many different outcomes which can be obtained by different uses of our many and increasing possibilities. This representation should be in pictures, according to the utopian tradition. For us, television now offers a new technique of exposition. A variety of modes of life which seem achievable can be displayed to the public in order to elicit its preferences.

Through an unprecedented kind of collaboration of the mass media, millions of people in the Region can learn that the problems which so often seem a fog of uncertainty or uneasiness or anxiety can be crystallized. They can *see* alternatives to sprawl and slum and squalor. They can *hear* their options publicly debated. But people in millions cannot be expected to go the rest of the way by themselves—discuss the questions, resolve their choices, mark their ballots and send them in.

To help them take part in the decision-forming, RPA is asking civic networks and neighborhood or community groups to help organize tens of thousands of town meeting hosts, and it will ask each of these to bring together 10 or more persons to look, listen, talk it out, and vote. Offers of help have come in from corporations, the League of Women Voters, civil rights groups, school superintendents, union leaders, churches of 10 denominations. By the time the first town meeting goes on the air for its dozen and a half showings in March, 1973, an audience of hundreds of thousands will be assembled.

Collectively we're the poor old farmer who was asked why on earth he didn't go get free government advice on how to raise more crops and cash on his land.

"Wouldn't do no good," he sighed. "Already I knows better than I does."

We knows better than we does.

—We know how to have more housing built and preserved.

—We know ways to eliminate poverty or alleviate its worst effects, both on the poor and on the rest of the Region's and the nation's people.

—We know, then, how to relax racial tension.

—We know how to save the world of Nature in which Man too often walks as a blundering stranger, how to reduce pollution, how to make more comely the things we have to build.

—We know how to bring the growth of highways under control and how to make mass transit work and prosper.

Of the world's rural and urban, wilderness and skull-busting discotheque, we can have the best of each rather than the worst of all.

But do we want to? What would it cost us, what would it take? Total regulation by a government that could scarcely avoid becoming totalitarian? Taxes eating the heart out of motivation and hope and pride?

Always we circle back to the making of choices. Looser rather than tighter zoning regulations, more free enterprise rather than less, may be all we need to put housing back in business. It is possible to clean the air and the water at lower cost than under the laws and regulations that grew out of the first ecological panic, to reduce to manageable terms the cost of acquiring the parklands that will be gone forever once they go.

We can show how a change in the way taxes are assessed and collected would broaden, more than an increase in taxes would, people's choices of where and how to live. By just such rudimentary bookkeeping we could save square miles of countryside from cookie-cutter housing, save hundreds of miles of roadside from strip-slum exploitation, save hundreds of blocks of housing in the cities from death and putrefaction.

We can show how the rational location of job opportunities can multiply the number of persons *choosing* to use buses and trains, without requiring or even suggesting that anybody give up using his car if he likes the ordeal of peak-hour driving twice a day.

Quite obviously, these are not the only choices.

In this series of town meetings we discuss school taxes—who should pay, for what, for whose benefit—knowing that education is a subject much larger than that. An entire series might be devoted to it, perhaps will be. We examine the way in which crime in the cities is driving out people and business and opportunity, the way it preys on the poor more than on the rich, knowing that crime and punishment deserve a whole series exploring nothing except their own dark depths.

RPA has ventured to raise regional planning questions this time, because on the solution of these overarching problems depends the solution of all the hundreds of problems that spill or trickle out of them.

Planning as such is not new to this country. In the New York–New Jersey–Connecticut Urban Region alone, 775 separate municipalities, including the five-county City of New York, and each of the 26 counties outside New York City, are planning. The three states and a number of interstate agencies are planning. But, looking at the mess, you perceive that people's decisions are made not according to plan but according to impulse or vague antipathies or intuitions that rise not out of clear reason but out of the mists and vapors of emotion of the human heart.

"Everybody knows drug addiction is one of the boss tragedies of this civilization," a man says. "But whenever we propose a Methadone clinic or any other kind of treatment program everybody turns out and yells, 'Not in my neighborhood!' Sure, people are afraid of ex-addicts. But addicts go into every neighborhood to mug and steal and push junk, not necessarily places with Methadone clinics, and nobody seems to see that when everybody shouts, 'Not here,' what they're really saying is, 'Not anywhere! Not any way!' "

Only when we contemplate the whole Region can we see that fear—of the stranger, of the poor, of people who don't look or talk like our sort do—has more to do with the lag in housing than does any failure of technology.

"What about brownouts in the city. Nobody can build a power plant. That's another 'not in my neighborhood.' "

"No. That's different. Power plants are opposed by people living all over the place. They may *really* be bad for everybody."

"O.K., but who should decide? Right now, nobody asks *me* what I want—enough electricity or save some mountain somewhere. Somebody just sends me a message —the subway slows down to a crawl on a boiling hot afternoon, and I get the message: 'We decided to save a mountain. Sorry!' "

What's going on here? Who's in charge, anyhow?

Nobody's in charge of the Region. Each person goes about his own business trying to get the best for himself and his family, but when it's all added up, not many people really get what they want. We don't seem to see how the decisions we are making as a resident of a city, town, or village, as a civic activist, or as an executive of a corporation, add up.

The purpose of these town meetings is to add all our decisions together and show what they are leading to, from the viewpoint of the Region as a whole. Then you can choose. You can be in charge because you'll know what you are doing to yourself and how you can change it.

Only as a Region can we find out what we want.

The town meetings' response to the questions presented can be the beginning of the political processes which can solve the problems the present political process has created or left unmet. It is a beginning. Through the magic of the great media we shall be made once more such a common conscience and common cause as was little Athens in its golden age. But this is not enough. After that, after the CHOICES FOR '76 have been made, we shall have to learn how to see that our governments hear and respond. They are established to serve us. How to ensure that they do it is the next great question.

We shall return to consult with you about that.

I. TOWN MEETING ON HOUSING

Housing in New York is in its most serious crisis of the century.   —*United Neighborhood Houses* (1972)

It is recognized today that city planning cannot remain strictly a municipal affair. By means of land, rail, water, and aerial routes, city planning is even the manifestation of national life.   —*Le Corbusier* (1937)

Our nation is moving toward two societies, one black, one white—separate and unequal.
    —*The National Advisory Commission on Civil Disorders* (1968)

Most cities by 1980 will be black and brown, and totally bankrupt.   —*The National Urban Coalition* (1971)

Why Housing Is the First Issue

Let's begin our search for solutions with the housing problem —or crisis, to use that sadly depreciated epithet once and be done with it—by seeing whether we can agree that the word "housing" does not accurately describe the thing we're talking about.

We're stuck with "housing"—it is embodied in the law and the usage of planners and bureaucrats and speculators and activists alike, and even the most fastidious among us find the word occurring in their speech when they're talking about houses collectively for people whom they do not know.

But it misstates the problem. Nobody lives in housing. Nobody saves up money or applies for a loan to buy housing for his family. If we're compassionate or intelligently selfish or foresighted enough to apprehend that the way people live tends to make them who they are and what they are, we shall glance at each other and nod this silent agreement that when we say "housing" we mean the untranslatable complex of walls and floors, shapes and colors and smells, memories, griefs and laughter, dreams and despair, that is home.

Everybody has a housing problem. Not quite everywhere in

the immense New York Urban Region that sprawls along the
Atlantic coast from New Haven to Trenton do people call it
by that name. If they like the house and the neighbors, the
town they live in, they'll tell you the rent or the mortgage payment and the real estate taxes are murder. If the taxes seem
just about right, it's because local government is letting developers swarm in with office buildings and shopping centers and
industries that pay high taxes but alter forever the relationship
between Man and Nature that people came here to have and
hold. People in the city fear that it is doomed. People in the
suburbs fear that people from the city will swarm over them.
On country estates, such gentry as is left worries about plagues
of strangers, about where its own children will live when they
grow up and get married, about where the gentry will go when
all the children are gone and the house is suddenly too big,
too much.

Ask any group of lower-income people to list their problems
and housing will top the list almost every time. Three quarters
of a million families are living in substandard housing. Many
more are living in neighborhoods they would leave if they
could. And in New York City more housing is being abandoned
than is being built or rehabilitated for those with lower
incomes.

We start with housing because enclosed within it are most
of the other dominant concerns of the Region. Until we have
made up our mind about where and how we live, about the
relationship between that and the way we work and play and
get from place to place, about the relationships between ourselves and people of a different race or ethnic heritage or income or age—until we've made some decisions about housing
and home, we can't have any clear idea of what we want to do
or have done.

Some of these decisions can be made by each individual or
family. But some we must make together. Choosing a home
is a decision each family or individual makes alone. But
whether the home is available where each family wants it at
a price it can afford depends on decisions we make together,
in our local areas and in the state we live in and in the nation
as a whole.

We start with housing because this series looks at the whole
New York Urban Region, and housing is a truly regionwide
issue. When New York City teachers went on strike, many
city people moved out of the city to get their children back
into school. They drove suburban house prices up all over
the Region, even 40 miles from Manhattan. At the same
time, the local zoning laws passed by towns all over the Region,

even 40 miles from Manhattan, are pushing New York City rents sky high. Home prices and apartment rents from New Haven to Trenton are tied together. Your housing affects my life and mine affects yours. In housing, this is one region.

Finally, housing is fundamental because it occupies most of the built-up urban land. Factories, offices, stores, schools, and other nonresidential uses take up only 17 percent of the land in urban development in the Tri-State Region; another 23 percent is taken up by streets and highways; the remaining 60 percent is devoted to housing. These proportions are similar in other urban regions along the Atlantic Seaboard: more than half of all urbanized land is devoted to housing. What housing is like and where it is located gives the Region its basic appearance. Housing location and the number of households per acre determine whether people drive their cars a great deal or walk and use transit, whether they feel they are part of a community or not, whether they stay close to nature or not. These last considerations will be discussed in later town meetings.

Now let's see why we're creating a housing shortage for ourselves.

Where We're At

There are 6.7 million housing units (homes, you know) in the Region, only about 40 percent of them in single-family houses, the rest in two-family and apartment houses. For the sake of reference, details on how much of that housing stock is located in New York City, and how much in the rest of the Region, as well as how much was added in the last decade, are given in Table 1.

Table 1. The Housing Stock in the New York Urban Region

Existing Stock, 1970 (in thousands)	Region Total	New York City	Outside New York City
Total Housing Units	6,760.8	2,924.3	3,836.5
In single-family houses	2,696.5	349.5	2,347.0
In multi-family houses	4,064.3	2,574.8	1,489.5
Change in Stock, 1960–1970			
Total Housing Units Added	+807.7	+165.7	+642.0
In single-family houses	+220.4	− 17.9	+238.3
In multi-family houses	+587.3	+183.6	+403.7

SOURCE: U.S. Census.

The table does show that some 800,000 housing units were added to the Region's stock in the past decade, but there are clear signs that this was not enough. First, the number of vacant houses and apartments in the Region dropped sharply, down to 3 percent. A low vacancy rate means that it is much more difficult to find a suitable house or apartment, and that prices are driven up. (In the late 50s, when the nationwide supply and demand for housing were in balance, the nationwide vacancy rate was 6.3 percent.) Second, the average number of persons occupying a house or apartment has not declined at the rate demographic trends would suggest, indicating that anywhere between 50,000 and 100,000 households in the Region are doubled up, and would move to separate quarters if they could find them. Third, in the past decade, the Region received 8.9 percent of the nation's population increase, but only 7.1 percent of the nation's increase in new housing units, indicating that we are falling behind the rest of the country in providing housing for our population.

Unfortunately, not being able to keep up with population growth is only part of the problem. An even greater problem is our inability to keep up with the obsolescence of existing housing. Definitions of what constitutes obsolete or substandard housing are notoriously subjective, but indications are that at least 750,000 housing units in the Region, or more than 10 percent, are substandard, and present renewal and rehabilitation programs have not kept up with the pace of deterioration. A lot of housing built during the boom years of 1890–1929 will be from 70 to 110 years old at the end of this century, and will require replacement. One Regional Plan estimate suggests that 2.4 million obsolete housing units will have to be replaced in the Region over the next 30 years.

If we add the needs of the new households that will form in the Region over the coming decades, the needs for replacing hopelessly bad housing that cannot be rehabilitated, the needs to replace housing lost by fire or demolition, and the need to have a less tight vacancy rate, we find that we should be building about 200,000 housing units in the Region each year. Independent studies by the Tri-State Regional Planning Commission, the official planning agency in the Region, and by Regional Plan Association, an unofficial group, agree on this figure. Compared to this need for the construction of 200,000 houses and apartments annually, our actual production has averaged slightly over 80,000 units a year over a recent six-year period, *less than half of what is needed.*

Some people suggest that if we cut our birthrate further, and slow down population growth in the Region, the housing crunch will be eased. Unfortunately, this is true only for the next century. The point is that people form new households, that is, move away from their family to live by themselves, or to get married, generally between the ages of 20 and 30. So, most of those who will be forming new households and will need new homes over the next 30 years have already been born, they live among us. If they have fewer children, their housing needs will be different, they will need smaller houses or apartments. But the total *number* of housing units they will need will not be much different. For example, if the birthrate stabilizes roughly at the present level, the Region's population will grow from 20 million today to 25 million in the year 2000; that will mean 3.4 million additional households. If, by contrast, the birthrate keeps declining at recent rates to reach zero population growth by 1985, the Region's population will be only 22 million by the year 2000; however, that will still mean 3.1 million additional households. To repeat, further declines in the birthrate will mean a smaller household size, smaller housing units (probably more apartments), but will not appreciably reduce the number of housing units needed over the next three decades. The housing we are not building today is housing for our own children.

So, the main question our first town meeting addresses is how we can build more new housing and save more existing housing than we are doing now.

Answering that question, we'll in fact be deciding five other issues:

1. What quality of housing we want.
2. What we want the Region to look like.
3. How much choice people should have in types of housing and in where they can live.
4. Whether people with incomes at the lower half of the scale will be able to find housing outside the older cities and whether people with incomes in the upper half will be able to find housing they like in the older cities.
5. Who should decide all these questions—local, county, state, or federal government, or the private market.

Part A. Allowing Private Enterprise to Build More Housing

The main reason why too few new housing units are being built in the New York Region is that new units are so expensive most households can't afford to buy or rent them. Only about one family in five can afford the lowest-cost housing unit that can be built now in the Region. We will first suggest ways we can bring down the *cost* of new housing so more households can afford to buy or rent a new unit without any government subsidy. (We'll talk about bringing down the *price* of housing with government subsidies later.) Just cutting the cost of new housing would increase the number of new units being built and help everyone who is looking for better housing. The added people moving into new housing would be moving out of older units; so these would be available for people now doubled up or living in worse quarters. Rents and house prices would not go up as fast as they have been doing, and they might even go down. A renter's market for city apartments would develop, and so would competition among owners to see that apartments were better maintained.

How can we cut housing costs to build more unsubsidized housing?

There are two ways.

—Change local laws that now prohibit construction of lower-cost housing than would otherwise be built by private enterprise for families with children—such kinds as town houses, garden apartments, two-family houses, and small one-family houses on small lots.

—Change local laws to let more mobile homes and other factory-built housing be used in the Region.

These two steps would cut the cost of new housing so sharply that almost three times as many families of the Region could afford to move into new housing as can do so now. (See Figure 2.)

Allowing More Attached Housing and Small Lots

One reason why we aren't building enough housing in the 13,000 square miles of the Region is that we don't see the Region whole and clear. We're looking at little tiny chunks of it—775 cities, villages, boroughs, towns, and townships, each considering its own needs separately, each a law unto itself. Some are just a square mile in size or smaller (like Hoboken, Great Neck Plaza, Pelham). Some are as big as many a county (like Brookhaven, Warwick, Franklin, East Fishkill). Large or small, few represent a real, whole community, a place that has within itself all the jobs, services, shopping, housing, and amenities or fun that the people within those boundaries need. Each surveys its own little universe and says: We'll take this kind of housing or industry, and we won't take that kind; we'll

Figure 2

FAMILIES THAT COULD AFFORD A NEW HOUSE IN THE NEW YORK REGION

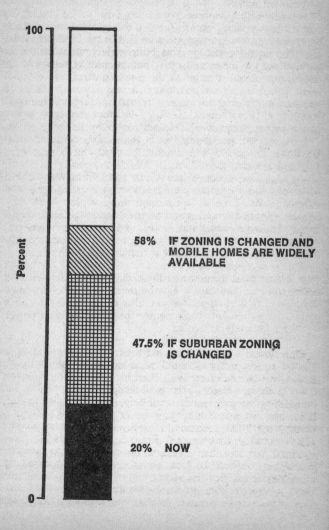

100

Percent

58%   IF ZONING IS CHANGED AND MOBILE HOMES ARE WIDELY AVAILABLE

47.5% IF SUBURBAN ZONING IS CHANGED

20%   NOW

0

let some other municipality take that and then we'll go and use it there or we'll let people travel from there to work in our community. Almost every municipality that has vacant land suited to housing construction at affordable prices is saying: Let the other town take it. And each one has the legal authority to make that stick.

Here's how it has worked.

Immediately after World War II the Region's housing stock increased very fast (in fact, twice as fast in the 1950s as in the 1960s). The new housing was built mainly on vacant land surrounding the developed cities and suburbs. Levittown, on inner Long Island, exemplifies the rapid construction of housing at that time. New homes swept across the potato fields of Nassau County and the celery farms of Bergen County—mainly four-room houses on 60-by-100-foot lots costing less than $10,000, "expandable" to six rooms by finishing off an attic. About half of all families in the Region could afford a new house in the 1950s, and about 120,000 units a year were built and bought. Even though little new housing was built through the Depression of the 1930s and World War II, still by about 1960 the housing shortage seemed well on the way to being ended. True, a half million units of New York City housing were considered unsatisfactory, but in the early 1960s New York City housing was increased so fast by builders getting apartments up just ahead of tighter city zoning requirements that many had to offer rent reductions to fill their buildings.

By this time, all the new housing outside the city had created a problem. In almost every new house there were children of school age. Suburban school tax bills skyrocketed. It didn't take long for residents to recognize they had the legal power to protect themselves: zoning.

Zoning was invented around 1916 to make sure that new buildings did not cut off light and air from buildings already up, and to protect residential neighborhoods against commercial intrusions. Zoning is an exercise of the "police power" of the state, delegated by it to municipalities, and constitutionally justified only insofar as it protects the *general* health, safety, and welfare. Zoning was never meant to empower a municipality to limit or forbid the housing builders wanted to build for families that wanted to buy it. But that's how it has been used for more than a decade. Nor was it meant to "protect property values." In fact, it was first vigorously opposed as an invasion of property rights.

Today, almost all vacant land suitable for large-scale home building is zoned precisely to discourage large-scale home building. On the average, each house has to have at least half an acre of land; on most of the remaining vacant land—two thirds of the vacant land in New Jersey—each home must have an acre or more. That's a lot of land compared to the seventh-acre each Levittown home has and the tenth-acre or less around typical homes in Queens. What it does is limit the number of families that can find space in each municipality *and* raise the price of each house, so the taxes paid by each new family are higher than the taxes paid by most homeowners already there. In fact, instead of protecting property values, it inflates them, to the disadvantage of all. It works to price property out of the reach of most people. The family who purchased a home for $18,000 in the 1950s is fooling itself when it rejoices in its present value of $40,000, because the next step up—the $25,000 house it hoped to move up to—now costs $75,000.

Right now the lowest price for a new house on vacant land in the Region ranges from $30,000 to $45,000, depending on the part of the Region. Considering high mortgage rates and real estate taxes, bankers generally require that a home buyer have an annual income about half the purchase price of the house before giving a mortgage. This means that only families with incomes of over $15,000 can afford a new house in the Region today. That includes only about 20 percent of the families. Four out of five families cannot afford a new house in the New York Region today.

If local governments allowed town houses, garden apartments large enough for families with children, two-family houses, and the Levittown kind of houses on small lots, they could be built for $20,000 to $30,000 or so, available to families earning $10,000 to $15,000 a year. About 47 percent of all families would then be able to afford a new home, more than doubling the effective demand and therefore the number of homes that would be built for families with children.

In other words, private enterprise, without government aid, would build more than twice as many homes per year in the Region as it is building.

Some privately financed new middle-income housing could be built even in the older cities (not high-rise apartments, construction of which costs about $40,000 a unit in New York City). New York City's Planning Commission has shown how low-rise housing might be built on vacant lots all around the city at a cost per unit of less than $30,000. This could help to bridge the housing gap over the next few years, but it could not long continue to meet the demand for new housing under $30,000 a unit. (The Planning Commission estimates about 450,000 units might be built that way, enough to meet an estimated 2½ years' housing demand in the Region.)

Altogether, new middle-income housing, if built without

massive government subsidies, will have to be built mainly on large tracts of vacant land beyond the older cities and towns. But this will require a change in laws and attitudes.

Necessary at the outset will be drastic change in the way school taxes are collected and distributed. For instance, the state governments might take over the whole of school financing. They'd levy the taxes according to some standard of ability to pay, and they'd allocate the money according to the children's need. State commissions in New York and New Jersey have proposed just this. At the same time, courts in a lengthening list of states and federal jurisdictions have crystallized the question by declaring the traditional method of school financing used in most states to be unconstitutional. It makes the quality of a child's education depend on the worth of his district's taxable real estate, and so discriminates against have-not districts and have-not people, according to these courts.

What makes this relevant to housing? As matters stand, municipal government has a vested interest in enacting and enforcing zoning laws which say in effect, "No children allowed." The more children, the higher the tax rate on the local real-property base—and the lower the life expectancy of the administration that lets the children in.

But if the state were levying and distributing school tax money, the major economic incentive for exclusionary zoning would collapse. Indeed, it might turn out that the incentive would be the other way around. The more children then, the more state money; the more state money, the bigger and better the schools, with all the breathtaking possibilities that opens up; and at last a municipal zoning ordinance might say what a town hopes to make of itself rather than what it fears the fair, decent, and satisfying allocation of land use would cost its voters.

The argument against state collection and distribution of school taxes is that it would reduce local school districts' control of the cost of education. The state would determine how much money each district could spend.* Opponents ask, "Why shouldn't a school district that wants to put extra money

* New Jersey's Tax Study Committee recommended that after the state taxes cover most school financing, school districts be allowed to spend some of their own tax money in addition. New York's commission on school finance (the Fleischmann Commission) recommended that local school districts be prohibited from spending their own tax money on schools. If local districts were allowed to spend much of their own money for schools, fiscal zoning—i.e., zoning for tax money rather than for land-use planning purposes—probably would not disappear.

into giving its children a better education be allowed to? Why should every school district have about the same amount of money for each child if some parents are willing to spend more? Is there anything better to spend money on than education?"

Next question: Whose rights are more important? The rights of local people to decide how much to spend on educating their children? Or the rights of children in poorer districts to have as good schools as Scarsdale or Ridgewood or Darien—and the rights of people who need lower-cost housing to find it in the Region?

As to what kind of state tax should replace local real estate taxes for schools, the reader can picture any kind of tax. We will discuss the pros and cons of different types of taxes, and the way they fall on different income groups, in the town meeting on poverty. The only issue here is whether taxes for schools, which make up the largest chunk of municipal budgets, are collected separately by each locality, or by the state as a whole.

CHOICE ONE: Would you favor or oppose replacing local taxes for schools with some form of a statewide tax?

FAVOR   OPPOSE   NO OPINION

A transfer of the collection of school taxes from individual municipalities to the state as a whole will reduce the incentive of municipalities to zone out children and lower-cost housing, and to zone in rateables. It will reduce it, but it won't eliminate it. For while the zoning barriers are, to a large extent, fiscal in nature, they have other reasons as well: racial prejudice, the desire to keep out families from a different income bracket no matter what their color, the desire to stop any growth and maintain the present degree of openness and greenery, the desire to maintain the existing neighborhood "character."

Now, the more legitimate of these objectives—such as density appropriate to the site—can be maintained even if most zoning decisions are, shall we say, in the hands of the county, rather than individual towns. There is no reason why the county or state would not want to preserve the positive values of existing development in *most places*. But change cannot be prevented in *every single place*, as long as the Region as a whole keeps growing. And we have already indicated—and will indicate in greater detail later—that even if we move toward zero population growth at the fastest imaginable speed, the Region will still keep growing for the next two decades, and hence many places will have to change. The question is: Who decides how? The residents of each separate place, separately? Or the residents of larger entities, together?

Building enough housing is not the only concern. Housing, as we will see in more detail in the fifth town meeting, relates to nonresidential facilities, factories, shopping centers, offices. How can these be located in a rational manner, if every one of 775 municipalities in the Region is competing for them not from the viewpoint of how these things are best arranged, but from the viewpoint that each municipality wants a piece of the taxes they will pay? If we transfer the bulk of local tax collections to the state, maybe no municipality will want factories, or power plants, or shopping centers anymore, but they still will have to be located someplace. So, local taxation goes hand-in-hand with local zoning.

We can change that too, if we wish. Constitutionally, the power to pass laws controlling the use of land belongs to the states. The states have lent the power to each municipality, but they can take it away with the approval of the legislatures and the governors.

Short of that radical surgery, the states, the counties, and the municipalities could arrange to share zoning powers. (This need not apply to New York City, which comprises five counties, complete community facilities, and a wide range of housing.) Leave to the local governments the local matters of laying out neighborhoods and local roads and making sure that one group of houses lives comfortably with the groups next to it. But leave it to the counties to plan the larger community—where facilities go that serve more than one municipality, e.g., the large offices and factories, major shopping, hospitals, colleges. Since they are needed by the whole county, it seems reasonable that people all over the county should have the main voice in deciding where they go. Then housing could relate to these facilities. The county could lay out generally where different types of housing would go and leave the details to each municipality. The state would make sure the county plan accommodates enough people of every income level.

We want to make clear that while this proposal aims at greatly increasing the Levittown kind of houses, future developments need not look like Levittown. Houses can be clustered so that most of the land allocated by zoning to a development can be preserved in its natural state or used for parks or lakes or golf links and tennis courts. We shall be looking at the choices for preserving open space in the town meeting on environment. For now, we simply want to leave you with the vision of a Region varied in types and densities of housing—not haphazardly varied but related in a way that works well and looks well. Sharing zoning responsibility among the state, county, and municipality can help this. Leaving zoning entirely in the hands of the municipalities cannot achieve this, because few municipalities cover enough area to interrelate all the facilities people use in their daily lives. They are not whole communities.

There are other ways to make sure that builders are allowed to build housing people want, but they all come down to one principle: the people who have a stake in how much housing of what type is built on vacant land—and almost everyone in the Region does—should have some voice in deciding what is to be built.

But the people now living in those localities that have vacant land say: "Don't let the county and state come into our community and tell us what has to be built here. We came out here because we like it this way. We don't want it to change. We want to control what happens. Let people go somewhere else." Because everyone says, "Let them go somewhere else," we have a housing shortage.

Several recent court decisions have limited the right of municipalities to restrict the kinds of housing they'll allow. For example, in Middlesex County, New Jersey, the Superior Court told Madison Township that it could not enforce a zoning ordinance that excluded 90 percent of the people living in the general area—outside the municipality as well as in. The general welfare, which the zoning ordinance was supposed to achieve, must include the welfare of those outside the township as well as in it, the court said. The United States Supreme Court has not spoken on exclusionary zoning but is expected to.

So what rights are more important? The rights of local people to control completely what is built in their general area? Or the rights of people in the Region as a whole who need better housing which private builders can produce? And the right of everyone in each county to have jobs and services closely related to transportation and housing instead of haphazardly planned or passively accepted by small localities each looking within its own invisible boundaries though its residents' lives range over a far wider area in their daily affairs.

CHOICE TWO: To allow the construction of more private housing, would you favor or oppose zoning more vacant land for less expensive housing (attached or on small lots), even if some zoning responsibility were shifted to county or state governments?

     FAVOR   OPPOSE   NO OPINION

Allowing More Mobile Homes

There is no land in the Region set aside for mobile homes, though some mobile home parks have been established with special permission of the municipality, mostly on the outskirts of the Region. Elsewhere in the country, mobile homes have become an important factor in filling the housing gap. Nationwide, 23 percent of all new housing units built in the country in 1970 were mobile homes.

The cost of living in a large mobile home suitable for a family of four is somewhat less than in, say, a new garden apartment; it would require an income of about $8,500 a year to live in a new mobile home large enough for a family of four (if there were sufficient sites and appropriate financing were available), compared to $10,000 to $12,000 a year for a new garden apartment or town house (row housing) of roughly the same size. General availability of mobile homes, in addition to the tax and zoning changes we have discussed, would increase the percentage of the Region's families that could afford a new housing unit from about 47 to about 58. (See Figure 2.)

However, a mobile home's satisfactory life is much shorter than a garden apartment's. The Mobile Home Manufacturers Association estimates it as over 20 years; others suggest about 10. A recent bank study found that after 15 years, mobile homes are worth 20 to 35 percent of the original cost. By contrast, well-maintained garden apartments could go on indefinitely.

Figuring the total cost per year, the mobile home may not be the least expensive form of housing, but for immediate filling of the housing gap without government subsidy, it would bring new housing within reach of an additional 500,000 families in the Region.

Opposition to mobile homes stems mostly from the fact that in the past "trailer parks" have usually been ugly. But with proper design controls and landscaping standards, they don't need to be. Recent experience indicates that mobile home parks can be designed and landscaped to form fairly attractive, even if temporary, communities.

CHOICE THREE: Do you favor or oppose allowing more mobile home parks in the Region, providing they conform to high design standards?

FAVOR   OPPOSE   NO OPINION

Other kinds of factory-built housing (sometimes called pre-fabricated or modular housing) are being tried by more and more industrial corporations, large and small, particularly through the U.S. Department of Housing and Urban Development's Operation Breakthrough. Unlike mobile homes, manufactured houses are meant to be permanent. They allow not only greater efficiency in production than is possible with houses built by hand on the site, but also open new vistas for the use of unconventional materials (new types of concrete, steel, plastics), of imaginative design and greater flexibility. "Why can't a man who has a growing family buy an extra bedroom and bolt it onto his house?" asks a General Electric executive involved in modular construction.

Because of the tastes of home buyers, most factory-produced houses built today are still made to look like conventional houses, and the savings attainable from factory production are not yet large enough to bring the cost down below the cost of housing of comparable quality built on the site. But industrial housing can be built more quickly, and progress on its economic potential is being made, according to the U.S. Department of Housing and Urban Development.

Twenty-seven states, among them New York and Connecticut, have passed statewide building codes that allow the construction of industrialized housing, and the national building trades have created new forms of labor agreements recognizing the peculiar nature of the industrialized housing process. Thus, political barriers, such as the multiplicity of restrictive municipal building codes, and labor opposition from the building trades, are being overcome. The remaining questions to be resolved before a mass market is created are largely technical in nature, and so we are not raising the issue as a "choice" in these town meetings.

Part B: Saving the Present Housing Stock

An odd perversity excites and infects much of our talk about saving the cities. Suddenly we are all utopians. New towns spring up on the horizons of our conversation, satellite cities swim into gleaming existence in distant Elsewheres, people in millions stream out of the festering ghettos to homes on green and peaceful parklands, and everybody lives within walking distance of the place where he works or plays, shops or fishes, or goes to school. Let no one deride Utopia; our ability to imagine it speaks well of our good intentions, and we have substantial reason to believe in technology's ability to produce just about anything for which a blueprint can be drawn.

It will then perhaps be noticed that in the process of saving the city we shall have made it into something else. What? A storage warehouse for the invincibly poor, the old and sick, the hard-core unassimilables? An amusement park? A gathering place for far-dispersed corporations' and exchanges' computers?

Let's be as tough and realistic as we can. Those regional Utopias aren't going to leap out of the hinterlands overnight. Cities can be saved not by any single fiat or legislative act or stroke of a statesman's pen but by billions of separate steps, an inch at a time.

How to Deal with Abandonment

Over the past six years, about half a million new housing units were constructed in the Region, but a fifth of that number of older housing units were abandoned to the rats and cockroaches and vandals. Right now, about 300,000 housing units in New York City alone are creaking toward abandonment. Elsewhere, there are other thousands of units that have not been adequately maintained over the years, and some rehabilitation, new forms of housing finance, and steps toward assuring neighborhood stability are urgently needed.

Since we are unlikely to produce enough new housing soon, and since whole communities in the old cities are at stake, it is merely sensible to consider how these existing housing units might, within this decade, be restored to decent life.

They range in quality and condition from some 300,000 old-law tenements (declared obsolete in 1901) and better-designed housing that nevertheless has been abandoned in places like Brownsville and East New York to some newer housing in places like Washington Heights and the Grand Concourse area of the Bronx which has been neglected so much as to threaten deterioration not only of the buildings themselves but of the whole neighborhood around them.

One common reason why housing becomes uninhabitable at a time when it is desperately needed has to do with the way it's financed. Management of the property usually devolves on one small businessman who sees it as an investment rather than as essential housing for the tenants. These small investors seldom have much money in reserve against setbacks—difficulty in collecting rents, say, or burst pipes, or an unforeseeable rise in taxes. When such emergencies do arise, the money must come from funds that had been set aside for routine maintenance. That's where maintenance stops and neglect sets in. The low incomes of the tenants simply don't allow them to pay enough rent to compensate the landlord for his expenditures, and banks are reluctant to lend money if they have little chance of recouping it.

In thousands of tragic little cases, the owners and the mortgage holders have decided it was not profitable to hold the building any longer, and they just abandoned it. The tenants no longer received services, one by one the apartments were vacated, and in many neighborhoods drug addicts moved into the empty rooms and turned the whole building into reeking pigsties.

About the rapid deterioration of these neighborhoods, the New York RAND Institute observed in 1970 that the main causes were rising maintenance costs and "landlord-tenant antagonisms" due to "rapid changes in the ethnic and social composition of the city's population," causing "open warfare: rent strikes and malicious mischief by tenants, discontinuation of building services and harassment of tenants by landlords." In many neighborhoods "both tenants and landlords suffer from growing vandalism, theft and burglary, arson and muggings in the hallways and elevators."

However the decline starts, it's hard to stop. Money for rehabilitation dries up. Insurance rates skyrocket, the city's own services degenerate. Everyone who possibly can moves out, leaving the most helpless households to cope with adversities that have defeated the strongest.

Many of the abandoned buildings remain sound structures. Though from the owner's point of view they were not worth keeping, from society's point of view, they could be rehabilitated into satisfactory housing for less than any other decent housing would cost. But how do we get the building promptly into the hands of those who could rehabilitate it? Where do we find the money? And how do we ensure that the neighbors and the tenants themselves won't bring the building's conditions back to havoc?

In a flurry of demonstration projects people are seeking the answers. One of the most successful anywhere in the country is in East Harlem. Some 8,000 persons who had been living in substandard housing are being rehoused in a mixture of new and rehabilitated buildings sponsored by the Upper Park Avenue Community Association (UPACA). By the end of 1972, nearly 450 households (about 1,500 persons) will have been rehoused; by the end of 1974, nearly 1,750 households (about 5,750 persons). The money is available, and the community is taking the responsibility for keeping the neighbor-

hood stable and the buildings well maintained. Two social
statistics associated in the public mind with problem neighborhoods insinuate that East Harlem's Upper Park Avenue would
be a poor risk for renewal: in about 65 percent of the households there is no adult man, and 40 percent of the households
are supported by welfare.

But two East Harlem housewives who head UPACA recognize the need to assure that tenants in the new or renewed
buildings will have help in solving the problems that plague
poor people more than others. So that tenants can be good
neighbors, UPACA requires applicants to take a 10-week
course, prepared by Cornell University, at which problems of
living together in an apartment and in a city are discussed. The
New York Medical College assists by trying to identify and
overcome mental problems that might strain relations with
neighbors. For most prospective tenants of UPACA's new
buildings, the process seems to have been successful. In some
cases, but only a few, applicants had to be rejected to protect
the other tenants.

Similar experiments in social organization of neighborhoods
and in different kinds of housing rehabilitation have been tried
elsewhere.

In order now to save and make satisfactory homes of the
cities' older housing, these steps appear necessary:

—Some legal method for taking over buildings promptly
when they are poorly maintained so that tenants do not suffer,
so that those who move out are replaced and no empty apartment is left to vandals, and so that deterioration in general
does not reach the point of no return.

—A community organization capable of commanding better
city services, managing buildings if necessary during their
transition to new ownership, and assuming responsibility for
the social services necessary to assure a good neighborhood.

—Where necessary, a process of organizing cooperative or
condominium ownership of apartment buildings or transfer of
ownership to a person who will live in the neighborhood, preferably of the same racial or ethnic background as the tenants.

—Financing for rehabilitation which, wherever feasible,
leaves the tenants within the building while it is being fixed.

—Public assistance to assure rents high enough to maintain
the buildings well where the cost is higher than tenants can
afford. This could be in the form of rent certificates to lower-
income families living in private standard-quality housing
which they would be unable otherwise to afford where that
housing is available.

Such devices as these do work, and there are pilot examples

to prove it, but carrying out such programs across all the old cities of the Region would entail widespread and rather radical change from private to public real estate investment and toward strong community organization control of housing and neighborhood affairs. It would also encourage the survival of segregation over broad areas, separating people by race, ethnic group, or income. About 55 percent of New York City's low-income people are black or Puerto Rican.

Furthermore, many of these neighborhoods would remain barely satisfactory places to live even when the buildings were made safe and sanitary. The old-law tenements and the older new-law tenements (built before 1916) might be the best available housing for the next few years, but such a best is none too good and should be considered simply stopgap housing to be used only until new construction catches up with demand. That means that the total cost of improving these buildings is high for the years of satisfactory housing they will provide. Even where the buildings are newer (built between 1916 and 1929) and better designed, many of the neighborhoods are more crowded than people would like—too little play space, parking space, and greenery; too much noise. Undoubtedly some money will be wasted—as has happened already in various parts of the country—in the repair of housing that will quickly be destroyed again and in payments to shrewd predators in a complicated program involving transfer of real estate ownership and subsidies.

On the other hand, there appears to be no immediate alternative way to maintain present housing quality or begin to raise it for lower-income families in the city or to keep vast areas of the older cities livable for moderate- and middle-income families, at least over the next decade or two, while housing demand is likely to exceed supply.

CHOICE FOUR: Do you favor or oppose public programs which encourage the transfer of management responsibility for deteriorating housing from private owners, to tenant groups and community organizations?

FAVOR   OPPOSE   NO OPINION

Housing Rehabilitation

Federal and state funds provided for rehabilitation of older housing are small compared to those allocated for construction of new subsidized housing—even though rehabilitation often can be done without removing the tenants and frequently costs as little as a third or a fourth of the cost of new construction in New York City. Many reasons for this continued emphasis on new construction are given, including the poor organization of the construction industry for rehabilitation so costs often rise or performance falls well beyond what is expected, tenant dissatisfaction in some early instances, the difficulty of rehabilitating a sufficiently large area to protect the neighborhood from vandalism and deterioration again, whereas clearance and reconstruction give a fresh start. Furthermore, the financing programs that do exist have recently been involved in scandals. Finally, many older buildings will not be considered satisfactory, say, in about 10 years, so the investment just for a few years may be substantial. On the other hand, many people charge that a conservative attitude by the Federal Housing Administration—not any strong reasoning—is the main reason that funds for rehabilitation have been limited. In any case, much more money was being released for rehabilitation in the New York Region toward the end of 1972.

The issue is that several hundred thousand apartment units in New York City alone need rehabilitation. Without rehabilitation and the kind of community organization described above, they probably will be abandoned over the next few years. With strong community organization and $5,000 to $25,000 a unit for rehabilitation, they could be made not simply livable but attractive—at least in the present housing market.

Public funds also would be needed in many of these buildings to subsidize maintenance so they don't require rehabilitation soon again. The cost of maintenance has been going up faster than the cost-of-living generally and faster than most tenants' incomes. RAND Institute suggested that this maintenance subsidy be in the form of rent allowances to the tenant so he or she could afford to pay enough rent to keep the place up.

Again, some waste and some misuse of the funds are conceivable. But the alternative is to let abandonment and vandalism proceed, tear down the buildings as soon as they become uninhabitable, exacerbating the housing shortage deliberately, as it were, in the hope that if there is not enough housing around, people will start moving elsewhere. Where, exactly, remains unclear.

CHOICE FIVE: Do you favor or oppose greater governmental (federal, state, or local) investment in rehabilitating and maintaining older city housing?

FAVOR   OPPOSE   NO OPINION

Part C: Building New Housing for Low-Income Families: Why and Where

Even if most of the existing low-cost housing in the cities is preserved while new middle-income housing is expanded rapidly outside the older cities by means of liberalized zoning, over the next decade or two most of the improvement in housing quality will go to middle-income families. It is unlikely to help many of the 150,000 households (between 400,000 and 500,000 persons) on the waiting list for low-cost public housing in New York City and the 7,000-plus on Newark's waiting list (about 20,000 persons) or the many people outside these cities living in housing not fit for rehabilitation.

Many people continue to believe the principle on which the public housing program was initiated in the United States: that good housing is essential for good physical and mental health and repays the public investment by reducing the public outlay in fire, police, and public health costs. Even when a strong maintenance and rehabilitation program has been established, it is estimated that 35,000 to 40,000 units of *new* housing a year should be made available to low-income families over the next five years out of a total of 200,000 new units that ought to be built in the Region each year. However, throughout the whole country in the 1960s the federal government subsidized an average of only 53,000 housing units a year for middle- and moderate-income households as well as low-income.

More recently, the number of federally subsidized housing units has spurted upward—197,000 in 1969 and 431,000 in 1970. In 1970, 21 percent of all housing units started in the United States were subsidized by the federal government. They constituted 40 percent of all housing starts in the New York Region, but because total housing construction in the Region is so low compared to the nation, that was far less than the Region's share of nearly 10 percent of the nation's population.

The 1973 federal budget provided $1 billion for public housing nationwide, compared to $626 million in 1970, but it is often pointed out that this is still only a fraction of the indirect federal housing subsidies for the well-to-do. The President's Fourth Annual Report on National Housing Goals indicates that homeowners received tax deductions on mortgage payments and property taxes totaling $4.7 billion in 1971 —and the higher the income, the larger the subsidy.

Over the coming decades, as the gap between housing

demand and supply is closed, is it more important (1) to improve housing quality for low-income households and enlarge their choice of where in the Region to live, or (2) to leave the housing market free to satisfy middle- and upper-income housing demands first?

If we choose to build more subsidized housing, a place must be found for it. Many projects planned and financed have been delayed by failure of communities to accept subsidized housing. And the whole Region is getting less than its share of federally subsidized housing because not enough satisfactory sites are available and those accepted are mainly in New York City where construction costs are very high so we get less housing for the money.

Of the Region's 2,700 square miles now developed, some 2,000 have few housing units which are likely to be priced in the near future for lower-income families without subsidy, yet nearly all the added jobs and population will be locating out there. For example, by 1985, Suffolk County on Long Island, Monmouth and Somerset and Morris counties in New Jersey, and northern Westchester and Rockland counties north of New York City will contain about 4.6 million people and about 1.35 million jobs. Unless some housing there is subsidized, those counties will be a huge continent where almost no lower-income people can live and compete for the jobs that will be going there. And the poor in the cities will stay poor because their jobs are no longer there.

In the beginning, in mid-Depression some 40 years ago, the responsibility for initiating public housing was delegated to municipal government. State and federal governments would put up the money, but local government had to want it and ask for it, and local governments, sensitive to constituencies' need where it existed, were glad to accept the responsibility.

But that was in the 1930s, when most cities were still whole communities, each an integral complex of place to work and place to live or play or shop, pretty much an island entire of itself. That which local government did was done for its own people, its own voters, and housing was supplied as cheerfully and naturally as was police or fire protection or water and sewerage. It could scarcely be foreseen then that home rule in subsidized housing would be perverted from being a way of liberating people to functioning as a way of confining them in ghettos far from where the jobs are—of locking them into the poverty cycle.

Now, when the urban community extends far beyond the municipality—spreading in this region over 775 separate municipalities—the competition among governments is to *avoid* public housing. In Dover, N.J., in Port Chester, N.Y., for example, widely supported plans for renewing the downtowns have been held up for years because the municipalities did not want subsidized housing to relocate people living in shoddy housing in the downtown areas. The attitude was: "Why should we be responsible for low-income households? Why not places nearby that have no low-income families at all?" In Westchester County only 13 of the 44 municipalities have any low-income housing, but three of the 44 have about 10 percent of all their housing units in low- or middle-income subsidized units. Yet Westchester municipalities are not whole communities. Harrison, with no subsidized housing of any kind, wraps around and relates closely to White Plains, which has the most. This is typical of the Region's counties outside New York City: municipalities surrounding Paterson, New Brunswick, and Bridgeport have little or no subsidized housing. They have none not because they are inappropriate locations but only because an accident of history made public housing a municipal function instead of a county function.

The federal government is trying now to encourage construction of low-income subsidized housing outside the neighborhoods and even outside the municipal boundaries within which the low-income families live. The purpose is to avoid enlarging the poor and minority ghettos in the older parts of urban regions—to slow America's rapid movement toward the "two societies, separate and unequal" against which the President's Commission on Civil Disorders warned.

Moreover, confinement of subsidized shelter to the aging downtowns is a rash extravagance. Most cities find it necessary to build high-rise public housing, far more expensive than lower apartments that could be built economically outside the city limits. High-rise apartment units cost about $40,000 each in New York City; the Urban Development Corporation has planned 900 units of low- and moderate-priced housing in Westchester that will cost about $25,000 a unit.

Finally, some people (including the chairman of the New York City Housing Authority) believe low-income families inevitably have more problems than higher-income families and that herding the poor together in a vast vertical project reinforces their problems and makes it harder for them to enter the economic and social mainstream if they want to.

Although new federal housing aids allow private builders and civic and church organizations to sponsor low-income housing anywhere in the Region (it is called 236 Housing, after the chapter number of the enabling legislation), communities outside the areas where low-income families live have strongly resisted the construction of housing for low-income families, even when the projects are small, low, and open to families with middle income. And up to now, most of the resistant towns have been able to keep out this subsidized housing by resorting to large-lot zoning.

Elsewhere in the country, where the federal Department of Housing and Urban Development (HUD) has succeeded in getting 236 Housing built outside the ghettos, there were instances in which poverty problems were brought out to the new project, causing problems for others there. HUD therefore has begun to require that all housing they subsidize for low-income families must be accompanied by adequate social services, and project managers must be trained in handling problems of poverty. Like UPACA's program, the aim is to solve problems so all those needing the housing can be admitted, but occasionally some families are rejected. (It is not unusual for public housing projects to set high standards of tenant behavior. The New York City Housing Authority has long had very high standards for admitting tenants; for many years, households without a father were not admitted, for example; and even now, though some of the requirements have been relaxed, so much care is taken to avoid admitting households that will include problem tenants that the New York Civil Liberties Union is suing the Housing Authority over some tenant rejections. The City Housing Authority points out that the crime rate in its projects is much lower than in surrounding neighborhoods.)

Examples of successful low-income housing projects in neighborhoods of higher-income families are in Mount Kisco, Westchester, and Huntington, Long Island.

Many low-income families oppose the idea of scatter-site housing outside the ghettos. Some black leaders argue that keeping the black community together would help it organize to solve its own problems. But can the two societies live peacefully side-by-side but separately when low-income neighborhoods are as large as they have now become in many parts of the Region? And can low-income people get a fair share of opportunities if they are separated in large ghettos?

CHOICE SIX: Where should most new subsidized (government-assisted) housing for low-income people be built?
A. Predominantly *in* ghetto areas
B. Predominantly *outside* ghetto areas
C. No more subsidized housing should be built
D. No opinion

If low-income subsidized housing were to be decentralized, how should we decide where it is to go?

Two possible formulas are:

1. Assigning a flat percentage of this housing to each municipality throughout the Region.

2. Distributing it according to a regional plan which guides the location of housing for all income groups in relation to jobs, transportation, and services.

If every town in the Region accepted a flat percentage of low-income subsidized housing, no part would have to accept much, and everyone would recognize that the distribution was fair and so would be more forebearing toward it; so goes the argument for this formula.

Massachusetts chose this approach. It required every municipality in the state to accept proposals for low- and moderate-income subsidized housing despite contrary zoning as long as no more than 10 percent of existent housing is of this kind and no more than 1.5 percent of all privately owned land is used for such housing.

Two problems:

a. This formula declares low-income households to be an odious burden, to be doled out so that everyone bears his calibrated share of the affliction. While this grim view of one's fellowman seems to be the attitude of many people right now, should it be incorporated in official policy?

b. Following a flat percentage formula ignores the needs and preferences of the low-income families. Are the sites near jobs? Near public transportation? Near social services? Shopping? Do the people want to live there—often in quite rural outlying places? Also, it ignores plans for regional and county development. Is the density appropriate there? Is this the best way to gain acceptance of low-income housing?

2. We could, instead, prepare a regional plan (or interlocking county plans) showing where housing of various densities should go—of whatever income level—and assuring that housing would be available at prices enabling all those working in the general area (e.g., the county) to live there. The states would empower themselves to assure that enough low-income housing was included in the plans to meet regional needs. Detailed local plans would remain the responsibility of the municipalities as long as they conformed to the county and regional frameworks. Governor Cahill has proposed something much like this in New Jersey.

The main argument for such regional planning is that it would achieve the optimum development pattern for everyone. Furthermore, it would treat low-income families the same as other families in that it would match their housing needs to the development pattern rather than creating them as a bitter medicine that no one wants.

Since some communities would end up with more low-income families than other communities, tax or federal grant adjustments would be necessary—to compensate for losses in otherwise prospective taxes.

This system would entail a healthy lot of public debate and negotiation among state, county, and municipal governments and the Tri-State Regional Planning Commission, and resistance to low-income housing may be so strong that the haggling over fair shares would cause political explosions—more than would a flat-percentage formula. But if it worked it would create a regional plan meeting many needs, not just the need to find the least objectionable places for low-income families.

CHOICE SEVEN: If low-income housing were to be located *away* from ghetto areas, what principle should govern site selection? (Check one.)
A. Require each municipality, regardless of location, to accept a "fair share" of new low-income housing
B. Place low-income housing only near jobs and public transportation
C. No opinion

Part D: Other Subsidy Issues

Housing Certificates: A Better Way of Subsidizing Housing?

The unceasing fights over the location of subsidized housing projects, the stigma attached to them in the public mind, raise the issue: Is building such projects the only way to provide new, decent shelter for families who cannot afford it on the private market? Many people are advocating and HUD is experimenting with the use of so-called housing certificates or housing allowances as a way of making unnecessary the construction of at least some low-income public housing projects. Housing certificates, like food stamps, would add to the money a family has available to pay for a necessity. A family of five that could afford on its own to pay, say, $100 a month for rent might get a certificate worth, say, another $100. Or a widow on Social Security might get a rent certificate worth, say, $25 a month. The recipient could then use that certificate to rent or buy any housing in the Region that is legally safe and sanitary, an attached house in the suburbs or an apartment in New York or an older house in Elizabeth or Passaic, just for instance. People could go shopping for shelter, and they'd have an incentive to drive a hard bargain.

The advantages:

Most important, a housing certificate drastically changes people's attitude toward each other and themselves. It makes the low-income family free to seek housing as other families do; it just puts in their pocket the extra money they need to rent or buy standard housing. It does not say: "If you're poor, live here and like it!" The public won't even know which families get assistance.

Some people feel this doesn't go far enough—that low-income households should simply receive enough money to live decently and let *them* decide how much to spend on housing. We shall discuss that more in the town meeting on poverty.

But two answers have been given to this argument.

First, RAND Institute and others observe that one cause of apartment abandonment in New York City has been failure of welfare recipients to pay their rent even though it was included in their welfare check. RAND, for that and other reasons, recommended rent certificates.

Second, everybody has a stake in everyone else's housing; so if the public is paying part of the bill, it might want to be certain that a reasonable share goes into housing, one of the purchases that most affects it.

The cost of housing allowances or certificates could be less than the cost of housing low-income households in subsidized housing projects—not right away, perhaps, but when the total supply of satisfactory housing has come closer to demand in the Region. Each household living in subsidized housing in the Region costs taxpayers about $2,600 a year. New York City public housing costs the taxpayer considerably more. So a housing certificate allowing families just half the average subsidy for public housing would total more than $100 a month. If enough middle-income housing were available, $100 a month probably would give low-income families extra money enough to find decent housing.

Why is the cost of housing certificates for an individual family cheaper? In part because when more public housing is needed, *new* projects are built, whereas most low-income families with housing certificates would find used housing. In part because most low-income projects are built in dense, high-rise neighborhoods and cost more. It also may be a matter of greater efficiency in the private economy than in public projects. Also, with apartment maintenance costs rising rapidly, families able to maintain their own unit could find it considerably cheaper to buy a house than to pay rent.

Another advantage in housing certificates is that no government has to go through the political agony of finding a site for low-income public housing. Families find their own home. And low-income families don't have to go through the agony of waiting while public housing is produced.

Of course, if a housing allowance program is implemented, it would have to go to most of the poor—not just the few lucky enough to get into public housing today. That will raise the total cost of the program—despite the lower per-family cost—substantially. For example, in New York City, 38 percent of all renter households are estimated to be eligible for public housing, but don't live in it; only 7 percent actually do.

In deciding whether certificates are a better device than publicly owned and operated units we should compare what is *possible* with public housing, not simply what has been done in the past. Public housing *could* be located throughout the Region in small clusters and *could* be mixed with housing for all income levels in new towns and neighborhoods. So even living in a project wouldn't mean that a family was getting public assistance (because others would be living there too). Public housing units could be sold to tenants who wanted to purchase, just as housing certificates could assist families that wanted to buy their own housing. And tenants could (and do in some places now) perform maintenance work for rent credits.

Public housing, then, if built on a large enough scale, could achieve many of the social changes enumerated in support of housing certificates and could achieve them with greater certainty and directness if governments really wanted them—particularly racial and income integration.

An experiment with housing certificates in Kansas City indicates black households that had been living in substandard housing did move out of the worst neighborhoods when they got more money for housing but tended to move into black neighborhoods nevertheless, whether by choice or because it was the easiest or because of discrimination. An added argument for continuing some public housing construction is that it can contribute to the renewal and stabilization of selected neighborhoods.

So the basic issues between housing certificates and public housing are these:

Housing certificates provide a wider choice for those to be

assisted. Whether to choose integration or segregation is for them to decide, not the government (though many obstacles might have to be cleared away to effectuate their choice).

Second, shifting to housing certificates takes governments out of the housing construction and management business. Some think this is good, others think lower-income people will get worse housing if they have to compete with moderate-income families for the cheapest housing in the private market.

Importantly, however, the success of a large-scale housing allowance program is predicated on a lot of new housing construction in the private sector, on building something like 200,000 rather than 80,000 new housing units in the Region annually. For, if the new housing supply is insufficient, if the housing market continues to be tight, all that housing certificates or allowances will do is drive up the price for existing housing, both new and secondhand. With more money in the hands of renters chasing the same number of available apartments, landlords will raise rents, and the federal subsidies, instead of helping low-income families, will simply provide landlords with a windfall profit.

CHOICE EIGHT: Would you favor or oppose a shift away from building public housing for low-income families toward providing them with a "housing allowance" that enables them to purchase or rent moderate-income housing in the private market?

FAVOR   OPPOSE   NO OPINION

Subsidizing Middle-Income Housing to Keep a Balanced City Population

The regional director of the U.S. Department of Housing and Urban Development remarked recently: "New York City has not faced up to the need for middle- and upper-income housing for employees of corporate headquarters. That's the reason corporations are moving away."

In fact, New York City has been losing middle-income families steadily over the past 20 years despite the difficulty of finding middle-income housing in the suburbs. If some such policy changes as we discussed above were adopted, enabling more middle-income housing outside the older cities, families with incomes of $10,000 to $15,000 a year, who find it very difficult to move to the suburbs now, would be able to do so.

At the same time, decent city apartments would remain expensive because maintenance costs for apartments are rising far faster than the cost of living generally and because the cost of building high-rise apartments will remain far higher than the cost of building garden apartments and town houses. With suburban zoning liberalized, a faster out-movement of middle-income families is likely, even of those who might prefer city living, simply because there will be better housing within their budgets outside the cities.

Like the last choice, this one should be made only after taking a long-range view. What is our idea of the good city and the good region? Can we dream a little of cities in which neighborhoods gradually are redesigned and rebuilt? Can we dream of a time when people who love city living can live in the city and will not have to flee because they think the schools aren't good enough for their children—or the discomforts, dirt, pollution, and general dreariness are too much for them—or simply because living in a decent building costs too much? Can we dream then of city neighborhoods in Paterson, Trenton, Bridgeport, Jersey City, Newark, and the rest in which people of all incomes *want* to live and are able to live?

Many people argue that few people want to live in cities, even pleasant cities; that almost anyone would choose roomier, greener neighborhoods if they could. George Sternlieb, one of the Region's best-known housing experts, said recently: "The only thing that is really gluing the central city population together right now is the housing shortage. And when and if we have very substantial housing development in the suburbs, I think we are going to see a major flight from the cities that will make the activities of these past 10 or 20 years take second place. It will be a flight of the blacks and whites, whoever can make it."

On the other hand, a large number of families choose to live in New York City despite all the problems. The persistence of consumer demand is illustrated by the high rents in the desirable neighborhoods and the new middle-income communities in Brooklyn's Park Slope, Cobble Hill, and Boerum Hill and Manhattan's Chelsea and Upper West Side.

But even if middle-income families prefer city living as conditions are improved, it will take subsidies to lower city housing prices enough to make them competitive with those of suburban housing, at least until new construction methods and new building maintenance methods are invented.

The question we are raising here is whether efforts should be made to keep middle-income families in the older cities at a time when they can find housing they can afford outside the cities without a subsidy. Should we worry about maintaining a balanced population in the cities and the threat to the cities' economies that the concentration of a heavily low-income low-skilled population implies? On the other hand, with so little subsidy money available for the hard-pressed lower-income family, should we really be spending subsidies on middle-income people who could—if policy changes discussed earlier come to pass—find privately financed, unsubsidized housing in the suburbs?

CHOICE NINE: To encourage middle-income people to live in cities, would you favor or oppose much greater subsidies for middle-income housing in cities?

  FAVOR   OPPOSE   NO OPINION

II. TOWN MEETING ON TRANSPORTATION

Concern for the quality of urban life has led to growing disenchantment with the automobile . . . and to increasing support for rapid transit. But the condition of urban transportation cannot be ascribed simply to the methods by which people move . . . much of the fault lies in the planless way that cities have been allowed to grow.
> —*Kermit Gordon, The Brookings Institution* (1971)

There has been congestion upon the transit lines almost from the start . . . the crowding during rush hours has resulted in indecent conditions . . .
> —*Committee on Regional Plan of New York and its Environs* (1926)

The deficit problem is huge. In the period 1972 to 1985, the Region will need $14.6 billion to finance mass transit operating deficits. In the same period, the Region will need at least $7.3 billion to finance capital outlay.
> —*The Governors' Special Commission on Financing Mass Transportation* (1972)

Private Choices Versus Public Choices

As individuals, we constantly make choices which affect the Region's transportation. We choose places to live. We choose places to work. We choose people and places to visit. We decide what time to leave and what route to take. We buy automobiles. We want rising wages, and in the suburbs we require large-acreage zoning, both of which demands have an impact on transportation. Yet as a society we don't like the consequences of these private choices. We oppose new highways. We don't like the rising cost of public transit. Still, untouched by our rhetoric, automobile travel continues to grow and public transit continues to decline.

Our private and our public choices are on a collision course. If we keep buying automobiles but stop building highways, we shall be producing larger and longer traffic jams. If we let public transportation fares rise step-by-step with rising wages in the industry, we shall guarantee further declines in ridership. If we keep putting most of our new housing on the outskirts of the Region and insist on large-acreage zoning, these new parts of the Region will permanently be precluded from having any public transit to speak of.

Clearly, we have to make up our mind. Do we really want those things we advocate publicly? If so, we have to change the ways in which we run the Region, so that our private choices do not forbid our doing together that which together we say we want.

Before we look at the possible changes and see whether they are worthwhile, let us see where we stand now.

Transportation Scale in the Region

Of the 20 million people living in the Urban Region of New York, New Jersey, and Connecticut, about 8 million work. That means that each weekday nearly 16 million trips are made to and from work alone. In addition, people travel for a variety of other reasons—to shop, on personal business, to go to school, to visit, or for recreation—with the result that some 40 million trips are made in the Region each day by some mechanical mode of travel.

Of these 40 million daily trips, 4.4 million are made by franchised bus, 4.2 million by subway, and 0.5 million by railroad. But the importance of subways and railroads in the total calculus is greater than the number of rides would indicate, because trips by subway (and even more so by railroad) are longer than the average trip in the Region (which is about 6.5 miles). Thus, if measured by total miles of travel rather than just trips, subways and railroads account for close to one fifth of all our travel. Measured that way, buses are less important because the average bus trip is short—about two miles even though trips on express runs to New Jersey and outlying parts of New York City are much longer. Travel by other modes—such as school buses, which perform a major portion of all public transportation in the suburbs, or the Staten Island Ferry—should also be taken into account. All told, travel by means other than automobile adds up to just about one quarter of all travel in the Region and auto travel to almost three quarters.

Compared to the 40 million trips within the Region, trips to and from places outside the Region are few. Intercity buses carry 20,000, long-distance trains slightly fewer than 20,000, and airplanes somewhat more than 100,000 passengers in and out of the Region every day. All told, this is about the same number as ride on the Canarsie line of the BMT subway.

This is not to deny the importance of intercity trips, because the Region needs efficient links to other parts of the nation and the world. Still, our focus will be on internal travel, because most travel occurs close to home.

One's choice of travel mode depends a great deal on where in the Region one is and where one is going. On the outskirts, in areas still largely rural, virtually all travel is by auto. In the older suburbs—Westchester, Nassau—the railroad is used for about one fifth of all trips to work, and a few trips are made by bus. In New York City, close to 60 percent of all trips are made by public transit—subway or bus. Finally, trips to the Manhattan central business district are 75 percent by public transit during the whole day and 90 percent during peak hours. Some 6.5 million trips in and out of the central business district (south of 60th Street) are made each weekday. They are much longer than average trips and account for more than one fifth of all miles of travel in the Region and more than half of all travel by public transportation. Other downtowns, as in Brooklyn, Newark, Jersey City, or Paterson, generate much of the remainder of public transportation trips.

We can see that public transit serves highly concentrated travel, travel concentrated in time (during rush hours) and in space (to downtowns). By contrast, the private automobile, which requires something like 15 times more space per passenger than transit, has difficulty entering the tightly built-up areas and works best when development is loose. In the loosely built-up areas the auto is inherently faster than transit simply because it does not have to wait for passengers to assemble in sufficient number to make the trip worthwhile and does not have to stop for passengers en route.

Thus, the kind of Region we build determines the kind of transportation we have. If buildings, particularly nonresidential buildings in downtowns, are tightly clustered, public transit will work well and auto use will be only occasional. If buildings are scattered far apart and there is no downtown to go to, we shall have no alternative to the automobile.

The possibility of public transit to areas that are now poorly served is not dependent on new hardware—monorails or air-cushion vehicles or magnetic suspension. It is a question of land use: how many people live within easy reach of a possible transit line and how many buildings are clustered at the other end of the line.

The issue is illustrated in Nassau County: the proposal to build a new high-rise downtown in the middle of the county on the abandoned Mitchell Field airport was unpopular among Nassau County residents; at the same time they wish they had better bus service or even some modern, lightweight transit system within the county. The two desires are, of course, incompatible: either you have a large place to go to, hence a workable transit system, or you have no particular place to go to and you subsidize a few anemic bus lines.

The suburban attitudes of Nassau County are by no means unique to that county; they reflect a direction the Region as a whole began to take some 30 years ago. The decision was that the Bronx, Brooklyn, and even Queens were outdated, and that, rather than try to build improved versions of them on vacant land, we would wrap a looser version of Los Angeles around New York City and the older counties of New Jersey. This is exactly what we did. In 30 years, between 1940 and 1970, 6 million people were added to the suburban counties of the Region, more than doubling their population, while the population of the older core (New York City, Newark, and Hudson County) remained stable, at 8.5 million. Moreover, to each resident in the newly developing areas was apportioned *15 times more land* than his counterpart had in the central cities.

There was no intention and no possibility to serve this kind of dispersed development with public transit except for service to Manhattan. On the contrary, as lot sizes increased from less than one quarter to one half and then one full acre, the urge to acquire second and third cars per family became irresistible. Today we find ourselves in a Region more than half of whose population simply cannot have access to public transit, except perhaps for trips to Manhattan. Lot sizes and shopping centers and factory locations are predicated on the assumption that everybody has an automobile.

Transit remains to serve only two kinds of people: those who are too poor to own an auto or too young or old to drive, and those who are able to drive but either work or live in one of a very few highly concentrated places, mostly in New York City.

That's where we are. Now, where do we go from here? Do we try to accommodate the auto? Do we make auto travel more difficult? Or do we try to reduce the demand for auto travel? Conversely with transit: Do we subsidize it to prevent ridership from declining further, and, if so, how much subsidy and who should pay? Where do we build new lines? And do we concentrate places of employment and give up large-acreage zoning so that demand for transit increases? More generally, how much mobility do we want, and what resources are we willing to spend for mobility? These are the choices to be dealt with.

Part A: What Pattern for the Region: Auto Versus Transit

The Region's population will increase from 20 million today to 25 million in the year 2000 if the birthrate stays at the present level. However, if present trends in the growth of income and the preference for scattered suburban housing and employment locations continue, motor vehicle registrations will double, from 7.7 million in 1970 to 15 million in 2000. Even if public transit ridership slows its decline and remains relatively stable, the balance between auto travel and transit travel will shift decisively in favor of the auto. *Transit travel, instead of amounting to one out of four trips in the Region, will amount to about one out of eight.* Is this the kind of transportation future we want?

A quick overview of recent history and where the current trend is taking us is shown in Table 2.

Table 2. Auto Versus Public Transit Trips in the Region

Year	Transit Trips	Auto Trips	Total Trips
	(Estimated trips on an average weekday, in millions)		
1950	15	15	30
1970	10	30	40
2000 (current trend)	8	60	68

SOURCE: Regional Plan Association.

Problems with the Auto

The auto would not have gained its worldwide popularity if it did not have a number of inherent advantages. It is the fastest available mode of travel on short trips within an urban region, even in congested areas. It does offer convenience, privacy, and freedom at a cost that all but the very poor can afford. It does enable a semi-rural life-style along with access to opportunities urban in kind. The arguments against it are largely environmental and social.

The most widespread environmental argument is that a very large share of all air pollution in the U.S. is caused by motor vehicles. Of course, one does not have to get rid of the automobile in order to reduce air pollution; since 1968, federal standards have required increasingly strict emission controls on motor vehicles, and the current federal goal is to reduce auto emissions 90 percent by 1976. Some spokesmen for the auto industry doubt this goal is attainable that soon. Even if it is, meeting the stricter standards will make the internal-combustion engine more complex and several hundred dollars more expensive, and will reduce its performance and reliability. "It is difficult to know whether this approach will be sufficient to stay abreast of the problem, as more and more cars appear and the performance of existing engines deteriorates with age," Robert U. Ayres writes in his book *Alternatives to the Internal-Combustion Engine.* Hence the search for alternative methods of automobile propulsion.

New types of engines, such as rotary (Wankel) motors and gas turbines, could be a partial answer, but their pollution characteristics do not appear to be dramatically better than present power plants. Theoretically, a great improvement could be made if internal combustion, as in the conventional motor, were replaced by external combustion, as in the boiler of a steam engine. Numerous experimental steam engines suitable for auto use are under development, but the success of this technology is uncertain. Besides, the boilers would still have to be fired by conventional liquid fuels, the supply of which is limited. This is a limitation steam propulsion shares with the fuel cell, a device that converts fuel directly into electricity. It is expected that by the 1980s, the United States will have to import more than half of its oil, and some scientists envisage a worldwide depletion of oil reserves in the early part of the next century. Making synthetic oil out of coal, which is much more plentiful, imposes its own harsh environmental costs (viz. strip mining). An electric auto, charged from a supply distributed by large nuclear generating stations, would seem the least evil. The big barrier here is the difficulty in development of a battery capable of storing energy enough to match the performance of the internal-combustion engine. The Ford Motor Company and others have high-energy batteries under development, but even if the immediate technical problems are solved it will be a very long time before all the related industries, which make up such a big chunk of the American economy, will be able to switch over to a completely new technology.

Even assuming a nonpolluting vehicle is eventually developed, arguments can still be made against overreliance on individual vehicles as against public transportation. Inherently, a system of individual vehicles will go on using up more land, more energy, and more of other material resources than a public transportation system. The world's physical resources are not infinite. We know that we must conserve what's left of space, energy, and raw materials. And we know that when we allowed the automobile to dictate the patterns of development in the Region we dried up the wellsprings of opportunity for people who can't or don't drive a car of their own—the young, the old, the poor. Finally, accidents and deaths due to the automobile are beyond comparison with any other mode of travel: 150 people each day are killed by the auto in the United States; the fatality rate in the Region is lower because auto use per capita is lower.

A further question is whether society needs as much mobility as it is getting from the private vehicle. It can be viewed as a cause of travel as well as a device for traveling. Next to income, the most important determinant in people's decisions to move around is car ownership. Households with one car in the Region travel twice as much as households with no car. Households with two cars travel nearly three times as much. The relationship holds for each income bracket. It can be said, though not proved, that much of this travel is not essential.

Of course, over the past four decades our urban areas were built so that it is hard to get around now by any means other than auto. If the auto were to disappear tomorrow, a large part of the U.S. population would be literally unable to survive, to get to work, even to buy food. But this may be an argument to start building our suburban areas in such a way that they are not monopolized by the auto, so that those who cannot drive or have no car would usually have a choice of public transportation.

CHOICE ONE: Should public policy in the New York–New Jersey–Connecticut Region encourage more reliance on public transportation?

FAVOR   OPPOSE   NO OPINION

Higher Versus Lower Density of Development

Increasing public transit use and slowing the growth in auto travel is primarily a matter of how the Region is organized— whether it is compact or spread. Regional Plan Association studies of the 1960 journey to work in the Region indicated that 62 percent of the variation in people's decision whether to take the auto or public transportation to work depends on the *density of development* at their place of employment and their place of residence. Only an additional 14 percent of the variation could be explained by such things as directness of public transportation service and its relation to the auto in travel time and travel cost. Thus, while good service is obviously important, the decisive element favoring transit use is high enough density of development.

Conversely, high density also discourages auto ownership and automobile use. Data from the Tri-State Regional Planning Commission, the official planning agency for the Region, complement Regional Plan findings: generally, the higher the housing density, the fewer autos are owned. Not only that; the higher the housing density, the fewer trips are made by the autos that are owned and the fewer trips by mechanical means are made altogether, because automobile travel is more difficult and because more places are within walking distance.

Thus, on the average in the New York Region, families living on two-acre lots have two cars; families living 15 to the acre (one-family houses on 30-by-100-foot lots) have one car; and families living at densities typical of Manhattan (more than 200 to the acre) have 0.2 cars. Likewise, automobile trips per person to and from home reach their peak on large-lot developments. Families living on lots larger than one acre make 1.8 such auto trips *per person* each day if they are high income, 1.5 if they are middle income, and 0.9 if they are low income. In the suburban world of single-family houses, these rates do not decline much as lot size gets smaller. As lot size declines from one acre to 1/10 acre, the amount of auto travel per person declines about 10 percent.

However, as soon as we move away from single-family houses and into urban housing such as attached houses and apartments, auto travel drops precipitously. By the time we reach a density between 30 and 100 families per acre—typical of Brooklyn Heights, Jackson Heights, Flushing, or Hoboken —auto trips per person decline 65 percent for the high-income group, 77 percent for the middle-income group, and 85 percent for the low-income group.

As auto use declines with increasing density, transit use grows. At densities of less than five families per residential acre, public transit—except for special services to a distant, large downtown (e.g., Westport to Manhattan)—is not possible.

With an average of five families to the acre (e.g., South Shore of Nassau County), occasional local bus service does become possible. This is a density at which dial-a-ride and similar systems might work: dial-a-ride, also known as a "demand-actuated system," is essentially a big taxicab, in which several parties may ride together part of the way, and which is dispatched with the assistance of a computer.

With an average of 10 families to the acre (e.g., outer Queens or Clifton, N.J.), regular local bus service (a bus about every half hour) becomes possible. Generally, this is the breaking point between urban, or transit-oriented, and suburban, or auto-oriented, development.

As densities rise higher, toward the 200 families per acre typically found in Manhattan or the Bronx, transit use increases sharply: greater density allows greater service frequency, makes access to transit lines more convenient.

Incidentally, at the higher densities, each person also uses less mechanical travel altogether: thus, New York City residents living above the low-income level make one-third fewer trips by all mechanical modes than their counterparts in the suburbs.

The message seems to be clear.

To achieve a dramatic, not just marginal, reduction in auto use and really convenient travel on foot and public transportation, we must pretty much give up the detached, single-family house and go back to building our suburbs at *urban* densities —like the streetcar suburbs of pre-World War I vintage. Are we ready for that?

A less dramatic, though likewise essential step would be to revamp local zoning on a county or regional basis in such a way that whatever higher density housing is built is clustered along bus lines and near rail stations, rather than splattered at random all over the landscape. After all, in the first town meeting we have shown that two thirds of the housing added to the Region *outside* New York City in the past decade was in multi-family houses. But most of it has been scattered beyond walking distance to bus or rail lines, missing the opportunity to provide clusters with viable transit service.

While most of the trips in the Region do begin or end at home, their other end is usually some nonresidential building —an office building, a store, a school, a factory. Dispersed as they are so often now, these nonresidential buildings can be approached *only* by auto. If they are clustered together, they can begin to support public transportation and thus reduce auto travel. Generally, the possibility of doing that begins to appear when there are more than 2 million square feet of nonresidential buildings in a square mile. Examples of places with roughly 2 million square feet of nonresidential building space are the downtowns of Greenwich, Hicksville, and Montclair. A tangible reduction in the proportion of auto travel does not occur, however, unless the center has roughly 10 million square feet of nonresidential buildings— examples are the downtowns of New Haven, Bridgeport, White Plains, and Paterson. Auto trips to centers of this size generally vary from about 85 percent of all trips to about 50 percent of all trips, depending on whether or not the centers have rapid transit service. However, it takes a downtown at least as big as Newark's, with 30 million square feet of different kinds of nonresidential buildings, to support a rapid transit service of its own, such as the Newark subway (the expansion of which is now planned). Office buildings generally account for one third to one half of all nonresidential buildings in a downtown area.

Figure 3 shows the top 100 square miles in the New York Urban Region arrayed in order of density (to show all 3,700 square miles for which data are available would have made the chart over nine feet long). Shown in black at the bottom of the chart are trips by auto to these square miles. It is evident that roughly the same number of auto trips—generally between 10 and 40 thousand—go to each of these square miles regardless of its density. *The surface of a square mile can only absorb so many auto trips.* The entire excess over that level— rising from less than 10 thousand to 750 thousand trips a day —is carried by public transit.

Another message is made clear. Auto dependency can also be reduced by putting more new nonresidential building, especially office buildings, into tight clusters, such as existing or new downtowns, rather than scattering them along highways and on open campuses. This goes for office buildings especially, but it applies to universities and shopping centers. The effect would be much more modest than that from raising residential densities, but the approach may well be more realistic. For example, Regional Plan Association has found that of all the office buildings that will be built in the Region in the next three decades or so, about 80 million square feet (equivalent to eight World Trade Centers) which would, if current trends continue, locate on dispersed sites along high-

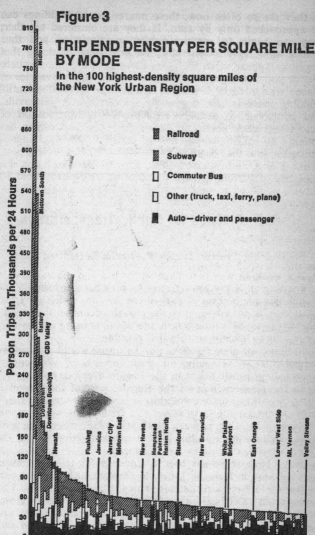

Figure 3

TRIP END DENSITY PER SQUARE MILE BY MODE

In the 100 highest-density square miles of the New York Urban Region

Legend:
- Railroad
- Subway
- Commuter Bus
- Other (truck, taxi, ferry, plane)
- Auto — driver and passenger

NOTE: Trip end density reflects the combined density of residential and nonresidential buildings.

ways throughout the Region, could be clustered in existing and new downtowns outside Manhattan. The effect would be to save the need for about 100 miles of four-lane expressway, plus a lot of other construction on local roads.

CHOICE TWO: To encourage more public transit use do you favor or oppose:

A. Building more townhouses and apartments—and fewer one-family houses?

      FAVOR   OPPOSE   NO OPINION

B. Clustering higher density buildings near transit stops?

      FAVOR   OPPOSE   NO OPINION

Part B: Policies for Public Transportation

Maintaining Present Transit Ridership: Subsidized Fares

The question why patronage on the bus and subway system in the Region is not growing has by now been answered. The population of the central part of the Region, which is served by transit, is not growing; all the growth occurs on the periphery, where there is little transit and where housing is so widely spread that virtually no transit is possible.

Building for higher densities in the future would bring more transit riders—eventually. But what about now? We actually keep losing transit riders in the Region every day. Why?

In the smaller cities of the Region, part of the reason is rapidly growing auto ownership in areas surrounding them, plus changing patterns of travel as a result. This was also true in New York City between 1947 and 1958, when riding on buses and subways declined by 36 percent. However, in the last 15 years, conditions have changed.

Since 1958 there has been a tendency for travel on buses and subways in New York City to *increase* during those years when the fare remained stable. This increase was canceled by declines in ridership during those years when the fare was raised. In 1966 the fare went from 15 cents to 20 cents, and subway ridership dropped by 4.9 percent; in 1970, the fare went to 30 cents, and ridership dropped by 5.4 percent; in 1972 the fare went to 35 cents, and ridership dropped again. Should the fare keep going up at this rate, we will have to pay about $1 a ride in 1980. Between 1946, the last full year

of the 5-cent fare, and 1972 the consumer price index in the
New York area went up 2.2 times, while the transit fare went
up seven times. Clearly, transit seems to be pricing itself out
of the market. Why?

The answer generally given by economists is as follows.
Our living standards are going up because productivity is going up in many industries. Technological improvements enable
people to produce more goods with the same effort, and they
get more money. But in most services (barbers, waiters) it is
difficult to improve productivity through new technology. Yet,
their workers legitimately expect rising wages, as does everyone else. Since they are not producing more, the price of their
product must go up at a rate higher than other prices. This is
precisely what is happening in urban transit, where increases
in productivity are often difficult to achieve—it is impossible
to have less than one driver per bus and impossible (with most
existing subway cars) to have fewer than two men on a subway train.

Meanwhile the wages of hourly rated transit employees in
New York City have gone from 93 cents an hour in 1946 to
$4.77 an hour in 1972, or more than five times. (Pensions
and other fringe benefits add about a third more to the 1972
wage level.) Altogether, the Transit Authority now spends
about 86 percent of its budget on labor and only 14 percent
on power, fuel, materials, liability, and miscellaneous items.

The question becomes: How can the costs be kept down?
And what about automation? It should be pointed out that
the Transit Authority has tried to keep costs down—by saving
on maintenance, by closing change booths, by providing less
off-peak service—and such savings are precisely the ones that
provoke public displeasure. Should public desires in these
areas be satisfied, the costs would go up.

As for automation, it seems to have little application to buses
(except perhaps in the field of maintenance). Economies in
bus operation are possible, but again public acceptance may
be questionable. Many bus routes of the Transit Authority are
very long (10 miles or longer), while their heavily used por-
tions are short (the average bus trip being about 2.5 miles in
the city). Also, many bus routes duplicate subway lines. On
the long routes, buses usually run empty near the end of the
line, while they are crowded in the middle of the line. Now,
if long bus routes were broken up into several short ones,
fewer buses would be assigned to the sparsely used stretches.
Long-distance riders could switch to the subway. Some small
cost savings would result.

On the subway there are two possibilities for automation,

one immediate, the other long-range. An immediate possibility
is to dispense with change clerks and install automatic token-
vending machines. Unmanned stations are operating on the
new Lindenwold rapid transit line from Philadelphia to southern New Jersey, and the Port Authority is introducing them
on its PATH system. In New York City, however, objections
would come from many riders who feel that it is good to have
stations attended for purposes of getting information and for
safety. These purposes could be served by television and telephone, but there is a feeling that life is already too mechanized
and that it is worth extra money to have real people in the
stations. Furthermore, there is a lot of unemployment around
and many wonder what benefit it would bring to throw 4,000
change clerks out of work.

Converting to unattended stations could probably save only
about 7 percent of the subway operating costs.

The longer-range possibility is to have the motorman control the doors and have no conductor on the train. This will
be possible when new cars, from which the motorman can
see both sides of the train, arrive in sufficient number. Since
a complete changeover of rolling stock takes about 30 years,
some conductors will have to be on subway trains for a long
time in any case. Automatic train operation, in which train
speed is regulated by computer and the motorman only goes
for a ride, does not in itself reduce labor requirements, beyond
eliminating a conductor, since one attendant is kept on the
train even on completely automated systems.

What savings are possible with automation? The first fully
automated transit line in the United States is the Lindenwold
line, mentioned earlier. One crude way to measure its productivity is to see how many passenger-miles daily it produces
per employee (a passenger-mile is one passenger carried one
mile). It should be stressed that the measure may not always
be fair because transit systems vary in their complexity, in
their age (which pushes up costs), and in the kinds of services
they have to pay for—e.g., some pay for policing, others don't.
In any case, the simple, rather small (14 miles), new, and
fully automated Lindenwold line is able to produce about
2,000 passenger-miles for every employee. The figure for the
New York City subways is about 1,000; one should add that
as recently as 1969 it was about 1,200, but since that time
new personnel have been added (for station upkeep among
other things, increasing personnel by 8 percent), yet passengers have declined—so the net effect is an apparent drop
in productivity. The index of passenger-miles per employee is

substantially lower for the commuter railroads (it is about 750 on the Long Island Railroad), and it is lower still on the bus lines (about 380 generally) since bus lines are inherently more labor-intensive. What this all amounts to is that savings from reduced labor requirements can primarily be effected on the suburban railroads, which still carry at least four men per train and where one motorman per train would be sufficient on electrified lines operating new equipment and having automatic fare collection. The Lindenwold experience suggests that labor costs on suburban railroads could be cut *roughly in half*. Experiments with automatic fare collection were successful on the Long Island Railroad but were given up because of objections from labor.

In sum then, a close look indicates that the possibilities for cutting operating costs on buses and subways are marginal at best, and that we are locked into spiraling costs. There are only two ways to cover them; raising the fare, or raising operating subsidies (or doing some of both). This calls first for a review of the present fare structure.

In many ways a flat fare as practiced on buses and subways in New York City is inequitable and inefficient. Why should a person going from Times Square to Grand Central, a distance of less than a mile, pay the same as a person going to Manhattan from Jamaica or Coney Island, a distance of 14 miles? The fare now averages 5 cents a mile—the same as an airplane ticket. Should not the one-mile trip be 5 cents and the 14-mile trip 70 cents? Why should those living at the end of the line be subsidized by those living nearer the center of the city? The subways, so the argument goes, would develop a lot of short-haul business if short trips were not overpriced.

Similarly with regard to time of day: off-peak, trains are running with many empty seats. No extra costs would be involved in carrying additional passengers. Therefore, the fare off-peak could be lower. But during the peak hours, every extra passenger costs a lot of money. Most of the trains have to be kept just to provide service during a few hours of a day, and they stand ready but idle the rest of the day and on weekends. That is a major reason why transit systems are losing money. So should not rush-hour passengers pay the extra costs they are causing? If they were charged more, there would be fewer of them and congestion would be relieved. Off-peak activities would be encouraged, because travel would be cheaper; it could even be free during the night, when demand is low.

The ideal fare may be one graduated both by distance and

by time of day. A zoned fare (without differences by time of day) has always been in effect in London, and has been introduced to the United States on the new Lindenwold and San Francisco transit lines. However, converting the New York City transit system to complex electronic fare collection varied by time and distance would not be an easy job.

On the suburban railroads, even though the fares are somewhat more responsive to distance of trip, the short-distance rider likewise subsidizes the long-distance rider. On the Long Island, the commuter traveling an average distance (20 to 25 miles) pays 5.4 cents a mile; the commuter going only 10 miles pays 9 cents a mile, one going 50 miles pays only 3 cents a mile. Also, the reverse commuter, who is not causing the railroad any extra cost (a lot of seats are running empty in reverse direction during peak hours) is not given any discount. This contributes to keeping some suburban factory jobs out of reach of city residents.

Charging each rider according to the cost of the service he personally uses guides us toward spending money only for services that people really value. But we also must be concerned about how they fall on different people with different incomes. With a 35-cent fare, the average New York City subway rider pays about 2 percent of his annual income to travel to work, slightly less than the 2.5 percent the average suburban commuter pays on the railroad. However, for the low-income worker earning the New York State minimum wage, the cost of going to work on the subway or bus amounts to 5 percent of his wages. And when he has to pay a double fare, going to work takes away 10 percent of his wages. For comparison, let's hear from the suburban commuter with a $20,000 a year income on being told he'd have to pay $165 a month for his commuter ticket.

There are two kinds of double fares in New York City: among different bus routes and between buses and subways. Free transfers from one bus route to another are very haphazard. There are none in the Bronx, a few in Manhattan, more in Queens, quite a few in Brooklyn. Since bus trips are so short, paying a double fare for a two- or three-mile trip is a true hardship.

The other kind of double fare is paid if one takes the bus to the subway. With few exceptions (where former transit lines were replaced by buses), there are no free transfers if one makes that change. This kind of a double fare is less odious, for two reasons. One, most of the poor areas are located close to subway lines; most of those who have to take a bus to the subway are not poor. Second, most of the double-fare zone is near the outer end of the subway line, so people who live there are making a longer than average trip by subway; requiring them to pay a double fare is similar to requiring them to pay more because their trip is long and costs more.

Eliminating the double fare among buses only and having uniformly free transfers would cost about $60 million a year or would raise the bus fare from 35 to 42 cents. Eliminating all double fares would raise all transit fares in New York City from 35 cents to more than 40 cents, or would cost about $130 million a year in subsidy.

In sum, there is plenty of room for reforming the public transit fares in the Region, particularly in New York City. But, while some of the reforms might reduce the need for subsidies somewhat, others would actually require more subsidy (i.e., eliminating double bus fares without a general fare increase). So, the need for supplementing revenue from fares with outside subsidies remains—unless we are ready to let transit price itself off the market, to become an exclusive system for the well-to-do. We will proceed to look at the question: How much subsidy?

There are those who advocate full subsidy, who say that public transit in cities should be free. Bronx Borough President Robert Abrams is one of them. He says: "In New York Governor Dewey established the doctrine that mass transit has to be self-sustaining and that theory I think was wrong, inequitable, immoral. It said that only the person who used it had to pay and the assumption was that he or she was the only person who got the benefit from mass transit, and that's not true." Employers, retailers, landowners, the public at large benefit from the access provided by mass transit. "Mass transportation is a basic service that can be provided by government out of general tax resources. We have clear examples of how services today are provided out of the general tax base. For example we have police, fire, sanitation provided without specific user charge. We have free public education. Now we know it is not free in the literal sense—it costs a lot of money to build schools, to pay the salaries of teachers. But we offer it without specific user charges because we believe this is something that all people should have access to. And we have come to the point where public transportation should be one such service."

Economists point out that financing out of general tax resources is appropriate to what are known as "public goods," such as police protection, street lighting, or the provision of open space, where the direct beneficiary is hard to pinpoint, and where one person's enjoyment of the benefits in no way denies these benefits to others. In this view, public transportation has some characteristics of a "public good," and hence deserves some subsidy, but not a complete subsidy. Dr. Dick Netzer, dean of the NYU Graduate School of Public Administration, says: "I think that transportation is quite different from many of the services traditionally provided without user charges. Transportation is not an end in itself. We do not want people to use more transportation pure and simple. We do want people to use more schooling pure and simple—really true. We want the children to stay to graduate. We want as many as possible to go through higher education. That's a wholly different kind of thing from transportation. We want to be mobile and to have jobs and houses and things accessible but we don't want people to use as much transportation as possible. That is basically the same argument as having user charges for electricity or telephone service or water service, namely, that you don't really want people to waste them."

There is no question but that abolishing fares on subways and buses would greatly increase ridership: Atlanta and other cities which have drastically cut transit fares (without abolishing them altogether) have all experienced large increases in patronage. While bus service can be expanded to carry more passengers at a relatively low cost, what about our overcrowded subways? Thus, while we may come to free transit eventually, such a scheme would cause difficulties immediately.

Moreover, calculations show that abolishing public transit fares would not cut auto use appreciably. The calculations were done in great detail for Boston (Thomas Domencich, Gerald Kraft, *Free Transit*), but would be even more true in the New York Region. The added riders would largely be new riders, or "induced traffic," those who do not travel now, rather than motorists.

Providing free public transportation for all cities in the United States would cost about $2 billion a year, at present prices. While this is less than half the amount spent on farm subsidies, the question is raised whether this kind of money would not be better spent on transit improvements. It could provide new lines, faster service, more frequent service, better maintenance, better equipment, and in general a new and competent kind of urban transit. Dribbled out in operating subsidies, such money would only perpetuate present conditions. So the argument goes.

Last comes the objection that as a means of transferring money to the poor, free transit is a very ineffective instrument. Most transit riders are not poor; in New York City they have an average income close to $10,000. If the objective is to help the poor, why not give them the money directly?

Over the past decade, the Region has been pursuing a middle course between making transit pay its own way from the fare box and making transit fully subsidized. The three states, the City of New York, other municipalities, and the federal government have all contributed to what were, in effect, operating subsidies in the past. What is different about the future is that the amount of subsidy needed is going to rise spectacularly. All the bus systems, subways, and commuter railroads in the Region received roughly $230 million in operating subsidies in 1970. The Yunich Commission on financing mass transportation, appointed by the governors of the three states, suggests that if inflation continues at a rate of 4 percent a year the deficit of all of these transit operations will rise to $530 million in 1975, $1 billion in 1980, and $1.9 billion in 1985. This kind of money will have to be scratched up each year merely to keep trains and buses going at their present level on present fares. The needs for new construction are separate —estimated at about $7 billion over the next 13 years.

CHOICE THREE: Should fares on public transportation be subsidized? (Check one.)
A. Just enough to keep up with the cost of living
B. Enough to reduce them
C. Enough to have free transit
D. Not at all

Who Should Pay for Fare Subsidies?

If it is decided that fares should either be free or subsidized, the question then is where the money should be coming from.

One source often mentioned is taxes on the automobile. Over the past 25 years costs of transit operation have increased about three times faster than the cost of living index, but automobile costs have increased at a much slower rate. The average price of a new car has just about kept pace with the cost of living. The retail price of gasoline has gone up slower than that; relatively speaking, gasoline is now cheaper than it was 25 years ago.

Auto taxes in the United States are low, and they declined

further after the repeal of the federal excise tax on new cars in 1971: they were 11.4 percent of all auto costs before and are 9.7 percent of all auto costs now. And some highway tolls have not gone up at all, which means, in the context of inflation, that they have become twice as cheap. Instead of a $1 two-way toll on Trans-Hudson facilities, the Port Authority would have to be charging a toll of $2.20 had it kept up with inflation, and a toll of $7 had it kept up with transit fares. One of the reasons why the auto is so attractive is that, relatively, it is getting cheaper. So, the argument goes, since this is to some extent what is pulling the rug from under transit, why not equalize the situation by imposing higher charges on the auto? The contrary argument is that the auto is more efficient in our kind of society, so why penalize it for this efficiency?

Another argument for automobile taxes to subsidize the common carrier is more direct, namely, that in places where auto and transit systems run side-by-side, such as New York City or inner New Jersey, raising highway tolls would cause some people to switch to transit and thereby free up the highways, benefiting the remaining motorists. In other words, the justification is the very high cost of providing added highways to crowded areas, compared to providing transit.

Figure 4 shows the daily profile—hour-by-hour—of traffic in and out of the Manhattan central business district. Indicated in black at the bottom are trips by auto, and shaded above are trips by transit. It is evident that auto use is fairly even for most of the day, from 7 A.M. to midnight, with only small bumps in the rush hours, while transit use peaks tremendously during two rush hours and is rather sparse for most of the rest of the day. If the auto were to handle the entire peak-hour load, streets and highways into the central business district would have to be widened more than *five times*. Clearly, that would be impossibly expensive and self-defeating: the entire surface of Manhattan would be barely sufficient to accommodate all that pavement. Moreover, it would be largely unused for most of the day, except for the rush hours. Transit, however, must live with such an inefficiency today—most of the plant is maintained all day for use during a rather short period. Which is one reason transit is losing money. Now, if the high peaks are required by the pattern of life in our society, why should only transit riders pay for them? Why not all travelers?

Finally, a related argument is that in recent years, more than half the federal tax dollars paid by motorists in the Tri-State Region were not used to build new highways in the Region, but rather to build highways in other parts of the coun-

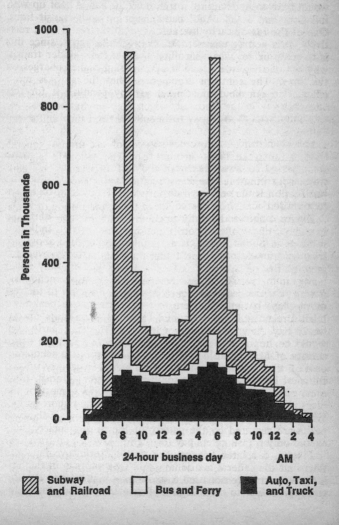

Figure 4

ENTRIES AND EXITS, THE MANHATTAN CENTRAL BUSINESS DISTRICT, TYPICAL BUSINESS DAY IN 1965

Subway and Railroad

Bus and Ferry

Auto, Taxi, and Truck

Persons in Thousands

24-hour business day

AM

try. In effect, because opportunities for new highway construction in the Region are limited, and because federal highway taxes have been earmarked for the Highway Trust Fund, we have been paying for highway construction in rural areas, instead of spending the money on our own transportation needs. Is that a reasonable arrangement? Should not each large urban region be deciding, on its own, how best to invest its transportation taxes? And spend them on public transit, if it cannot spend them on highways?

Of course, proponents of the automobile can reverse this argument and say, Of what possible use to motorists in outer counties of the Region like Sussex or Sullivan (with no rail and few buses) is it to pay for new trains on the Canarsie line BMT? Perhaps they would much rather pay for an unnecessary highway in the Midwest, which they might use once on a vacation trip, than to pay for a subway train they will never use?

This then brings us to other sources of tax funds—general taxes, rather than taxes on motorists. The rationale is, first, that just as highway taxes should not necessarily be earmarked for highways, so transportation taxes should not necessarily be earmarked for transportation. If we want political freedom to decide how best to spend taxes, the raising of taxes should be separated from the spending of them. The rationale is, second, that if the smooth functioning of urban areas, and hence good public transit, is a "public good" to some extent, the public should pay for it, rather than one class of citizen— the motorist.

Assuming that is the case (or perhaps assuming that is to *some extent* the case), the question is only, general taxes collected over what area?

Until recently, municipalities in the Region—ranging from the City of New York to the City of Norwalk—have themselves coughed up the money to subsidize fares on local transit lines. (One of the oldest subsidized operations is the Staten Island Ferry, which costs $1.20 for a round trip, but charges a fare of only 10 cents.) The Port Authority has been subsidizing PATH, and the states, starting with the State of New Jersey, have been covering deficits of rail lines which threatened abandonment. Lately, New Jersey began supporting local bus lines, and counties have gone into local bus operations: Mercer County and Nassau County are examples. In all of these cases, the immediate area primarily served by the system needing subsidies has come up with the first subsidies.

There are two reasons this arrangement may not be able to last long. One is, municipal and county lines frequently bear no relation at all to the service areas of transit systems. The other is, the municipalities may simply lack the resources. Can Newark pay for a bus system that in large part serves suburban commuters to its downtown?

So, the next logical step would be for the Region as a whole to collect the tax. But we have no regional government; each of the three states in the Region, in effect, plays the role of regional government. Hence the argument that the primary responsibility for subsidizing public transportation should be at the state level. Now it is possible to set up within the state transportation districts or regional agencies to which the state gives various financial powers. It is possible (as has been proposed in New York State) to have a number of districts, with a separate transit tax in each, supplementing the state income tax. But the state has to set up such an arrangement.

Of course, taxes are odious, and an arrangement like that is likely to run into political conflicts between those parts of the state where transit needs are large, and those where they are small. Besides, the states of New Jersey and New York (but not Connecticut as of this writing) are already contributing toward covering local transit operating deficits. But the federal government is not. So, should not the federal government chip in, not only with monies for planning and construction, but also with monies for operating and maintenance costs? Another argument for primarily federal subsidies is that federal taxes are most progressive—fall most heavily on the well-to-do, whereas state taxes are more regressive. In the end, probably all levels of government will have to contribute, so our Choice Four is not phrased as an either/or proposition, but rather in terms of who should pay most, some, or not at all.

CHOICE FOUR: If public transportation is subsidized, who should pay the cost?

	MOST	SOME	NONE
A. The motorist			
B. The municipality or county			
C. The state and/or region			
D. The federal government			

Improving Transit Service: What to Build?

So far we have considered mainly the needs for operating public transit. More money for operating transit can result in numerous improvements which are wanted by the public but precluded by tight budgets: more frequent schedules, better maintenance of stations, more convenient transfers, and so on. More fundamental improvements and an expansion of transit (as opposed to merely holding its own) will, of course, require new construction.

The current program of building new subway lines in New York City was approved by the city and the state in 1968, and is now under way. Its priority elements are three: (1) a new tunnel from Manhattan under 63rd Street to Queens, with a high-speed bypass track to relieve the overcrowded Queens Boulevard subway; (2) a subway under Second Avenue from downtown Manhattan to Harlem and into the northeast Bronx, to relieve the overcrowded Lexington Avenue line and provide faster travel from parts of the Bronx; and (3) a spur to southeast Queens, connecting to the Jamaica railroad station and the center of Jamaica, replacing about two miles of the Jamaica Elevated line. The cost of these projects is estimated at about $1.5 billion. They will be completed, if all goes well, around 1980. Several additional lines in Brooklyn, Queens, and the Bronx are also planned. On the New Jersey side there are active plans for extending PATH to Newark Airport and from there southwest, as well as building new connections to Pennsylvania Station in Manhattan, which would allow direct service by Jersey Central and Erie-Lackawanna trains.

While the subway construction program for New York City and for some rail improvements in New Jersey is pretty well committed for the rest of this decade, what happens after that is open to choice. That choice has to be made soon, because the lead-time in transit construction is so long. What do we do next, after the Second Avenue subway (55 years after it was first planned!) and the 63rd Street tunnel are built, and Jersey trains from several directions run into Penn Station?

Transit improvements might be concentrated in any of four rings of development in the Region, and it is unlikely that money will be available to emphasize all four. Which ring of the Region is chosen for early rapid transit and railroad improvement will shape development in important ways.

First, one plausible next stage of transit investment would be not to add any new subway lines, and not to extend present ones, but rather to rebuild the existing chambers of horror or correct environmental deficiencies—whichever words one prefers. That is, put emphasis not on serving new areas of New York City but on rebuilding stations on existing subways and removing as many as possible of the 70 or so remaining miles of elevated lines, which blight the city's environment. While it it is neither desirable nor realistic to replace each elevated line with a subway mile-for-mile, by locating new subways between the elevated lines to be torn down, the same areas can be served, mostly in Brooklyn and the Bronx, so that most elevated lines can be removed. Stations can be rebuilt to provide more comfortable and wider stairways, to have openings to daylight and street life, to have open sunken courts with access to adjacent buildings, to have stairways off-sidewalk so they do not interfere with street circulation. Stations at important locations can be air-conditioned in summer. Hand-in-hand with such a program of rebuilding the existing system could go accelerated replacement of old equipment—for example, faster introduction of air-conditioned cars. At the present rate of replacement (about 200 new cars each year), it will take 36 years before all cars on the subway system are renewed.

This could trigger a general renewal of the inner parts of New York City, making it a much more attractive place to live for people of all income groups, so that many of those who work in the Manhattan and Brooklyn central business districts would live closer to their work.

A related emphasis is on circulation within Manhattan: providing moving sidewalks or other "people-mover" devices to replace, for example, the 42nd Street Shuttle, providing subway access to the West Side, building other crosstown "people-movers" near 48th Street, linking Penn Station and Grand Central, and providing another crosstown "people-mover" in downtown Manhattan near Fulton Street. These kinds of projects are expensive, but because the number of people they serve is so high (10 million trips on foot are made daily in the central business district) they can be well worth while.

However, an articulate pressure, coming from peripheral parts of New York City, is to keep extending subway lines into these outer areas, where people now have to depend on buses to get to the subway. The northern Bronx, eastern Queens, and southeastern Brooklyn are examples. These areas are generally more than 10 miles from Manhattan, and are built up to a large extent with one- and two-family houses. Subway extensions will encourage redevelopment to apartments. However, unless the extensions are part of a new trunkline to Manhattan, the travel times to these areas will remain slow. Moreover, as one gets farther out, subway lines, which are like spokes of a wheel, become farther and farther apart, meaning that many people will remain in a "double fare" zone, i.e., will still have to take the bus to the subway. Per-passenger cost of many of these extensions on the periphery of the city is very high because of the limited passenger load: for example, the proposed Utica and Nostrand Avenue extensions in Brooklyn would cost anywhere from $16,000 to $23,000 per daily rider, whereas the Second Avenue subway is estimated to cost only $3,300 per daily rider.

This second set of transit improvements would result in higher densities—more high-rise apartments, probably—along the extended subway lines. Generally, it would spread more people outward from the closer-in neighborhoods. While express buses could be a much more efficient way to serve these areas in general, there are some legitimate needs here, which can be accommodated at relatively low cost on existing rights-of-way, such as service to Co-Op City, or to Rego Park, or to Canarsie on the Bay Ridge railroad right-of-way. Some such routes could be coordinated with the program of removing elevated lines.

With regard to suburban railroads, we have a similar choice: interconnect and expand them at the center, or spread them further out. Thus, a possible third set of improvements is to build up close-in suburban rail service—for example, converting several little-used railroad lines to inner New Jersey (i.e., the West Shore and Susquehanna lines) to rapid transit operation similar to the Lindenwold line. Such suburban transit service would not have to dead-end in Manhattan as current plans of the MTA and the Port Authority propose, but could run through, say, from Mineola or Port Washington, under Manhattan (with a couple of stops there), to, say, Paterson, or to Rockland County. This way, trips from suburb to suburb would become possible by train, and Manhattan would no longer be a barrier to east-west travel in the Region. Combined with these additions to rail transit in the inner ring of suburbs around New York City and Newark might be higher frequency and speed of service on existing rail lines into Manhattan from close-in suburbs.

By putting money into improvements in the inner ring of suburbs, the spread of population outward would be somewhat slowed, new areas in the older suburban counties probably would be open to apartments, particularly along the new rail transit lines, and close-in urban centers surrounding Manhattan–Newark, downtown Brooklyn, Jamaica, Paterson, Passaic, Hackensack, White Plains, and Stamford almost certainly would be strengthened as business hubs and suitable locations for apartments.

Finally, the fourth option is extending electrification and high-speed rail service as far as possible into the hinterland.

Electric commuter service now generally does not go beyond 40 miles (except to Trenton and New Haven); it could be pushed to 60 miles or more. Then the development of such areas as eastern Suffolk County, northern Fairfield, Orange, and Dutchess in New York, and Warren, Hunterdon, Monmouth, and Ocean counties in New Jersey would be accelerated. This long-distance service would come into dead-end terminals in Manhattan such as Grand Central, and the proposed terminals on 3rd Avenue and on 8th Avenue near 48th Street.

This would enlarge Manhattan workers' choice of where to live, which might somewhat take the pressure off housing prices closer to the center, offering wider urban opportunities to these areas, and possibly strengthen the office industry in Manhattan (which, however, all of the earlier options would also do).

CHOICE FIVE: What new rail construction should get next priority?

	FIRST PRIORITY	SECOND PRIORITY	LAST PRIORITY
Ⓐ Rebuild existing subways			
B. Extend existing subways			
C. Link up suburban railroads at the center			
D. Extend suburban railroads into outer areas			

Part C: Policies Concerning the Auto

To Walk in Dignity, or Taking Care of Pedestrians

A policy of building higher on less land, which we have discussed in the beginning, would tend to reduce the growth of auto travel in the long run and would create a market for public transportation. But, while building to higher densities would tend to slow the growth in the *total amount of travel* in the Region, the *concentration* of travel by auto in particular high-density places is likely to get worse unless some controls are adopted.

Thus, federal emission standards for automobiles, proposed

for 1976, will not become fully effective in less than a decade, because it will take that long for all the old cars, not equipped with the pollution control devices, to get off the roads. In the meantime, if strict federal ambient air quality standards are enforced, reductions in auto and taxi travel in Manhattan and perhaps some other downtowns of the Region may become necessary just to comply with the federal standards for clean air.

Even independently of air pollution standards, the idea has been gaining popularity that we should design some refuges from the automobile where people would not have to be exposed to noise and the danger of accidents and could enjoy that basic mode of transportation, walking. If the auto can have its limited-access expressways, where by law none but motor vehicles can travel, why should there not be limited-access pedestrian environments?

The conflict between pedestrians and vehicles, the problem of sheer pedestrian congestion, is nowhere worse than in downtown areas. Pedestrians do need room to feel comfortable, so that they don't bump into others, so that they can freely choose the speed at which they go, so that they can pass other pedestrians or walk in a different direction, so that they can walk in a group and talk to each other. Studies done by Regional Plan Association suggest that to feel comfortable on an outdoor walkway a pedestrian needs roughly 130 square feet of room around himself (20 times less than an auto); to give a sense of activity on busy shopping streets, this space can be cut in half, but preferably no lower.

In an existing downtown, additional room for pedestrians can be created in many ways: by setting buildings back farther from the building line and making sidewalks wider; by building arcades through buildings; by building pedestrian bridges above ground or pedestrian mezzanines underground. Unfortunately, most of these methods have to await the replacement of existing buildings, which takes decades. Some are highly expensive. So, if added room for pedestrians is to be provided quickly, the roadway now used by vehicles is the obvious place to go: this is how the idea of the pedestrian mall emerged. Transforming a street into a mall not only creates instant pedestrian space; it also reduces conflicts between vehicles and pedestrians.

The main problem with the mall is that by shutting off vehicles you could be shutting off some of the very vehicles that bring pedestrians to the mall in the first place. So a careful analysis has to be made of alternative approaches to the mall and who benefits and who suffers. Such an analysis has been performed by Regional Plan Association with regard to Midtown Manhattan.

Briefly, the argument is as follows:

If one subtracts the space needed for trucks and buses, which do account for about one quarter of all vehicle traffic in Midtown, then the remaining space is about equally divided between sidewalks and that portion of the street pavement assignable to cars and taxis. Yet during 12 daytime hours pedestrians in Midtown produce twice as much travel as cars and taxis. During midday, they produce 3.8 times as much travel. If one compares people and vehicles at midday directly instead of measuring miles of travel, the contrast is even greater: *for every auto or taxi in mid-Manhattan there are 11 pedestrians.* This suggests that allocating more space for pedestrians on those avenues where congestion is worst is reasonable. Take Madison Avenue: closing it to motor vehicles (other than buses) would divert exactly 3 percent of all motor vehicle traffic in the central square mile of mid-Manhattan, involving, perhaps, 20,000 trips by individuals, while an estimated 200,000 pedestrian trips a day along the avenue would be benefited directly and another 600,000 on crosstown streets indirectly, because their crossing the avenue would have been made easier. An added benefit would be the attraction to the avenue of walking trips which, because of congested conditions, are now not made. The attraction of about 20,000 such pedestrian movements can be estimated. Generally, the experience of some 100 cities in Europe and North America does indicate that malls increase retail sales and improve business conditions, not merely enhance amenity and attractiveness.

Still, some attention should be given to that 3 percent of the vehicular traffic which will be diverted by closing the avenue to taxis, autos, and through trucks. Many former taxi passengers will undoubtedly switch to bus, since buses will move faster and be more convenient. Some auto trips will probably not be made; after all, about 40 percent of all private auto traffic in Manhattan is only moving *within* Manhattan and another 35 percent comes from the neighboring boroughs, which do have subway and bus service; only 25 percent comes from outside the city, and the persons constituting that traffic possibly have no reasonable alternative to driving.

It is highly unlikely the exigencies of business dictate that all of the traffic coming from within the city absolutely must go by car; much of the traffic is there because the street space is there; remove the street space, and the trips, rather than not being made at all (which is a fear often expressed), will simply be made by other means of travel.

Individual street or avenue closings, illustrated here on the example of Madison Avenue, are, of course, small steps, affecting a tiny fraction of vehicular traffic. More far-reaching proposals for creating vehicle-free pedestrian precincts have been made—for example, creating a large pedestrian island in Midtown Manhattan from Lexington Avenue all the way to Broadway, with only side streets open for delivery vehicles. Even more ambitious schemes have envisaged banning the private automobile from high-density places such as Manhattan.

On a moderate scale, proposals like that can be implemented in any high-density area which has good public transportation access or adequate garage space within walking range. However, any large-scale proposals will have to take into account the disruption of regionwide travel which they would cause and the harm to those who have no alternative to travel by auto. Thus, a large car-free precinct in Manhattan would undoubtedly require bypass expressways under and around the central business district, as well as some peripheral garages. While projects of this type may be desirable in the long run, they are very costly.

CHOICE SIX: Do you favor or oppose improving pedestrian amenities by:

A. Converting selected streets into pedestrian malls?
          FAVOR   OPPOSE   NO OPINION

B. Banning cars from entire precincts in cities?
          FAVOR   OPPOSE   NO OPINION

Managing Congestion

All of the measures enumerated above, whether building to higher densities or creating pedestrian islands or building many more public transit lines, can somewhat *slow the growth* of auto ownership and hence auto travel, but they will not stop it as long as income and population keep growing.

In the past decade, motor vehicle registrations in the 31-county region of New York, New Jersey, and Connecticut increased from 5.5 to 7.7 million. More motor vehicles than people were added to the Region. Compared to the previous two decades, 1940–60, the growth in motor vehicles per capita slowed somewhat in New York City but actually accelerated in the suburban counties. Our appetite for more cars is not abating, even though we now have one motor vehicle for every two people in the suburban counties and one for every 4.5 people in New York City. Most of these motor vehicles—some 90 percent—are passenger automobiles.

Autos are not bought to stand idle; each is driven on the average about 9,000 miles a year. To run up this mileage they need pavement. The supply of pavement on our local streets is pretty well fixed—it expands very slowly, mostly when new streets in subdivisions are added or an occasional road is widened. So we come to a crunch. Cars, growing in numbers very fast—doubling every 20 to 30 years, are pressing against a supply of street pavement which is increasing very slowly. This spells increasing congestion. What do we do about it?

One approach is to do nothing and rely on the fact that people's tolerance for losing time in traffic jams is limited. Stuck many times, they will either start avoiding that particular route, take public transit (if it exists and offers comparable travel time), or stop making the trip altogether. Traffic never really seems to grind to a halt because of congestion for any long period of time. Traffic moves at eight miles an hour in most of our downtowns—not just in Manhattan; apparently, if it gets any slower, people stop driving through downtown. And we do have examples of highways in the Region which reached their capacity some 35 years ago and whose traffic has not appreciably increased since: the West Side Highway or the Pulaski Skyway are examples. Of course, this passive approach—deliberately letting congestion reach its "natural" limit—is painful and frustrating. People have adjusted their habits and expectations to an assumption of ability to make certain trips. They have chosen jobs or houses or in-laws on this assumption, and now they will be finding that the trips on the basis of which they made their choices are getting more and more slow and difficult—that their range of choice is being narrowed. This goes contrary to the notion that the purpose of the urban region is to expand opportunity and choice. If one's choice is limited to the part of the Region close to one's place of residence and other parts of our huge region become inaccessible, there may be no point in living in a region as large as this to begin with. One may prefer to move to a smaller urban region where the choice may not be much more limited but where traffic frustrations are fewer. Thus "deliberate congestion" may be a growth-retarding device.

An improvement on "deliberate congestion" is "regulated queuing." Experiments are in progress to apply it to expressways, where it is known as "ramp metering." There's a traffic light at every on-ramp. If the speed of traffic on the expressway falls below some predetermined figure, such as 30 miles per hour, the lights turn red and cars at the ramps have to wait in line until there is room enough for them on the expressway. Instead of waiting in the jam on the expressway, you wait before you get on, at which point you have the option to use local streets.

Instead of increasing the time it takes to travel, which is what queuing does, we could increase the cost of travel. Travel can be discouraged with toll charges if these charges are sufficiently high, say, several dollars. The method of "congestion pricing" has been suggested many times and implemented on occasion. The simplest method is to install toll booths at critical locations and raise the toll during peak hours, so that those who value traveling at that particular time very highly pay a premium price, while those to whom traveling at 5 P.M. is not very important and who can wait until 6:30 do change their time of departure and pay less or even nothing at all (at night). A similar system could be implemented on summer weekends, when highways to recreation areas around the Region are heavily congested. The airlines use this control with their higher weekend and summer rates. A more sophisticated system of congestion pricing has been proposed. Each car would have a meter which would click at a different rate, depending on whether one was traveling on a road in high demand (such as the New York Thruway on a Sunday night) or on a sparsely used road; at the end of the month one would pay a bill for user charges, depending on what the meter showed. Highway display signs would indicate the current rate per mile. Electronic technology makes such devices feasible. How bad congestion would have to get before they become acceptable to people is another question.

Without necessarily going all-out for such a comprehensive system, the principle of congestion pricing does have attractive features. In essence, it views the balance between traffic and the space available for it as a balance between demand and supply. If it is difficult to expand the supply, the other option is to cut demand. And the classic economic way of cutting demand for a good is increasing its price.

Higher prices for travel during peak hours would encourage people to stagger their work hours, and generally their times of travel. Highways usually are crowded only on short periods during the week, primarily during the trip to work. If work periods were systematically staggered, more cars per 24 hours could flow along the same pavement. If work times were staggered over the week's seven days, even trip-to-play peak periods (now Friday evenings and Sunday nights) might be overcome.

The major criticism of congestion pricing is that it discriminates against the poor, particularly low-income workers whose car may be their only means to get to a job and who cannot choose when their shift starts and ends. To this, economists retort that the poor should be given money directly rather than indirectly, through subsidizing their transportation. We see again how interrelated urban problems are—eliminating poverty could be a prerequisite to one solution for congestion.

One must realize, however, that if congestion pricing is only applied selectively, and not as a universal principle, such arguments tend to become academic. Let's take an example. Say commuter tickets are no longer honored on the George Washington Bridge between 7 A.M. and 11 A.M., and the toll is raised to $2. This would hit suburbanites driving into New York City in the morning, and encourage them to use public transit. The low-income worker driving from the Bronx to a factory in New Jersey in the morning would go free, just as he does now, when there is no westbound toll. In the evening, coming back, when he pays the toll, peak-hour prices would no longer be in effect and he would pay the same amount as now. With devices like this, tolls can be tailored to the specific flows of traffic, if one takes the trouble to design them properly. Of course, there can be limitations—such as morning westbound traffic on the Bridge getting to a point where it also needs congestion pricing. Still, there is a difference between viewing tolls simply as devices for raising revenue, which is the traditional view, and looking at them as valves to regulate traffic flow.

CHOICE SEVEN: Should higher prices during peak hours and lower prices during off-hours be used to reduce travel congestion?

      YES   NO OPINION

How Much Further Expressway Construction, and Where?

A more traditional prescription for highway congestion has been, for decades: decentralize. Use the unused capacity of roads now in being on the outskirts of the Region. This pre-

scription has helped push us into the suburbs. The trouble
with it is, it works fine for the first fellow moving out. But
when others follow, the local roads, scaled to sparse demand,
quickly become overcrowded. It becomes clear that expressways are needed to catch up with the travel demand created
by the new development.

Before the current anti-highway revolt, for three and a half
decades, building more expressways was the ultimate answer
to auto congestion. In fact, the expressway (they call them
freeways in California) was invented in the Region; its early
predecessor was the Bronx River Parkway, opened in 1921, and
the first road to conform fully to modern freeway or expressway standards was the Meadowbrook Parkway on Long Island, opened to traffic by Robert Moses in October, 1934,
seven months before Hitler opened his first *Autobahn*. Until
1950, the Region had more expressways than the rest of North
America.

Today we have some 1,600 miles of expressways in the
Region. Though they represent less than 3 percent of all road
mileage, they carry almost 30 percent of all motor vehicle
traffic. They can do this because they are more efficient—they
have no grade crossings, no traffic lights, and no access from
abutting properties. Their purpose is to save time, reduce
accidents, reduce travel on parallel streets in their vicinity, and
enable longer trips by auto which would not be made if the
traffic had to meander through local streets. They do expand
our opportunities for travel; they do enable us to live farther
out and to use far more space around us. They provoke opposition because they disturb the natural environment, dis-
place houses, bring noise and fumes to an area, break up
neighborhoods, and—by making more travel possible—they
do create new traffic. They provoke opposition because too
many expressways in the past have been rather brutal in design
and appearance, even though we know how to build elegant
ones, if we spend some effort and money.

Balancing the pros and cons, how many expressways should
we build? Right now, we have about one mile of expressway
for each 5,000 motor vehicles in the Region. If we were to
decide that expressway construction should keep up with
motor vehicle registrations, which are closely related to motor
vehicle travel, we should have to add about 45 miles of
expressway each year. In the past five years we have, in fact,
been doing just that. This, however, *may not* keep driving
conditions at the present level; they may get worse. The reason
is that new expressways generate trips that otherwise would

not be made, generate what is called induced travel. One calculation—not confirmed by some other evidence—suggests that in the Region, about one third of the travel on expressways may have been created by the expressways themselves.

A case can be made not just for keeping up with traffic but providing more expressways, so that auto travel in the Region as a whole is made faster. This case is usually justified by what are known as benefit-cost studies. Such studies start by assuming how much time-savings are worth to people. This can be measured in different ways, for example by the time-savings people buy when they consciously choose faster toll roads in preference to slower toll-free roads. All indications are that people value the speed and directness of an expressway trip very highly—a figure of 6 cents per person (in 1972 prices) for every minute saved seems to fit behavior in the Region, suggesting an average value on time of $3.60 an hour. Of course, poor people, of necessity, value time less, and well-to-do people in a hurry value it more, but this seems a reasonable average.

Once a value of time is assumed, one can convert the anticipated time savings of a proposed expressway into dollars. One can add the anticipated dollars saved in accident costs and then compare these benefits to the costs of investment and future upkeep. If the benefits exceed the costs—for example, yield a better than 10 percent return on invested capital—the project can be considered advisable, according to this approach. With this kind of calculation *more than doubling* present expressway construction in the Region can be justified, even when some money allowance is made for environmental and community damages.

Actually, for any individual user the time savings resulting from greater expressway supply appear small. For example, *doubling* the expressway supply from 5 percent of all pavement to 10 percent of all pavement would increase the average speed of all travel roughly from 21 mph to 25 mph and save the average driver about 12 minutes a day. However, considering the number of cars in the Region, and assuming a time cost of $3.60 an hour for the driver plus half as much for the average half passenger, this would yield an annual benefit of $3 billion for the Region as a whole, which would in turn justify an immediate investment of some $25 billion, given a 10 percent rate of return. The figures given in this example are not anybody's recommendation but are merely presented to show how cost-benefit analysis works.

The question is: Would an average increase in auto speeds

from 21 mph to 25 mph really be worth some $25 billion in highway construction? Our own behavior on the highway indicates that it would. But two arguments may be raised against this approach. One is that we are willing to pay for speed as long as the highway is there but we may not have wanted the highway in the first place. The other is that we may have better things to do with our money than pay for saving time in highway travel. Some other investment may repay even greater benefits.

Rising opposition to new highways, the defeat of transportation bond issues in New York State and New Jersey, the approaching completion of the Interstate System, make it more than likely that expressway construction will fall behind the growth in automobiles in the Region, perhaps even grind to a halt in the near future. As a result, the degree of congestion which in the past was typical of highways aimed at Manhattan (such as the Long Island Expressway) will gradually spread to ring roads and bypass routes as well. This is already happening on such routes as the Cross-Bronx Expressway and parts of the Garden State Parkway.

While many of the people composing the traffic on the routes aimed at Manhattan do have the option of using public transportation but prefer congested driving because it is more convenient in particular cases, such an option is unrealistic for the bypass routes. The origins and destinations of this suburban traffic are so dispersed that no public transit line would find enough customers following the same path. In sum, if we keep auto registrations growing at the present rate, cutting down on expressway construction will mean seriously greater congestion in the built-up parts of the Region. In the outlying parts, where there is room for more traffic, cutting down expressway construction will have less serious consequences: it will simply mean that improvements in travel speed and in accident rates will be foregone because travel that would have moved on faster, safer expressways, if they existed, will plod on ordinary highways.

Since the very early 1960s the Port Authority has stated flatly that it would provide no expansion of trans-Hudson vehicular capacity into Manhattan, and in 1966 a regional policy decision was made *not* to build any new expressways where they would directly compete with public transit, particularly on routes leading into Manhattan from the east. The argument was very simple: in those days, it would have cost $22,000 in tunnel construction for a highway and its approaches to deliver an additional commuter to the Manhattan central business district (CBD) by auto; it would have cost only $1,400 in tunnel construction to deliver him there by subway or railroad. Costs have gone up since, but the relationship still holds. Another argument can be added: between 1927 and 1957, as new highway approaches to Manhattan were built, highway traffic rose to fill the available capacity of the entryways and of local streets; most of these added motorists who had been using railroads, subways, or streetcars. Since 1957, no new highway approaches have been built, and the growth of highway traffic into Manhattan has slowed down substantially.

The case against added highways *into* Manhattan seems settled. But what about auto travel within it, under it, and around it? What about travel through Brooklyn—a city of 2.6 million people (the nation's third largest, if it were not part of New York) with the least expressway access? What about travel through Hoboken and Jersey City? There may be ways to make some of these peripheral trips by transit, but fundamentally transit serves downtown travel, not the travel that has to go around the downtowns. Then, there are trucks. Because many people-trips in the core of the Region are taken off highways by public transit, the streets and highways have an unusually high proportion of trucks. In mid-Manhattan, more than 20 percent of all motor vehicle travel is by trucks, and they have to crawl, along with everything else, at eight miles an hour. Trucking delays, if drivers' wages are considered, do represent a real economic loss, which contributes to the out-movement of industries from New York City and to increasing blue-collar unemployment.

There are environmental considerations. More than 4,000 trucks a day are fighting their way across Midtown in the vicinity of 34th and 42nd streets only to go from New Jersey to Brooklyn or Queens and back. Both streets seem to be better suited to be pedestrian malls than interstate truck routes. Both streets could be closed to vehicles if a tunnel expressway under Midtown took care of through traffic. Similarly, the environment of Brooklyn and access to its industries too would be improved if some abandoned or little-used railroad right-of-way were used for truck-oriented expressways.

From a regionwide view, theoretically, the network of expressways should be closely meshed where development is dense and sparsely meshed where development is sparse. If a particular square mile has a high density of development and hence attracts many trips by trucks and autos (for example, the downtown of a Stamford, Paterson, or White Plains, or a piece of Brooklyn or Queens), an expressway should be near it, so that vehicles destined to that particular square mile do not waste too much time getting to it from the expressway on slow local streets. On the other hand, if density of development is low, local users going to that square mile will be few and the speeds on local roads will be good; so the expressway can be farther away, serving only the longer trips.

Calculations based on cost and time savings suggest that the closest reasonable distance between two expressways is about two miles. Even if development is very dense, as in parts of New York City, the saving derived from building expressways closer together than that wouldn't offset the high cost of relocation and construction in such an area. Also, the design of ramps and interchanges becomes inconvenient and complicated. This two-mile spacing has been pretty much reached in the Bronx, which could hardly take any more expressways, and in northern Queens. Brooklyn, by contrast, would need more expressways according to that rule, and so would Hudson County in New Jersey. In the compactly developed suburbs, desirable expressway spacing increases to about four miles, and in the sparsely peripheral counties of the Region, such as Orange or Dutchess, to more than 10 miles. Of course, in any one of these areas clusters of development should have closer spacing, areas where development is not to be encouraged sparser spacing.

In reality, our existing expressway system, because of past history (availability of right-of-ways, fights over location, shortages of money, timing of development), is not too well related to development density. In some areas several expressways run right alongside each other without serving any development cluster. The virtually adjacent locations of the Long Island Expressway and the Northern State Parkway in Nassau County and the New York Thruway, Sprain Brook, and Saw Mill parkways in Westchester are examples of bunching too much expressway in loosely developed areas while nearby clusters of development, such as Hempstead and White Plains, are not well served. Moreover, largely because of the poor relationship between land development and expressway supply, extravagant variations exist from county to county with regard to such things as proportion of travel on expressways, average travel speed, average accident rates, and average costs of driving. Generally, the northern counties of the Region within New York State have the best service, followed by Connecticut, Long Island, and New Jersey, in that order.

These discrepancies can be viewed as being inequitable. Some people do not get enough for their highway tax dollar, and some get too much. However, there is also the opposite view that inequalities in expressway service among otherwise similar parts of the Region are not a bad thing and contribute to preserving the character of particular areas. Thus, Bergen County might lose some of its character if it were bisected by one more expressway for the sake of equitable service and even spacing.

Curiously, political opposition to highways through built-up areas often has an effect exactly the opposite to what opponents intended—limiting highways and cutting down driving. If a planned expressway in a built-up area is strenuously opposed, the money is very often reallocated to a rural or semi-rural area, where fewer people live and the need is less but whcrc fewer people seem to object. In an open area, many more miles of highway can be built for the same price. Thus, opposition to a seven-mile interstate stretch near Elizabeth made possible the construction of 32 miles of what is called an interstate highway in Monmouth and Ocean counties. Similar examples can be cited for New York. New expressways through open, rural areas, of course, accelerate spread and scattered surburban development, totally dependent on the automobile. Thus, by reducing auto travel in one area slightly, auto travel in other areas is greatly inflated. We build expressways where none are needed, and we don't build them where the need is great.

One of the reasons for opposition to new highways in developed areas is the consequent need for relocating homes and businesses. Let us assume, for the sake of discussion now, that relocation payments are raised and procedures for relocation improved so that persons whose business or home must be taken are not hurt but they are paid and assisted sufficiently so they do not object.

CHOICE EIGHT: How many expressways should we build and where? (Check one in each column)

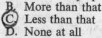

	√ IN BUILT-UP AREAS	IN OPEN AREAS
A. Just to keep up with additional cars		
B. More than that		
C Less than that		
D. None at all		

Part D: What Do We Want from New Technology?

Disenchanted with the ecological costs of the automobile, and with high labor costs of public transportation, many people pin their hopes on new transportation technology. Sunday supplement fashions—from monorails to hydrofoils to personal flying machines—fire the public's imagination but run into limits which are in the nature of the physical reality surrounding us. A monorail is inherently clumsier than a duorail, i.e., conventional train, for the same reason that a person who tries to walk on one leg is inherently clumsier than one who walks on two. Sure enough, a number of new systems have been built, and some of them can find specialized applications. But the kind of total revolution in mobility, such as was caused, in sequence, by the train, the auto, and the airplane, does not seem to be on the horizon for the near future.

However, government research into new possibilities for transportation is picking up speed, and ideas as well as experimental systems are proliferating. In fact the number of proposed new systems is getting to be so large, and issues involved in their evaluation are so complex, that it would be futile to display them to the reader or TV viewer with the question: Which do you like best?

Rather, a more relevant question for public debate is: Which kind of transportation job do you think needs more attention? After we know what objectives we want to achieve, what kind of urban living we want, then we can judge the various systems from the viewpoint of how well they are suited to do the job.

So, several different new technologies we mention here briefly are given purely as examples of doing particular kinds of transportation jobs. The jobs can be classified, very roughly, as fast service over long distances, fast service over intermediate distances, public transportation for smaller urban areas, and the improvement of private vehicles.

Discounting air travel, which is always likely to remain superior to ground travel for distances longer than about 300 miles (and perhaps even for shorter distances), fast service point-to-point can today be provided by rail. The Japanese New Tokaido line is capable of 160 mph top speed and has a normal running speed of 125 mph. Our own Metroliners between New York and Washington are capable of 150 mph top speed, but in fact average about 75 mph because the track is not sufficiently smooth and because of speed restrictions due to sharp curves, drawbridges, stations, and so on. Our new "Jersey Arrows" and "Metropolitans" on suburban railroads in New Jersey and New York are capable of 100 mph top speed, and could, with stations spaced five miles apart, achieve an average speed of 60 mph, again, *if* the track were rebuilt to high standards.

So far, we have not spent the money needed to rebuild the tracks to top-notch standards, and hence our gleaming new trains are performing far below what they are capable of. A barrier to upgrading the railroad tracks is not just the cost of rebuilding them but also the very labor-intensive matter of continued maintenance. The Japanese are employing large teams of workers on continuous night shifts keeping the tracks of the Tokaido line in perfect alignment.

It would seem that developing more maintenance-free tracks would be a reasonable research priority, but in fact our technologists have decided to go one step further and concentrate on a wheelless vehicle; the tracked air-cushion vehicle, or TACV. Their arguments against railroad wheels, apart from the fact that they shake up and misalign tracks, are that they cannot provide very fast acceleration and that they tend to be noisy at high speed.

The French have operated experimental tracked air-cushion vehicles since 1966. Development work is also going on in Britain, and the American urban tracked air-cushion vehicle (U-TACV) starts operation on a test track in Pueblo, Colorado, in 1973. It is the largest single experimental project of the Department of Transportation. What is the U-TACV and what will it do?

It is a car, seating 60 passengers, which rides on a cushion of air, supplied by on-board compressors, about one eighth inch off the ground. The pavement on which it rides has to be smooth, but because the air-cushion spreads the weight of the rather light vehicle, it does not shake or beat the pavement. Forward propulsion is supplied by a linear electric motor (LIM), which consists of magnets on board the car, and a large aluminum rail attached to the guideway pavement; the magnets and the rail interact much like the rotor and stator in a regular electric motor. The vehicle can achieve a top speed of 150 mph (though another one for 300 mph is planned) and accelerates at 3.2 feet per second,[2] comparable to an electric streetcar. Specifications are for a noise level that would not interfere with speech. To maintain a reasonable average speed, stations on the urban TACV must be no less than five miles apart, and 10 to 15 miles are preferred by the designers. Considering the shortness of the average urban trip, such a spacing can attract very few travelers.

It is evident that in a downtown-to-suburbs or city-to-airport situation, the U-TACV is not much different from a high-speed railroad in performance. It is somewhat faster, perhaps somewhat quieter, and needs a less expensive roadbed. But its disadvantages are serious. First, with 3,420 horsepower on board, the vehicle needs nearly *eight times* more electric energy per passenger than the Metroliner. Second, due to aerodynamic problems, it is not contemplated to run the vehicle in trains. Which means that the passenger capacity is only about 1,800 passengers per hour—comparable to an expressway lane, and about *one twentieth* of what is possible on a railroad. Third, and perhaps most serious, because of aerodynamic problems again, it is not possible to operate the vehicle at high speed in tunnels—it has to run at grade or on elevated structures. Thus, it will have difficulty entering built-up downtown areas. Its only contemplated application so far is to and from the Dallas–Fort Worth airport.

An approach quite opposite from TACV is Gravity Vacuum Transit, or GVT. It seeks to minimize environmental impact by operating underground, and to economize on energy needs in two ways: using the gravitational pull of the earth for more than half of its energy needs, and using, rather than fighting, atmospheric pressure for propulsion.

GVT in its urban configuration consists of trains, each seating, say, 1,600 passengers, which fit snugly into steel tubes; the tubes (a pair of them) are placed in an underground tunnel. Inside the tube, the trains are supported by specially designed wheels. The trains have no motors on board to propel them. Rather, they pick up speed by rolling downhill (the tunnel has a roller-coaster kind of profile) and lose speed by climbing uphill to the next station. Since this gravity action alone is not enough, the train gets an assist from air pressure: when the train is in a station, the tube in front of it is being evacuated (air is pumped out of it by electric compressors); when the train is ready to go, a valve opens and it is sucked into the near vacuum of the tube. It is pushed by atmospheric air from behind, until the closing of the valve behind it and the compression of some remaining air in front of it insure its proper stopping at the next station.

A most interesting aspect of GVT is that the passenger does not feel that part of the acceleration imparted to the train by gravity; therefore, the acceleration and hence total speed can substantially exceed those of *any* system that operates horizontally. With stations spaced one mile apart, the average speed (including station stops) is 45 to 57 mph compared to 30 mph with the best conventional trains; with stations five miles apart, 122 to 144 mph; top speed is 250 mph. The capacity is 38,000 passengers per hour, if no stations are spaced farther than five miles apart. The system is scaled to augment and partly replace older subways and elevated lines in the New York Region, as well as to provide service to airports of outlying centers, like TACV. It could whisk you from Staten Island to Wall Street (in a deep-rock tunnel under the bay) in four minutes, or from Co-Op City in the Bronx to Midtown Manhattan in 12 minutes, and open completely new horizons for the rebuilding of the older, inner parts of the New York Region. However, unlike TACV, GVT is not receiving any federal funding, and its development is currently inactive.

An active area of research and development, however, is personal rapid transit (PRT), which comprises a multitude of different systems, sometimes loosely called people-movers, or horizontal elevators. The notion here is to serve smaller cities and activity centers, which do not have the high concentrations of passengers needed to support conventional rapid transit. Small vehicles (seating, say, six passengers each) would be moving automatically on a grid of special guideways (at grade, elevated, through buildings, or underground, as needed). The speed would not have to be high (say 30 mph) because, ideally, each trip would be nonstop: upon entering the vehicle, one would push the button for the selected destination and be routed there without stopping for other passengers. Sophisticated electronic controls would insure that the vehicles can run very close together—much closer than automobiles can with manual operation. Such an ideal system, of course, is far off, because of the complexity of the controls needed, but a simpler experimental installation of small, automatically guided transit vehicles is operating on a university campus in Morgantown, W. Va. Its development and installation cost was high (more than $50 million a mile), and some calculations indicate that a comprehensive personal rapid transit system for an urban area would be substantially more expensive than an automobile system. However, short of replacing the automobile, simple automatic systems of small vehicles could fill a transit need in and near small- and medium-sized urban activity centers. A system of larger vehicles of this type is the Westinghouse "skybus," operating experimentally in Pittsburgh.

Lastly, a still different approach is, instead of starting with a personal transit vehicle which is trying to out-perform the auto, to start with the auto and to change its stripes. As we indicated earlier in this town meeting, electric propulsion for automobiles, which is likely to be needed eventually not just because of pollution but because of the limited supply of fossil fuels in our earth and the environmental cost of extracting them, runs up against the problem of batteries powerful enough to store up energy for a day's driving. Now, if the auto could also run on fixed automatic guideways, much like trains do now, two problems could be licked: (1) it could receive its power from a third rail, needing the battery only for short hops around one's neighborhood, and (2) automatic control would increase the capacity of a guideway lane far above what is possible today with manual operation on an expressway: that is, much more traffic could be accommodated on the same amount of pavement. This then suggests a "dual-mode" vehicle, which operates like an auto at each end of its journey, but runs on an automatic guideway most of the way. The so-called Starr-car, developed experimentally in the Boston area, is an example of a dual-mode vehicle.

Whichever of these research and development directions we choose to emphasize, new hardware won't change the fact that living close together is a prerequisite for public as against private transportation. A Stanford Research Institute study, *Future Urban Transportation Systems,* in 1968 put it this way: "the automobile has encouraged patterns of urban development and travel that cannot be satisfied by other available modes of transportation . . . the most serious challenge will be to design public transportation systems that are economical enough to accommodate the low volumes that are common in urban travel and will remain so . . ." If they really "remain so," the challenge may very well turn out to be impossible, and we should start thinking about changing our settlement pattern to fit a transportation system that will be more socially and ecologically responsible in the long run.

Admittedly, the evidence is anecdotal and unscientific, but most of those interviewed at random on the streets of Manhattan for the film accompanying this town meeting stated that walking would be their ideal mode of travel. And walking in a complex, interdependent society is only possible in high-density environments, be they patterned after historic cities or after the "arcologies" of Paolo Soleri. If a workable moving sidewalk (with an accelerating belt) is ever developed, it also will function only in high-density urban environments, environments that conserve natural resources and increase human face-to-face interaction.

CHOICE NINE: What should be the main objective of new transportation technology?

	MOST IMPORTANT	IMPORTANT	UNIMPORTANT
A. High-speed surface travel *between* urban centers			
B. High-speed underground travel *within* large urban areas			
C. Public transit for smaller cities			
D. New power and guidance systems for private vehicles			

III. TOWN MEETING ON THE ENVIRONMENT

At the core of the new situation is the interaction of increasing numbers of people, all using or seeking to make use of more energy and more materials, all tending to draw together in closer proximity in urban regions, all concentrating to a wholly new degree the by-products of their activities—their demands and consumption, their movements and noise, their wastes and effluents.

—*Barbara Ward and Rene Dubos,*
"Only One Earth" (1972).

Selecting the Issues

The environment is a word virtually as broad as the universe: chemicals in your food; the design of your chair; the climate control in your house or apartment; the purity of the air outside; the dirty water in the river—or in the ocean—several miles away; the balance between vegetation and water runoff; the food cycle of a river estuary or coastal wetlands; the preservation of historic buildings; the conservation of minerals in the earth's crust; the protection of animals threatened with extinction; the heat balance of the earth; cosmic—and manmade—radiation; the capacity of the earth to support human population, and perhaps even the littering of the solar system with wrecked or abandoned space vehicles, these are but a few examples of subjects that fit under the general heading "environment," as it concerns the designer or the conservationist, the scientist or the citizen.

Clearly, we cannot deal with all of them in this town meeting. We will have to select a few subjects that most directly affect the quality of the environment in the Urban Region, how fine a place it is, and raise some questions of who should pay for it.

The character—though not necessarily the quality—of a place is most obviously affected by how many people live there. So we will have to start by talking about population growth in the Region. What really messes a place of human habitation up is what we throw away. So, the management of wastes will have to be a major emphasis in our discussion. Nature, more or less unspoiled, remains the source of our biological sustenance, as well as the major link to our primordial environment. Therefore, the preservation of nature in the man-made Region, both for our own recreation activity, and for its own sake, will be our third point of emphasis. Obviously, many important things will be left out. But we had to leave important things out in the town meeting on housing (the quality of housing design), and on transportation (air travel and the airport issue, or exclusive bus lanes). Bear in mind that in these town meetings, we are not dealing with issues in a world or national perspective, but in the somewhat parochial perspective of one urban region. Our concern is broader than that of a block association, a neighborhood group, or a municipal society, but it is not as broad as that of a national or world organization.

It will be objected, as it has been, that a mainly cost- and region-conscious approach to environmental problems is fatally defective. It will be objected that sober scientists like the ones who were convened by the United Nations in solemn high conference at Stockholm in June, 1972, agree a global crisis is imminent; that something heroic must be done, preferably by yesterday at the latest; and that coolly anatomizing costs and benefits at a time like this is on the same idiotic level as asking whether we can really afford to survive.

The sincerity of the objection and the good faith of the objectors are granted. We are all of us citizens of the world. But it makes no sense to start preaching to the world, if our own backyard is messy. The issue before us right now is our own backyard.

We further have to face the objections of those who suspect the middle class of having conjured up the proposition that the physical environment is in trouble as a diversionary strategy. The conspiracy theory holds that, lest precious tax money and even more precious land surface be squandered on relieving the lot of persons who don't matter, the have-got middle class invented the ecological crisis to excuse the concentration of resources on gladdening the lives of the affluent in ways that mean little or nothing to the poor.

And it is a fact that in the Region, the quality of one's immediate physical environment is closely related to how much money one has. The "nice" (read better off) neighborhood will not only have more carefully manicured lawns, or the super will sweep the sidewalk more often, but it is also going to have, on the average (there are exceptions), cleaner air, and it's likely to be closer to trees and parks. What this says is that in designing programs to improve our physical environment we cannot be naïve; we have to ask the question, whose interests will be helped the most.

Everybody pays for the degradation of earth and air and water. "The citizen pays either as consumer or as taxpayer or as victim," say Barbara Ward and Rene Dubos in "Only One Earth," a report commissioned by the Secretary-General of the United Nations Conference on the Human Environment. "The political and economic problems raised by this inexorable and unavoidable price spring from the fact that different citizens are involved in the problem in quite different degrees," Miss Ward and Dr. Dubos continue. "The taxpayer may be out of reach of the major pollutions and have no direct incentive to clean them up. Yet poorer citizens can hardly welcome an increase in consumer prices for daily necessities even though they might be glad of cleaner air. The calculus of who shall pay for what improvements is *the* political issue . . ."

There is also a related issue, namely that if one has money, one can afford to be environmentally responsible, but one is also able to be more irresponsible than anyone else. A few powerboats or snowmobiles can wreck a fragile lake or mountain much sooner than hordes of swimmers or hikers. A wealthy society, which produces more, throws much more away, and it is thus no accident that the environmental movement started in the most developed, rather than in a less developed country. Spending money on the environment is a price that wealth has to pay for wealth, if it is not going to wreck the chances of survival for the descendants of today's rich and poor alike.

The two kinds of poverty—the acrid festering poverty of the indigent family, the vast inclusive poverty of a nation or indeed a world that is running out of pure air and clean water, out of natural resources and peace and quiet—the two kinds of poverty are but two frontal sectors of the same war.

And they involve us all.

The first question, before "Where do we want to go?" may as well be: "Where do we stand?"

Let's take stock.

A Stay Against Degradation

Some of the evidence is reassuring. Evidently when we try, no matter how unsystematically the effort is organized, we can indeed stop or reverse the environment's drift into degeneracy. Item: Consolidated Edison is increasingly substituting low-sulfur fuel for the stuff that used to account for much of the sulfur dioxide in our air. Item: the federal restrictions on automobile exhaust emissions are beginning to take hold. Item: New York City had 61 good days—days of clean, clear, utterly breathable air—in 1971 as against none, not one, in 1970. Air quality was acceptable 198 days as against 86, unsatisfactory 80 against 196, unhealthy only—only?—26 against 79.

The lower Hudson River and its tributaries are still open sewers, the Passaic a disaster area that will take a long time to redeem, yet they are being cleaned, and in response to the cleaning, fish that had been driven out of them years ago are coming back.

The pluses are modest, but they begin to add up. Within the past decade, open space—the amount of outdoor recreation land open and accessible to the public—has been increased by roughly one third in the Region.

We're trying, and it is beginning to show. But colossal problems remain; one of the most immediate ones is the problem of what to do with the garbage and rubbish we're generating at a rate much faster than population increase. Per capita, a ton a year and going up! Nowhere in the Region has a wholly satisfactory solution been devised or even proposed, and a reason for this stems from the fragmentation of our decision-making.

The decisions on abating air and water pollution have been made piecemeal, seldom with a clear picture of what we were buying with the $10 billion a year the nation is spending on it. The full cost and who would pay the cost have seldom been publicly explored. Nor have we looked very hard at whether it might be better to cut down on the wastes we are creating—faster every year—rather than increase spending to treat the wastes after we create them. At the same time, the many groups trying to prevent environmental damages by blocking new power plants and highways are not asking who would gain and who would lose if these projects are not built.

Open countryside is being invaded by houses and factories, highways and shopping centers at a fast rate. As of now, about 2,700 square miles out of 12,750 in the Region are urbanized. Each year, between 40 and 50 square miles are added to the built-up area.

The decisions to penetrate more open space for every added person in the Region have not been conscious ones. Each was a decision of separate municipalities on the advancing edges of urbanization, made when they tried to keep out school-children and raise the price of new housing—as discussed in the first town meeting—and when they set out to attract tax-profitable offices, factories, and shopping centers to string along their highways or be enthroned on broad campuses using ten times the land area that would have been needed in a moderate-sized downtown.

By reason of spreading housing, jobs, and services far more broadly on the landscape than ever before, everyone is forced to travel longer distances to get where he wants to go, and more and more trips can be made only by car—as we discussed in the town meeting on transportation. While the emission control devices mandated for motor vehicles after 1976 will cut down on pollution, they are likely to increase, rather than reduce, the consumption of fuel. Our fast-dwindling petroleum reserves will be further depleted.

Nor is higher energy consumption at low density related only to transportation. All kinds of energy requirements per capita, including heating fuel and electricity, rise as the density of settlement declines. We used to consider this immaterial when energy was cheap. It is still cheap, and getting relatively cheaper in dollars and cents. But we have learned now that that is not only the cost. Higher density urban environments are energy-conserving environments. Should that be one of our considerations in deciding how to build, and how much land to take?

Furthermore, while the overall rise in public recreation land in the past decade is dramatic, two of the places needing it most—New York City and Essex County (covering Newark) —gained only 8 percent and 17 percent, respectively.

To make considered decisions, let's look at the alternatives with the costs and benefits laid out. Many of our decisions will depend on national policy developments, but some can be made within the New York Urban Region now.

Part A: Slowing Population Growth in the Region

Why Concern About Population Growth?

The historic lesson—perhaps the most important lesson of the past 400 years of accelerating worldwide population growth—that we have begun to learn in the past decade is the rather simple one that growth cannot continue forever in a finite environment. In its 1967 report, *The Region's Growth*, Regional Plan Association stated: "Clearly, the current, unprecedented growth rate of 2 percent annually cannot continue for too long, for if it did, world population would multiply a thousandfold to 5,200 billion in 370 years [after 1990]. Such a population would settle the entire land surface of the earth, including mountains and polar icecaps, at the Manhattan density of 100,000 persons per square mile." The report continued: "Assuming modest reductions in the birthrate, the 1965 world population of 3.3 billion will nearly double to 6 billion in the year 2000 and triple to 10 billion before 2030. If one assumes, merely for purposes of illustration, that after 2000 the growth rate will start declining at the same pace it has been increasing in modern times, world population would begin leveling off at about 30 billion."

While an urban pattern accommodating 30 billion people, or ten times the present world population, can be fairly readily imagined (it would occupy one tenth of the habitable portion of the earth, with densities averaging 20,000 per square mile, typical of Queens, N.Y.), the technology and the resource base to accommodate so many people at a tolerable standard of living are much harder to visualize. In fact, given present technology and resources some scientists believe the earth to already be overpopulated. Biochemist H. R. Hulett of Stanford University estimates that "about a billion people is the maximum population supportable by the present agricultural and industrial system of the world at U.S. levels of affluence." With continued technological inventions, that maximum will rise, but the availability of food, of nonrenewable resources, of uncontaminated environment, and eventually of sheer space will impose harsh limits, and growth may well overshoot the carrying capacity of our planet—unless deliberately brought under control. In the words of the Club of Rome, "man is forced to take account of the limited dimensions of his planet and the ceilings to his presence and activity on it."

This is the world context of population growth.

The issue of growth, however, begins to look quite different if viewed from the perspective of the Urban Region in New York, New Jersey, and Connecticut.

First of all, the population of the Region is growing at a much slower rate than that of the world. We don't have to face a doubling of our population in 30 years, but rather an increase of 25 percent, if the birthrate stays at the present level: an increase from 20 to 25 million.

Second, assuming, again, that the birthrate stays at the level of 1972, the Region will attain a stationary population—of around 28 million—by the year 2020. Should the birthrate continue the steep decline that it has followed between 1957 and 1972, a stationary population of around 22 million would be reached as early as 1985. Unless we start having more babies than we are having now, zero natural population growth is coming in the Region and in the nation, and discussions of regulating growth in the interim pertain to detail, rather than to principle.

Third, probable ceilings on growth in the Region, imposed by technology and the immediate physical environment, are much higher than the realistically foreseeable amounts of growth. For example, one set of calculations by Regional Plan Association indicates that, theoretically, the total employment in the Manhattan central business district could triple—from 2 million to 6 million—and we could still provide much more pedestrian space and more pedestrian amenity in that area than is now available, as well as access by public transit at more comfortable standards. Now, the possibility of Manhattan tripling in the number of workers is most unrealistic; chances are it would grow *at most* by one fifth. For another example, if one third of the land in the Region that is now not urbanized were set aside for permanent open space (some 3,300 square miles of open space), and the remaining 6,700 square miles were developed at an average density of two families per acre (i.e., half-acre lots for everybody, on the average), some 13 million people could be added to the Region. Should trends and policies encouraging higher densities of settlement take hold, that number could easily go much higher. For a third example, the availability of water could pose constraints on growth in some parts of the Region, but only if we insist on raising our consumption rates and using existing systems of delivery. Do we really need 140 gallons of fresh mountain water or ground water per day now, and 170 in the future? Richard L. Meier has suggested that in a resource-conserving economy "the critical fresh water demand . . . can be reduced to 4–5 percent of the American level, if necessary, and still permit the city to operate efficiently."

In sum, we see that when we deal with the desirable growth rate and ultimate size of this Region, we are not dealing with the rigid limits that are facing the world as a whole. *Our* limits to growth are more a matter of values, since we are unlikely to exceed the growth limits imposed by the world.

Before we balance these values, let us look at some recent facts.

Recent Growth Trends

Population growth is the result of three factors: the birthrate, the death rate, and the migration in or out of an area. Of these, the death rate is the easiest to predict, short of truly catastrophic events. The migration rate fluctuates more, depending on changing economic conditions in an area. In-migration into the Region has been declining slowly, but steadily, and most estimates assume that it will dribble out by the end of this century. Even if such forecasts are off, they cannot be too far off. By far the most volatile and unpredictable, but also the most powerful factor is the birthrate. Changes in it have completely scrambled demographers' forecasts twice in the past 30 years. From the beginning of this century and earlier, until about 1936, the birthrate was following a long-term decline that continued through to the boom of the 20s and the bust of the Depression. Then in 1939 the birthrate turned upward and by 1957 reached a peak comparable to pre-World War I levels, contrary to everybody's predictions. The latter part of this was the famous baby boom. Then, before anybody heard much about ecology or the limits to growth on this planet, the birthrate took a sharp turn downward. Between 1957 and 1965 it dropped from 123 births per 1,000 females aged 15 to 44, to 100 births. The latter figure corresponds more or less to a three-child family, and the set of projections of the Region's growth made by Regional Plan in 1965 assumed a three-child family; it would have meant a population of 30 million in the Region by the year 2000, compared to 20 million now. However, in the intervening seven years the birthrate kept declining continuously (the figures quoted are nationwide), and by 1972 reached an all-time low of 75 births per 1,000 women of childbearing age. This represents roughly a two-child family and means that when those born today live out their lives the nation will have zero population growth—discounting in-migration.

Assuming that the birthrate stays roughly at the present level, the Region's population will be 25 million in the year 2000, not 30 million as it would have been with a three-child family. And, as we said, by about 2020, the Region's population could stabilize at about 28 million. But, in the light of past experience, such an assumption has to be compared to others. If the birthrate continues to decline at the same rate that it has between 1957 and 1972, then by 1985, there will be more deaths than births in the nation and in the Region, population will attain zero natural growth with a one-child family and the number of inhabitants in the Region will be 22 million. But conversely, in view of the rather wild fluctuations in childbearing and a possible "echo boom" to our earlier baby boom, the possibility of a resurgence, and of a large family coming back into vogue, should also be considered. That would result in a regional population of 28 million by the year 2000.

Which one of these futures will actually happen? That question will be decided by women entering the childbearing age between now and the end of the century. For purposes of planning, where it is sensible to err on the safe side, we have adopted the figure 25 million people in the Region by the year 2000 as a probable one (two-child family the rule), knowing full well that the possibility of anywhere between 22 million and 28 million is not excluded.

Figure 5

PROSPECTIVE POPULATION GROWTH 1970-2000

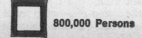

800,000 Persons

Now, 5 million people is still a lot. It could nearly mean wrapping another Los Angeles around the Region—almost repeating what we have done in the past 30 years. True, nearly a million of these people would be likely to settle in the far-out reaches of the Region—in Ocean County, in New Jersey counties along the Delaware River, at the foot of the Catskills, and in Litchfield County. But the other 4 million would likely fill the close-in suburban counties.

To give the reader a feel for what an increase of 5 million people would probably mean for parts of each of the three states in the Region, Table 3 compares the 1970 population to the amount of increase over the past 30 years, between 1940 and 1970, and to the projected increase between 1970 and 2000. Also, Figure 5 shows the location of the prospective growth schematically: about a million in the northern New York counties of the Region, somewhat over a million on Long Island, half a million in western Connecticut, and 2¼ million in New Jersey.

Table 3. Population in the Region by State Sector, 1970,
with Past and Probable Future Growth
(Assuming Current Birthrate).

	Total Population	Added Population	
	1970 (in thousands)	1940–70	1970–2000
		(in thousands)	
Connecticut sector (3 counties)	1,682	+ 690	+ 500
New Jersey sector (14 counties)	5,800	+2,340	+2,500
New York State sector (14 counties)	12,270	+3,155	+2,000
Region total	19,752	+6,185	+5,000

SOURCE: U.S. Census and Regional Plan Association.

Is this amount of growth good or bad?

Should or should we not take deliberate steps to further lower the growth rate?

The Pros and Cons of Population Growth in the Region

Our growing disenchantment with growth stems not just from a rational analysis of the balance between population and resources; it has more immediate, emotional roots, a feeling that growth has outpaced our decisions too often, that it has produced results we did not expect, that it expanded quantity at the expense of quality. But growth, in moderate doses, can be impetus for improvement, a lever through which desirable change can be achieved. No growth at all favors the status quo, and not everyone in our society is enamored with the status quo.

Certainly, a declining population growth rate can ease a number of problems confronting the Region, but it will by no means eliminate them.

With a smaller population, which also means a smaller household size, the new housing units we will need can be somewhat smaller, perhaps consume somewhat less land, but the total number of new housing units needed over the next 30 years is not going to change much, no matter what happens, simply because most of those who will form new households during that period have already been born. This we showed in the town meeting on housing.

With a smaller population, we will need somewhat fewer new highways, but we will likely still need additional highways as long as our rising income leads to more auto ownership. In the past decade, only 30 percent of our 2.2 million increase in motor vehicle registrations was due to population growth; the remaining 70 percent was due to rising income and lower densities.

With a smaller population, the task of controlling pollution will be made somewhat easier, but here again, it is not just the increase in population that increases pollution. Rather, it is primarily the fact that each of us is producing more wastes and using more energy every year because of rising incomes. While New York City population has been pretty stable since 1950, its electric energy consumption has been growing fast. Each of us wants more mechanical slaves.

Thus, most of the problems of growth in the Urban Region stem from our inability to manage our growing income, and not from our relatively slow population growth as such. At the same time, it can be argued that added population growth could be a powerful lever to change the Region for the better. If we channel a big chunk of the new population and employment growth into our old, decaying urban areas, and into their immediate vicinity, this growth could improve life in many parts of the Region. It could provide more new office jobs for the Region's older cities, it could make for bigger, and hence more viable and more vital, metropolitan-scale subcenters in established cities like Trenton or New Haven, Paterson or Stamford, Newark or Jersey City, Bridgeport or Poughkeepsie. It could provide more urban opportunities (health care, higher education, shopping) to the peripheral, still largely rural counties of the Region, such as the mid-Hudson Valley or south-central New Jersey. If properly arranged, this growth need not make the Region feel more crowded: congestion is all too often a result of inept design, not of overall densities or numbers of people.

Still, there is widespread skepticism: many people feel that while it is theoretically possible to guide growth so it will create a better Region, that chance, given our past performance, is remote. And since most of the possible 5 million new inhabitants of the Region over the next 30 years will be our own children, the place to start reducing population growth—if that is what we want to do—is by deliberate policies to lower the birthrate.

Reducing the Birthrate?

The 1970 National Fertility Study by the Office of Population Research at Princeton investigated, among other things, the incidence of unwanted births. It found that 15 percent of all births in the nation between 1966 and 1970 were unwanted and would not have occurred if access to and the reliability of family planning techniques were good. Another 29 percent of all births were wanted, but unplanned, i.e., wanted at a different time. This suggests that if contraceptive techniques are perfected, disseminated more widely, especially among lower-income families, and if abortion is made more widely available, roughly a 15 percent reduction in the birthrate can be expected, compared to recent levels. That means that, roughly speaking, the population increment in the Region over the next 30 years could be brought down from 5 million with present birthrates to about 4 million. Of course, this assumes present preferences of women concerning the number of children they want. The number has been declining sharply for 15 years now, and further declines in the number of children desired, could, as we pointed out earlier, make a much bigger difference than merely the prevention of unwanted births. Still, systematic availability of birth control measures remains a prerequisite for such a decline.

Several advantages of a further decline in birthrates can be listed. The major one is higher per-capita income, and less need to spend money on children, whether privately, or through school taxes. In theory at least, that money could be reallocated to all kinds of pursuits improving the "quality of life"—urban modernization, open space acquisition, public transportation, cultural activities, mental health services, income redistribution. With a greater proportion of the population at work, we could create more wealth, or have more leisure, or have some of both.

Other advantages would be in the areas listed earlier—somewhat reduced need for land, highways, energy and so on in the near future, and in the longer future, an earlier onset of population stability. As we indicated, population stability for the Region is not a very pressing issue. Much more farmland along the Atlantic Seaboard is being abandoned than urbanized, and populations much higher than those projected could be accommodated here. But a smaller ultimate population will obviously preserve more open space around the Region.

On the negative side, the absence of growth will bring new, unfamiliar problems, the most apparent one being a rapid aging of the population. Half the population would be over 37, instead of over 27, as now. The age distribution would be similar to that of St. Petersburg, Florida, known as a place where people retire. How soon we want to face a culture dominated by the middle-aged and the old is a question to be considered.

Possibilities for changing the settlement pattern of the Region dramatically in the long run will be lost. But the possibility to help the older cities of the Region and to build up their downtown areas in the near future (say, over the next two decades) will not be greatly affected by further reductions in the birthrate. The reason is that the need for additional office buildings, colleges, retail outlets, cultural activities and apartments—the building blocks of urban centers—will, in the near future, be determined by a population that has already been born. Smaller families and a greater emphasis on the working age population, particularly working women, should favor location in central, higher density areas. The three-child family in the post-World War II era was one of the forces that created "spread city." A two-child or smaller family could be a force favoring more compact development—depending, of course, on how we will decide to spend our rising income.

So, in essence, we have three possibilities to consider:

A. Put all efforts into further reducing the birthrate; this could, if we merely prevent unwanted births, reduce the Region's population from 25 million to 24 million by the end of the century. With still further declines in the desirable family size—a less than two-child family—the Region's population could conceivably attain zero natural growth by 1985, with a population of only 22 million.

B. Accept the current, moderate growth rate based on a two-child family; that would mean 25 million people by 2000 and zero growth by about 2020, with an ultimate regional population around 28 million.

C. Go back to the three-child family over the next several years; this would put the Region's population at 28 million by 2000, and at 33 million by 2020, with continued fast growth beyond, unless large-scale out-migration from the Region takes hold.

Encouraging Out-Migration?

There is a rather strong body of opinion which holds that while added growth will do little good in the large urban areas of the country, it could be helpful to the rural parts of the country, remote from New York, Chicago, California, or Texas. Rural parts of the country have been losing population for decades, and smaller, isolated metropolitan areas have not grown much: between 1960 and 1970, metropolitan areas with fewer than 100,000 people did have a large net out-migration, and have grown somewhat only because of natural increase. It was the metropolitan areas of the 1 million to 2.5 million size that grew the fastest.

Why not reverse the trend, and let people flow from the big urban areas into the small ones, and into underpopulated parts of the country? The problem is, it would be somewhat like asking water to flow uphill. The economy of the nation is becoming increasingly white-collar, and white-collar activities naturally gravitate toward large metropolitan areas, where the chance of finding all the specialized people they need is the best, and where the energy of human interaction is the greatest. The settlement of new areas of the continent took place when the economy was largely resource-based, related to agriculture, mining, manufacturing. The continuing settlement of open areas in South America or Siberia today and the development of their new cities is also largely resource-based; new white-collar centers in the wilderness, such as Brasilia or Novosibirsk are induced exceptions. In the United States, the location of employment is no longer dictated by the location of materials, but rather by the location of other people, and this resource is most abundant in large urban areas.

It is true that with enough concentration of government money for research, manufacturing, or education facilities, with enough subsidies to private firms, with sufficiently attractive wages and relocation allowances, and proper transportation, new "countermagnets" of urban growth could be established in the United States as well. With the inducements of high labor demand and high wages, they could attract enough new immigrants. After all, 19 percent of the American population is changing its residence every year, and 4 percent is moving across state or national boundaries. So, it is possible to deflect the migration streams to particular places with enough inducements, without any forced resettlement. This can create a predictably high rate of growth in a new metropolitan area. But what about the places these people would migrate from? That would be less predictable. Chances are they would be coming from all over the country, not just from the New York Region. Moreover, chances are, those that are coming from the Region would be of a special type—as most migrants are. Namely, they would be young, recently married, highly educated, and accustomed to moving. The more inert parts of the population—the older, the less educated, the poorer—would tend to stay behind.

This is one aspect of encouraging out-migration that should be considered. The other is that to create big "countermagnets" in open parts of the country would be very costly not only in terms of construction, and of the costs of getting there, but also in terms of subsidies that would have to be given to enterprises to lure them into places which they have avoided in the free market. The question is—Would that money not be better spent on improving our existing cities?

CHOICE ONE: Without considering the necessary policies, would you prefer the Region's population to: (Check one.)
A. Stop growing in 15 years, with an average of 1 child per family?
B. Stop growing in 50 years, with 2 children per family (present trend)?
C. Continue growing indefinitely, with 3 children per family?
D. No opinion

CHOICE TWO: Do you favor or oppose these policies to slow the Region's growth?
A. Take additional steps to reduce the birthrate

    FAVOR   OPPOSE   NO OPINION

B. Use federal aid to attract jobs and people to other parts of the country

    FAVOR   OPPOSE   NO OPINION

Part B: Quality of the Environment and Control over Wastes

What Environmental Quality Can We Afford?

Whether or not population is allowed to increase, the Region's people still can pretty much make up their own mind as to the kind of environment they want. Underdeveloped countries may be forced to lower the quality of their environment in order to feed their people and lift them from an income level that is a small fraction of what we call the poverty level. But in the Region—the wealthiest human settlement in the history of the world—we do have a choice. We can simply spend more on improving the public environment instead of spending more on private possessions.

We seldom think of it that way. One of the hundreds of thousands of Americans who annually tour the places of environmental quality in Europe was sitting in Venice's St. Marks Square one day when a fellow American remarked to him, "Isn't this a wonderful place? Too bad we can't afford one." But the Italy that financed St. Marks Square was infinitely poorer than we are.

The Possibilities. And we continue to increase our wealth. Money income in the Region in 1970 averaged about $3,860 per person, up from $2,900 in 1960 (in dollars of the same value) and 3½ times the real income per capita in 1940. By 1985 money income per person is expected to average about $6,400 (in today's dollars), under the two-child family assumption of growth. Clearly we could afford higher quality in public places over the next 15 years without lowering our spending on private goods and services.

The Choice: Public Versus Private. Even now, we can afford an environment better than we have. We say we don't have money enough to keep city streets clean, brighten subway stations, and let in light and air, quiet the din—generally make the places were people congregate pleasant and handsome. Meanwhile, however, we have been increasing our spending on other things—cars and vacations, housing, food and drink, time-saving appliances, whimsical gadgets, and fancy packaging. It is partly a question of how much people want to invest in the public world—the spaces and places they share with many

At the end of World War II, nearly everyone in the New York Urban Region lived in tightly built cities

around the port, as in Hoboken here and in Newark and New York,

or in outlying cities like New Brunswick here or Paterson, Hackensack, Bridgeport, Yonkers.

By then, highways had penetrated beyond the subway and between commuter rail lines, as on Long Island, and in Bergen County, western Essex, Middlesex.

They paved the way for homes to spread rapidly; half the Region's families could afford one. (Center)

Levittown, Long Island, symbolized postwar suburbia. (Bottom)

FAIRCHILD AERIAL SURVEYS

Services followed people,

almost anywhere highways crossed, as in Paramus, New Jersey.

Facilities clung to the cloverleafs, as below, in Milford, Connecticut—easy to reach by car, but not by public transportation.

The development homes of the 1950s, cheap to construct and purchase, proved expensive to the towns in which they settled.

They attracted children, spiraling local real estate taxes for schools.

By the late 1950s, towns with vacant land were outlawing these developments; their zoning ordinances required five to ten times as much land for each house. That meant fewer houses in their towns and fewer children; higher house costs and so higher assessments.

Many want homes on small lots, but zoning prohibits.

Only 20 percent of the Region's households can afford houses on the large lots that are allowed.

Nearly half our households could afford attached houses, but local zoning allows almost none. States hesitate to take away local zoning and school tax powers, "home rule," despite the housing shortage and high rents.

Meanwhile, hundreds of thousands of city apartments are deteriorating due to complex financing, absentee landlords, and tenants not used to city living.

From this neglect, some 150,000 New York City apartment units have been abandoned, though community and tenant groups with government help have rehabilitated some.

Lower-skilled workers have been bottled up in old cities, while distant suburbs attracted factory jobs to help pay school taxes.

DOUBLEDAY & COMPANY

So many factory jobs can be reached only by car—and a majority of residents of the old Core cities don't have cars.

Cities — like Bridgeport — are working to remain job and service centers with urban renewal, new stores, and, particularly, office jobs.

Office jobs will nearly double by 2000. If city downtowns attract the offices and become again the centers of urban activities, opportunities can be opened to city residents; public transportation and the countryside can be saved. But now it is easier and safer to scatter facilities.

others—compared to their investment in the private world of their family.

It is true that public spending has been rising rapidly, too—the federal, New York State and New York City budgets were all about 2½ times higher in 1972 than in 1965—and some public expenditures might be shifted to improving the environment. The kind of long-range needs represented by environmental quality issues should be weighed alongside other priorities in the annual governmental budget process. But a larger difficulty comes in deciding whether to shift spending from private to public goods.

In America, taxes are considered bad and private spending good. The United States spends less of its Gross National Product in taxes than many other developed nations:

Taxes as Percent of GNP, 1970

Sweden	48
Norway	43
Netherlands	42
United Kingdom	39
France	38
West Germany	38
Canada	35
Italy	33
United States	**31.5**
Switzerland	28
Japan	21

This often blocks us from getting better "public goods" like parks, well-designed public places, and good public transportation, which we may want more than additional factory-produced goods. If we do choose to spend money on "public goods," it is hard to make that decision effective—to tell government officials you would rather have a lower-priced car and spend the extra money on more attractive highways to drive it on, for example. One observer has called the result private affluence and public squalor.

Not spending money on public places actually induces people who can afford it to spend more on private goods. For those who have the money, the answer to poor public parks is a large backyard with a swimming pool or a second home in the mountains or at the sea. The answer to dirty, undependable, uncomfortable subways, buses, and trains is more driving.

Revulsion from dreary and congested downtowns, where nothing is green except the money, causes people to scatter downtown in pieces through the countryside, in privately built shopping centers and office campuses. Some of these pay for good landscaping and design. It comes out of corporate budgets, but eventually we all pay for it.

For those who can afford a good private environment there are undeniable advantages to private spending over public spending. Though we cannot entirely avoid the public environment no matter how well off we are, most people seem to have developed a knack for living in it with blinders on until day after day they can retreat to the private world in which they can think they control their environment.

It is a form of retreat that may have weakened or dissolved the sense of community.

More and more people seem to be ready to turn from accumulating private goods to alleviating the dreariness of the public environment—the air, the rivers, the endless urban sprawl—and they are suggesting that some of the tremendous productivity of our economy be directed to that.

CHOICE THREE: Would you be willing to spend more of your income—either in taxes or higher prices—to improve the public environment of the Region?

YES   NO   NO OPINION

As of now, we have no easy way to register our opinion on how much should be spent to improve the environment and who among us should be charged or how. The rest of this town meeting will deal with specific ways this might be done a little better. First we shall deal with handling wastes, then with preserving open space.

Standards of Cleanness for Air and Water

Until recently many factories, power plants, quarries, mines, farms, and communities used the air and water as free sewers. Into these common properties they dumped their wastes or with them cooled their machines, and let the people and other forms of life (e.g., fish) downstream and downwind pay all the cost in damages. There were some laws against thus levying against the community the cost of doing business, but they were not generally enforced. It was a low-cost way of doing things—or so it seemed. But no one gave people the chance to say, We would rather use less or pay more for paint or gasoline or electricity and not have so much pollution.

Now, in a frenzy of new laws, court cases, and sewage plant construction, we are beginning to close the free sewers.* We have not paid much attention to the total cost or to the benefits we're going to get from it. Literally billions of dollars will be spent to clean up the Region's waterways. Do we know what benefits we shall derive?

Similarly, new federal regulations require 1976-model automobiles to reduce emissions of carbon monoxide and nitrogen oxides about 90 percent. This will require a device for each new auto now estimated to cost about $350. By comparison, a $240 device is believed likely to achieve a large measure—but not all—of what the $350 one will accomplish. Is the extra cost worth it?

Decisions like these are being made without public scrutiny of benefits compared to costs. Many people might feel that any money spent to abate pollution is well spent, but will the general public continue to support all the money needed? Isn't it important to make every dollar do the most it can? Already there are signs of a growing attack on the "environmental quality above all" philosophy that has dominated the discussion in recent years. "A man out of a job is not really concerned about the possibility of getting lung cancer in 10 years," wrote the *Long Island Commercial Review* in its ecology column.

What priority should antipollution measures have in the nation's spending?

---

* One observation about the confusion resulting from the rather sudden energetic clean-up campaign from the 1971 annual report of the Interstate Sanitation Commission, which works on air and water quality in the New York Urban Region: "In December 1970, an Executive Order of the President broadened the administrative applicability of the Army Engineers permit system under the Refuse Act of 1899. That statute was a little known enactment requiring permits for the discharge of wastes into navigable waters of the United States, except for discharges from municipal waste disposal facilities and street runoff. Despite the sweeping nature of the law, it had not been enforced, except in a few geographic areas and on a very small scale . . . The sudden appearance of the new program and its magnitude have combined to make the past year a difficult one characterized by much confusion." The reincarnation of this act has caused similar confusion and controversy in the Delaware River Basin.

What procedure should be devised for deciding the value of individual projects compared to their costs, and who should pay?

Fixing the level of quality we want in air and bodies of water generally is difficult because what is broadly called pollution consists of dozens of different wastes. In the air drift nitrogen oxides and carbon monoxide, acids and lead from automobile exhausts, sulfur dioxide from electric generator smokestacks, soot and dust and many gases from incinerators and furnaces. Each of these inflicts a different amount and kind of damage or discomfort, and the degree of discomfort or damage depends on the weather, on the time and the place, and on people's physical idiosyncrasies. On breezy, clear days many wastes may do little damage at all; on days of air inversion, when cold air squats on top of warm air and traps the gases close to the ground, wastes in the supercharged air have speeded death for some people, caused eye smarting for many, were generally disagreeable, and deteriorated buildings and clothing.

Definition of the water quality we want creates the same complexity. Some forms of water pollution are measured by the amount of oxygen they demand to oxidize the material (BOD, or biochemical oxygen demand rate), and sewage treatment plants are rated by the percentage of BOD and suspended solids they take out. Dozens of different substances are being dumped into the Region's rivers and streams; some cause little damage because they are dumped at places where there's enough oxygen in the water to decompose them. But the same wastes might cause a great deal of damage at different times and places. A swiftly flowing stream can normally repair itself, if it is not overloaded with wastes. When a great deal of wastes come together, much more damage is done than when the dumping is spread out more evenly.

All this means is that it is mighty hard to set up general standards of air and water quality, put price tags on each level, and ask the public which level they choose. Because of this and limits on what can be presented clearly on TV and the ballot, we will not ask this directly. But you may want to consider it in anticipation of the next environmental bond issue vote.

We are now spending an estimated $10 billion a year in taxes and private investment—1 percent of a trillion dollar Gross National Product—to clean up air and water in the nation. Assuming population continues to grow in the United States at the relatively slow rate of the past few years, we shall need to spend about $25 billion a year in 2000 (in dollars worth the same as they are now) just to keep up with rising population, production, automobile driving, and use of electricity according to one estimate by the Washington-based Resources for the Future, Inc. To achieve the standards now set by the federal government for improvement in air and water cleanness would cost about $35 billion a year. There might still be a few days a year of really bad air in the large cities, but dust and soot would largely be gone and most rivers and streams would be pleasant if not swimmable.

For an additional $10 billion a year, $45 billion, it is likely that heating of rivers from nuclear power plants would be eased and safer methods of handling radioactive wastes could be devised, enabling greater expansion of nuclear power and replacement of more air-polluting fossil-fuel plants. There would be somewhat fewer days of bad air, particularly as a result of auto exhausts.

In considering whether we should improve air and water quality by spending as much as 2½ times, 3½ times, or 4½ times what we are spending now, we should recognize that our incomes are expected to go up considerably too. Instead of the present trillion dollars in total goods and services now produced in the nation (the Gross National Product or GNP), in 2000 we can expect some $2.5 trillion. So we should compare the 1 percent we're now spending out of GNP on antipollution measures with the same 1 percent in 2000 if we spend only $25 billion, or the nearly 2 percent if we spend as much as $45 billion a year by 2000.

A Process for Setting Standards

Many people will doubtlessly object that we are not going about this discussion the right way at all. Air and water should be clean—that's all, clean!—regardless of cost; many people say: Man has no right to throw his wastes into air and water, and any step we can take to eliminate those wastes should be taken, almost regardless of cost.

But there are leftovers from virtually every physical activity of man, and the cost of removing them soars as one approaches the ideal of absolute purity. For example, while it might cost $10 to remove 50 percent of the pollution from a sugar beet plant per unit of output, it may cost $55 to remove 90 percent, and $100 to remove all of it. Is virtually doubling the cost to remove the last 10 percent of pollution really justified?

How should standards be set and enforced? And who should pay?

The Present Process. Under present legislation, the federal government has offered to pay up to 75 percent of the cost of new sewage plants. Priorities for grants go to localities where the U.S. Environmental Protection Agency sees the greatest need. Public sewage plants must provide secondary treatment by 1977, eliminating about 90 percent of the BOD and suspended solids. Manufacturers dumping wastes directly into public waters must be using the "best practicable control technology currently available" by 1977 and by 1983 the "best technology economically achievable" as determined by the Environmental Protection Administrator.

As to air pollution, the federal government allows fast tax write-offs to private companies for installing air pollution abatement equipment and is setting standards of air quality for all areas which, somehow, these areas must meet. In some areas, cars might have to be banned to achieve the standard. The federal government has directly ordered auto manufacturers to install pollution-control devices on their 1976-model cars that will eliminate about 90 percent of the carbon monoxide and nitrogen oxides. It is estimated that the new device will add about 1 cent a mile to each motorist's costs, around $100 a year for the typical car.

Altogether, there is no consistent policy about who gets the bill for depolluting. In some cases, the federal government pays most of the cost (i.e., all of us pay in federal taxes, mainly income taxes). The manufacturer pays the full cost in some cases (i.e., all of us pay in the price of what we buy, rather like a sales tax). In other cases, the manufacturer might demonstrate he cannot feasibly clean the wastes at all right now (i.e., those near the production site pay in suffering the pollution). In still other cases, the cost to the manufacturer is modified because he dumps his wastes into a federally subsidized waste-treatment plant or uses tax-abated air cleaning equipment. The motorist will pay the full cost of cleaning his engine's wastes.

Now, there are disadvantages to this rather random approach. And a method has been proposed for enforcing clean air and water standards to get around these disadvantages. The proposal is to charge each source of pollution for the damaging wastes thrown into the air or water. First, a standard is established of air quality for an area and water quality for each body of water. Then a charge is levied against the polluters for each unit of waste they discharge—for example, 10 cents a pound of BOD or suspended solids. The charge would be set high enough to get rid of enough wastes to achieve the desired standard. This process cannot be followed in every detail in all cases, but the principle can be adapted to most situations—he who pollutes pays and pays promptly until the pollution is cleaned up.

Here is what is expected to happen in response to a charge for pollutants.

First, if the cost is placed on those dumping the wastes, there is an incentive to find the least expensive way of eliminating the pollution. In many cases, the cheapest way is to eliminate or cut down the wastes rather than simply clean them up. This was demonstrated recently by the Dow Chemical Company plant in Midland, Michigan. Each production division was charged the full cost of treating its wastes in the plant's own sewage treatment system. To save that charge, supervisors went over their production processes and found ways to avoid creating wastes or reusing what they had been throwing down the sewer. In one instance, a supervisor found ways to save $100,000 worth of materials just because he was ordered to pay $30,000 for treating those materials when they were considered wastes and thrown down the drain. Total saving: $130,000—a saving not likely to have been made if the sewage treatment process had simply been subsidized by the federal government.

Some cities have charged manufacturers the full costs of handling their special wastes, often with similar results—the wastes were gradually eliminated.

Second, charging for the wastes rather than simply ordering them cleaned up puts *immediate* pressure on the polluter. There need be no haggling over what's technologically or economically feasible to eliminate wastes. There is an incentive for polluters to figure out some way to *make* it feasible to eliminate their wastes. This can be applied to localities as well as to manufacturers.

If polluters had been charged promptly many years ago when localities were ordered to clean up their sewage, they might have achieved faster progress. A number of key sewage plants ordered by the federal government to be built or upgraded years ago have not even been begun. The reason: the localities have been awaiting promised federal grants—and there was no penalty levied against them for waiting. In other words, federal subsidies and a simple order to clean up—without charging localities immediately for *not* cleaning up—has resulted in years of delay for many sorely needed sewage plants. Ironically, inflation in the construction industry has been so steep that most of these localities will be paying more out of their own money to build their plants now, even with substantial federal aid, than they would have paid if they had built them promptly *without* federal aid.

Priorities have been askew, too, because of the present process. Because New York State voted bond money to prepay the federal share before the federal government appropriated the money, some New York State plants that are not of the utmost importance in the Region have gone ahead, while many New Jersey plants that would make a great deal of difference are not begun. The Hudson River above Spuyten Duyvil is safe to swim in, though few people do swim there because it is muddy. Nevertheless, the Westchester Yonkers plant that will clean that portion of the river is going ahead. By contrast, Raritan Bay is scarcely swimmable because of pollution and is a potentially valuable recreation area for literally hundreds of thousands of nearby residents. The shellfish industry there is closed because of pollution. But the key plants for cleaning Raritan Bay are not begun, awaiting federal funds.

Finally, setting the same standards for every discharge has had costly results. All sewage plants must provide secondary treatment, clean up about 90 percent of the BOD and suspended solids. The program for cleaning the Lower Hudson, Upper Bay, and Long Island Sound will cost about $3 billion. It probably would have been less expensive to achieve the standard desired by charging for pollutants and letting the people charged decide whether to clean up their wastes or continue to pay.

For example, the North River Pollution Control Plant in the Hudson River alongside Harlem will cost about $850 million. A plant designed to be built for about half that cost in 1966 was the choice of the city and the Interstate Sanitation Commission. They claim that the river and bays can attain a satisfactory quality even if this particular plant is allowed to work at a lower standard than the presently required 90 percent. Furthermore, the plant is not likely to achieve the full benefits of its high standard much of the time because of storm water running into it. The money could have been spent on far more beneficial steps toward pollution abatement, according to Thomas R. Glenn, Interstate Sanitation Commission Director.

Another possibility for more effective waste management through charges for pollution is to adjust the charges roughly according to the environmental damage done. Wastes of the same chemical, physical, or thermal kind do different amounts of damage depending on time, place, and weather. The factory or village dumping wastes into a river far from any other waste outfall may not be causing much damage at all because the available oxygen can decompose waste before any real damage is done. The same wastes dumped near a cluster of other outfalls might do irreparable damage by overwhelming the stream's reserves of oxygen and oxygen-producing plant life. Similarly, an electric plant smokestack in a rural area where plenty of wind blows to a clear horizon might cause little, if any, harm most of the time; the same plant in a large city would be a public health hazard.

With variable charges, a company in a rural place might not need to compete for the expensive and relatively scarce low-sulfur fuel that New York City plants need.

So, we can sum up the advantages of charging for pollutants:

1. By putting the cost on the polluter, better ways to handle wastes than simply treating them will be found—perhaps not producing the waste at all.

2. Pressure to clean up the wastes is immediate and continuous, until all wastes are eliminated.

3. The government does not have to argue with a manufacturer or locality about whether cleaning up the waste is feasible.

4. The most economical way would be found of achieving the standards set for air and water. Estimated benefits would always exceed expected costs.

Then Why Don't We Do It? The main objection to charging for environmental damages rather than setting a high standard of cleanness and requiring everyone to meet it is that such a charge is, in effect, a license to pollute. Man has no right to dump his wastes into the air or water, objectors say, and public policies should not appear to be allowing this—even if the result is faster clean-up of air and water. It is a moral issue, they say, and should not be treated exclusively as an economic issue.

Second, following the principle that he who pollutes must pay would put heavy costs on poor localities, the older cities which have neglected sewage plants and incinerators over the years and now will find it hard to pay the bill. (However, general aid for poor communities might get around this problem.)

Third, small plants charged the full cost for disposing of their wastes might leave sites in older cities, where their jobs are much needed.

Fourth, administering the system would be complicated. Setting the same standards for sewage plants and building them as fast as we can and setting industry-wide standards of what is feasible for manufacturers probably is simpler. The Region is on its way to improving air and water quality significantly. Perhaps we should leave well enough alone.

CHOICE FOUR: Which approach to improving air and water quality should be stressed? (Check one.)
A. The present approach of enforcing standards and sub-sidizing treatment facilities.
B. An approach that achieves standards by charging for pollutants dumped.
C. No opinion.

The Special Problem of Electricity

The people of the Region—just like their counterparts across the country—have been increasing their use of electricity at a fast pace. For example, Consolidated Edison's customers in New York City and Westchester have doubled their power consumption about every 15 years; Public Service Gas and Electric customers in New Jersey have doubled their use in 10 years. Long Island Lighting had to increase its output nearly *2½ times* between 1960 and 1970, and Orange and Rockland Utilities well over *three times.*

Yet, in the past decade, many new power plants in the Region have been delayed or blocked.

Some objectors argued that one proposed plant would add excessively to the air pollution in Queens, another would deface Storm King Mountain and possibly damage fish life in the Hudson, a third might endanger lives in the vicinity of a proposed nuclear plant at Shoreham on Long Island, a fourth would disturb an unusually valuable natural area in New Jersey, Sunfish Pond; and so forth. Others have argued that new transmission lines needed to bring power from distant locations would mar the scenery, and that barge-mounted nuclear plants offshore might endanger New Jersey's beaches.

The delays caused by these objections are one reason the Region has suffered from power shortages. Of course, some blackouts and brownouts have been due to distribution breakdowns, and construction delays have also plagued the utility industry. The overall effect has been periods of inadequate power supply that have slowed subways and elevators, limited air conditioning, interfered with computer operations, reduced the effectiveness of some appliances, and even kept people from cooking dinner.

Instead of promoting the use of more electric power, utilities are beginning to counsel against waste, and urge their customers to Save-A-Watt. Yet, demand grows, only in part because of growing population, and it becomes increasingly difficult to find acceptable locations for power plants and transmission facilities. Clearly, an increase in power demand anywhere near the rate of recent years cannot be satisfied unless much more power capacity is built. Yet, cutting demand will hurt most people. Even the strongest conservationists would like to use more electricity for some purposes, such as public transportation, sewage or solid waste disposal and recycling. And these are heavy power users.

In this short discussion, we cannot go into the details of environmental standards for power plants. The technical issues in dispute fill volumes of testimony. Rather, we ask the general question: What do we do now?

Should we follow standards of environmental protection that allow enough power to be produced to meet the expected rise in demand? Or should we insist on a higher standard of environmental protection and risk producing less power over the rest of the century than people will want? If we don't produce as much power as people will want, we have a second dilemma: should we just tolerate more and more random brownouts and power cutbacks or ration the use of electricity —for example, by raising rates so people choose to use less. Raising prices is a standard way of limiting the purchase of goods that are in short supply. Most studies show, however, that the cost of electricity would have to be raised very high to limit its use. The cost of electricity is such a small part of most budgets, family or business, that unless the rate increase is very substantial, people don't cut the amount they use. However, two changes in the way electric charges are made have been suggested to help to discourage the use of power: (1) increasing the charge during periods of highest demand, and (2) charging everyone the same rate per unit regardless of how much electricity he purchases, rather than lowering the price as more power is bought.

The rationale for peak period pricing is that the supply of electricity is adequate most of the time: shortages occur mainly at peak periods. Roughly the same amount of power is potentially available all day and all night. There is little demand in the middle of a cool night, but the plant capacity must be available for the middle of a hot day. When Con Edison urged its customers to conserve, the company stressed savings in air conditioning which accounts for nearly half its summer peak. So we might save money as well as adjust demand to supply if we could discourage people from using electricity during certain hours of certain days of certain seasons. It has been suggested that this might be accomplished by charging higher than normal rates during peak periods, the steaming hours when demand is greatest. Those who could put off using power probably would do so. In addition the rates for those who use a lot of power could be raised more. Under the present rate structure, the more power a firm or family uses, the less it pays for each kilowatt-hour. There is little economic incentive for the large user to conserve energy. And smaller families and firms have much less opportunity to conserve.

So one point of view says that a possible solution might be a combination of substantially raising peak-period rates and placing a flat charge on electric power regardless of how much each customer uses. This would increase the cost on large users. It would keep the cost of electricity from rising much for lower-income families and accomplish some reduction in energy demand.

But the choice is not a clear one. For one thing, measuring electric use at peak times for most utility customers would require the installation of millions of costly new meters. Current residential meters are not designed to do this job.

And the question arises—whom do we hit when we hit the big user? Among Con Edison's biggest customers are the City of New York, the Metropolitan Transportation Authority, and the New York City Housing Authority. Increased electric costs for them will inevitably be reflected in higher taxes or higher fares. And by increasing the cost, will we inhibit beneficial uses of electricity which essentially everybody wants?

What of the millions of underprivileged in the Region? Will a shift in rates at this time restrict the "have-nots" in their efforts to achieve equal status with the "haves"?

Already, the utilities contend, electric costs may have been pushed up by environmental protection requirements beyond the benefits achieved. They urge a closer look at whether the huge financial expenditures invested to achieve relatively small additional benefits to the environment might not better be directed to the improvement of other urban concerns—health care, housing, public transportation. A case in point is the shift for electricity production to 0.3 percent sulfur content oil, which is costing New Yorkers an additional $60–75 million per year. Only the proven scientific validity of such measures can justify them, the utilities say.

The solution the utilities offer is a combination of energy conservation, improvement of current operating methods and technology, and large expenditures for research and development for cleaner, more efficient ways to produce electricity. The latter two will inevitably be reflected in higher rates for the customer.

In fact, any effort to improve the environment while at the same time insuring an adequate and reliable supply of power is going to be reflected in higher cost to the consumer.

The answer may lie in a combination of steps. But we'd like to know in which direction you are leaning:

CHOICE SIX: Would you: (Please check only one.)
A. Increase the cost of electricity either at peak times or across the board to reduce electricity consumption?
B. Require utilities to spend more for research and development (which would require higher electric rates) to seek cleaner, more efficient ways to produce electricity?
C. Not allow environmental protection standards to impose an increasing burden on the costs and capacity of electric production?

The Solid Waste Problem

While progress in air and water quality is measurable, the decent disposal of garbage and trash—solid wastes—is literally a mounting problem throughout the Region.

If recent trends and present policies continue, the amount of garbage and trash shucked off by people of the New York Urban Region will be nearly twice as much in 2000 as it was in 1965.

To picture the problem at its most picturesque, the solid wastes generated by New York City residents over the next 30 years could cover Central Park to the height of the adjacent General Motors Building. That doesn't include the cars they'll junk.

In 1965, about 4 percent of the 17 million tons of solid wastes collected in the Region were salvaged or recycled, about 30 percent were burned, and the remainder, roughly two thirds of all trash and garbage, was dumped in landfill. We are actually building garbage mountains in parks—not in Central Park, but in others: in Pelham Bay, in Jamaica Bay, in Fresh Kills, on potential parkland in the Hackensack Meadowlands. But the remaining marshland, which traditionally has been the favorite place for landfill, is getting scarce in areas that are most accessible to the Region's garbage-producing population; and pressure from conservationists to save this marshland because of its biological value for aquatic life and wildlife is growing.

We could grind more of our solid wastes through disposal units and flush them down the sink—but that would put more of a burden on sewage disposal plants, and would only take

care of a tiny fraction of our solid wastes. We could reduce its
volume by burning more of it—but incinerators do contribute
to air pollution and are costly, especially if elaborate scrubbers
are built to wash their exhaust; the scrubbers also require
water. We could, with elaborate and likewise costly precautions, build garbage islands at sea, and ferry solid wastes out
there by barge. Lastly, we could reclaim or recycle more of
our solid wastes, but that, too, has its costs. Only ferrous
metals can easily be extracted from garbage by magnets. Separation techniques for other items are less than perfect and
require a lot of hand labor. Separation in the household, with
separate storage and collection, would likewise cost a lot in
labor, energy, and materials. In fact, some experts have suggested that the environmental cost of recycling domestic garbage can easily be higher than that of disposal. Besides, materials like glass, aluminum, or iron, found in domestic refuse,
are among those most abundant in the earth's crust, whereas
those in short supply—copper, tin, lead—are likewise difficult
to find in domestic garbage.

Whatever balance between landfill, incineration, and recycling is eventually arrived at, dealing with the mounting
quantities of solid wastes will not be cheap. And we might
ask ourselves the question we asked in connection with automobile traffic or electric power: Do we really need that much?
Do we really need so many throwaway things?

Paper and paperboard constitute (by weight) over half
the solid wastes picked up in the Region. Packaging of all kinds
of goods is increasing, for your convenience in shopping and
in using the product (separated cheese slices, boil-in-a-bag
vegetables), or to save store costs. Similarly, the use of disposable products is increasing—paper napkins and towels,
paper cups and plates. They are convenient—but this is the
stuff garbage heaps are made of. We can keep expanding our
capacity to deal with this refuse—or we can try to cut down
on its production: discourage the use of paper and of cardboard boxes, use less packaging, fewer bags, fewer disposable
paper products.

For example, a bill has been considered in the Senate that
would impose a 1 cent per pound tax on any manufactured
product that ultimately must be discarded. The aim is to stimulate recycling and encourage companies to design more easily
disposable products. The idea is similar to the effluent charges
we have discussed earlier.

Do we want this town meeting to send a message to manufacturers and retailers and lawmakers that we would prefer to do without so much packaging and so many throwaway items? Or is this a trivial issue?

CHOICE SIX: To deal with the mounting problem of solid wastes, would you reduce convenience packaging and other "disposable" consumer items?

FAVOR   OPPOSE   NO OPINION

Governing Waste Policies

Responsibility for setting and enforcing policies on wastes now is scattered through every level of government in the New York Region. Standards for air and water are being set by federal, state, regional, and local governments; enforcement is distributed among all kinds of governments; subsidies for waste treatment are paid by federal and state governments without any clear set of priorities.

All three states in the Region are increasing their planning for solid waste disposal, and New York and New Jersey are energetically encouraging counties to take charge. The states chip in some state aid as well as planning and technical assistance. But few counties are actually taking over that responsibility. So it remains with the municipalities. In some places solid waste disposal is still a private enterprise, though in New Jersey private landfills are regulated as a public utility and the environmental and health effects of landfills are the province of the Department of Environmental Protection.

Interlocking Waste Problems. Demand for rising standards of air and water quality complicates the solid waste problem. Having come to understand the importance of marshlands in maintaining animal and vegetable life in the oceans and bays, officials are reluctant to fill the wetlands of the Region with solid wastes, as has been done for decades. Some marshland is still being filled with wastes—most notably, the Hackensack Meadowlands across from Manhattan in New Jersey. The commission governing the Meadowlands is required by law to accept 30,000 tons of solid wastes a week from New Jersey municipalities. But generally, steps have been taken to save the remaining wetlands.

At the same time, higher air-quality standards have halted the proposed construction of a huge incinerator in New York City, and there is strong opposition from clean-air groups to an immense incinerator in the Hackensack Meadowlands, even though incineration would save some of the marshland there from destruction.

Similarly, in raising water quality by building more sewage treatment plants, we are producing more sludge—the viscous residue of sewage treatment and a stubborn solid waste problem.

We might clean the air somewhat by shifting from coal, oil, or gas-fired electric plants to nuclear energy. But handling the radioactive wastes remains a problem that troubles scientists.

The classic example of the error inherent in dealing with only one piece of waste management at a time occurred when New York City's Department of Air Pollution Control pushed through stricter controls on the gases emitted by apartment house incinerators. Instead of rebuilding old incinerators to meet the new standards, apartment owners closed them down and put all the refuse in garbage cans, to be picked up by the Sanitation Department, which was not at all prepared for this added burden. So the strict air pollution control was relaxed.

Therefore, One Waste-Management Agency? Experience suggests that large advantages would derive from setting policies and standards for all three types of wastes—solid, liquid (producing water pollution), and gaseous (producing air pollution)—together. It does not imply that a single regional agency must pick up all the garbage and inspect all the smokestacks and sewage plants. It does imply that one organization, responsible to the public, should work out solutions to our waste problems so that public choices can be registered.

What trade-off do we prefer among the three kinds of wastes, e.g., is it less damaging to fill a particular marsh than to build an incinerator? How much are we willing to spend to raise environmental quality, to recycle wastes instead of burning or dumping them?

A second advantage of a large-area agency responsible for wastes is that large sewage plants and incinerators are more efficient than small ones, not only saving money but also producing less pollution. Recycling is economically feasible only where the operation is large and located near manufacturers who can use the recycled materials. Furthermore, many innovations in waste-handling are being tried now—machines that separate types of waste, pipelines that take sewage sludge where it can rebuild the soil, and many more. This suggests that a major waste-management organization is needed to follow research or commission it, try out models, and adopt those that work.

But making one agency responsible would raise sensitive governmental issues. Would we be willing to give such an agency power to decide where an incinerator or sewage plant serving several municipalities should be located, without approval of the government in the town where it is to go? (No one loves an incinerator.)

Would we let a single regional agency levy charges for handling wastes or penalties for polluting?

To what constituency would a regional agency be answerable? Would it function as an ombudsman—an impartial judge of complaints—or as a remote and inaccessible bureacracy?

Which seems most important in the Region now: establishing a less confusing and more highly coordinated system for waste management and getting off on a strong, clear course that the public understands? Or is it more important to leave local governments freer to adjust to the various standards set for them?

If we choose one agency, should it cover the whole Region, including parts of three states? The present program for cleaning up the harbor area depends on action in both New York and New Jersey, yet sewage agencies in the two states have been allowed to move toward the common goal at different speeds.

Another example: to avoid adding pollutants to its air, New York City rejected a proposed incinerator for its solid wastes. But now New Jersey, from which the prevailing winds blow across New York City, is planning a huge incinerator that could affect the air New York breathes.

On the other hand, now that the states have moved strongly into environmental protection, perhaps we should await the results of their activities before talking about a super-agency.

CHOICE SEVEN: Would you approve or disapprove of a single governmental waste-management agency setting policies and enforcing disposal standards for air, water, and land throughout the Tri-State Region?

APPROVE   DISAPPROVE   NO OPINION

Part C: Open Space

Public Open Space: The Same Basic Issue?

Important as are clean air and water to the quality of our environment, saving open space in the right places is equally important:

- to preserve conditions needed for natural processes, such as water runoff and prevention of soil erosion
- for outdoor recreation
- for amenity, for sheer beauty
- and to mark off communities

At the same time, where *not* to have open space is important.

The function of urban areas is to bring people together, and scattering neighborhoods or letting them sprawl—i.e., having too much unrelated open space in an area—eliminates the possibility of good public transportation and increases the number and length of auto trips. It skyrockets the cost of sewage collection and discourages other ways of handling or preventing wastes efficiently.

The basic question in acquiring open space is the same as in waste management: What quality do we want, who should pay, and who should benefit? Like waste management, open space is sometimes considered a middle-class concern. To the new suburbanite, keeping all the land open that he sees on his first day in the suburbs is a high priority. But families with rats in the house and little more than food money may have other priorities for government spending, despite greater need for public green spaces in their neighborhood than in the suburbs where most families have their own.

However, paying for open space involves a calculus different from buying cleaner air or water.

Open Space for New Developments

New neighborhoods, whether built outside the cities on vacant land or on a large city tract cleared for urban renewal, can have their open space without taxpayer cost. The method has many names, the one generally used being "clustering." Open space zoning, density zoning, and Planned Unit Development (PUD) are among other terms commonly used. As we said in the town meeting on housing, the typical suburban zoning ordinance in the Region requires an acre or a half acre of land for each new one-family house. In clustering, an overall density is set for the area which could be, say, a half acre per house on the average, but the developer is allowed to arrange the houses and open space in a design that puts the houses closer together and puts most of the open space together; the developer's costs are reduced, and the community gains a park.

PUD allows all types of structures—apartments, town

houses, one-family houses, and nonresidential buildings—to be mixed in a complete neighborhood or new town. Zoning ordinances that do not allow for clustering require that every building in a proposed neighborhood be of roughly the same height and have the same amount of space around it.

In a city, open space can be gained at no cost to the government by means of so-called zoning bonuses. The small, well-publicized, and well-used pedestrian parks in Manhattan illustrate the value of small open spaces in dense areas. But they are very expensive. Similar results are being had without public payment from builders of new projects under the present New York City zoning ordinance which encourages builders to provide plazas at the ground level by allowing them more floor space at the top of the building.

Advantages of Clustering. On vacant land outside the cities, the builder of a cluster would find it to his advantage to avoid steep slopes, stream valleys, marshlands, stands of trees, and other places that should remain in their natural state to protect soil, water table, animal and plant life. On the rest of the land the same number of housing units would be built as zoning had declared to be reasonable for the entire site; so the builder would lose nothing. In fact, his costs usually are lower if he can design what he builds to fit the terrain. And the space lavished on streets often can be cut almost in half.

In several neighborhoods designed as Planned Unit Developments (PUDs), children don't ever cross a street to get to school. In addition, enough land can be put together for playgrounds. Neighbors can share the cost of maintaining the space and equipment. Natural open space outside the cities can be left in continuous strips, protective of plant and animal life and enjoyable for hiking and bicycling. Long, continuous, natural pathways are possible, best for nature, enjoyable for man.

When several Planned Unit Development neighborhoods are grouped, you get a new town like Columbia, Md. A new town can have a wide greenbelt around the whole community and green in the town center, as well as natural open space in and around individual neighborhoods.

Clustering can provide free to the taxpayer all of the open space needed for new or renewed neighborhoods and local communities.

Why Clustering Is Not Widespread. Clustering is being used increasingly on Long Island, a recent survey by the *Long Island Commercial Review* shows. But it is not yet very common in the Region. Why not? Builders approve—the National Association of Home Builders has even made a film promoting it.

Conservationists have argued for it over many years. All three states of the Region allow municipalities to use Planned Unit Development ordinances. Yet clustering is being resisted.

The main reason seems to be suspicion. Local groups are suspicious of builders generally and of any change in zoning specifically, which they see as their only defense against letting too many families into town. (Some cluster ordinances do allow higher overall densities, but that is not a necessary part of the clustering idea.) And some citizens are afraid of lowering housing costs, therefore prices, drawing in families of lower income than they like—though few would admit to that publicly.

The most frequent objection is that clustering would leave large sections of land without any houses on them, and some builder might talk the local authorities into changing the zoning and letting him build on the vacant surfaces.

There are several answers.

First, it has not happened. A cluster development was built during World War I in Bridgeport and remains one of that city's most sought-after neighborhoods, with the open space intact. Radburn, in Fair Lawn, N.J., new town movement pioneer built in the late 1920s, still has every bit of its open space. It is controlled by the Radburn Association, a cooperative of all the homeowners. (Sometimes the open space is controlled by the neighborhood through an association, sometimes by the municipality as a public park.)

Second, there is actually less chance to add houses after a cluster development is built than would be the case if the same number of houses were put each on its one-acre lot. The leftover land could be sold for more housing only with the approval of the homeowners' association or the local park agency (whichever owns the public space).

In addition, the zoning ordinance would have to be changed to allow more houses to be built on that tract. So there is a double protection. If houses were built the usual way, each on its own large lot, all it would take is a change in zoning to allow each homeowner to sell off part of his land for added houses. Since it would give homeowners a windfall (say $20,000 if one-acre zoning were changed to one-third acre, for example, allowing each homeowner to sell a lot on each side of his house), such a change isn't entirely unbelievable, especially as the neighborhood ages.

Third, the land a builder would leave in open space in a cluster subdivision would be the land hardest to build on; so it would not be particularly attractive to a later entrepreneur.

Nevertheless, local communities seem to feel safer standing pat. Many residents don't trust their local officials to judge the cluster plan. Few local suburban governments retain continuing professional planning and landscape architecture advice, and it certainly is possible for a slipshod builder's poor site plan to be accepted by amateur local officials. Others are concerned about maintenance of the common open space. And many builders have small firms that do not have the capacity to design a neighborhood in a persuasively attractive and suitable way. So they find it easier to conform to the old rigid zoning ordinance. Others would prefer to build PUDs, but they don't want to spend the hours, days, even months it takes to win local approval.

CHOICE EIGHT: Given the same number of people to be housed on a piece of land, how should most new neighborhoods in the Region be built? (Check one.)

A. Clustered, with some land left open for neighborhood or public use _____

B. Completely divided into private yards, with no open land shared by the whole neighborhood _____

C. No opinion _____

Buying Open Space: Immediately or Gradually?

No one could object on cost grounds to obtaining neighborhood open space by clustering. All that is necessary is that people be willing to live in somewhat less private space in order to gain public open space. Indeed, the public cost for sewers, water, gas, electricity, and streets is lower.

But what about open space that cannot be acquired free, that would have to be bought by the public? All the wetlands that might otherwise be built on, the wilderness areas that would be invaded by second homes or hotels, oceanfront and lakes and river valleys? What about parks and green squares in the older cities and suburbs that are not ready for wholesale renewal and so would not get free open space through clustering?

How Much Is Open Space Worth to Whom? There are two ways to buy open space. One is to float bonds and go out and buy it now, while it's there to be had. The other way is to buy it with funds appropriated every year or every few years, contrasting the benefits of each appropriation with the benefits that might be had from spending the same money for some other project, such as a sewage plant or highway or subway extension. That is the usual way to appropriate public funds.

In Favor of Buying Immediately. But buying open space is different from other public spending.

First, land bought to remain open does not lose value over years as something constructed does; the land gains value, particularly as land around it is developed. In fact, land prices in a growing urban area usually go up faster than other prices. Precise measures are not available, but one builder put it this way: "Anyone investing in land anticipates that he can at least double his money in seven years—and you know how much land speculation is going on in this region!" With state bond interest hanging around 6 percent a year and important parcels of land going up in price at more than double that rate, it would cost less to purchase the open space desired immediately with government bonds than to buy it piecemeal over an extended period. The land recommended for park acquisition by the Tri-State Regional Planning Commission, the official planning agency for the Region, would have cost $2.5 billion if bought last year, it was estimated. If bought in small pieces year by year for 15 years, the price of that land might be double that or more. The saving by reason of immediate purchase with a bond issue would be about $1 billion, including interest on bonds.

This would not be a case of our mortgaging our children's future for our benefit, as some bond issues are said to be, but the opposite—assuring that our children would have an irreplaceable asset of growing value.

In fact, the use of land so strongly affects the next generation that one might feel it immoral to make the decision about its use on the basis of any year's government budget. If, by permitting building in the wrong place, we lose an inch of topsoil, it will take many decades to restore it. Drain a swamp, and it can never be the same. It takes very little development to spoil a large tract. Unusually valuable apple orchards in Ulster County—50 miles and more north of New York City—are threatened today, even though there is abandoned farmland of much less value all around. The Lake Minnewaska tract of the Shawangunk Mountains, a little farther away, is one of the most spectacular landscapes in the nation, but fragile. It could not accommodate masses of people or construction. Two years ago this tract was about to be sold for a colony of second homes, and it was saved only by extraordinary effort of a number of cooperating organizations and finally by New York State, which bought it for the public. Even this unusually vigilant effort probably would not have succeeded if the landowner had not been sympathetic to saving it from development.

More often, land identified as especially valuable is lost before it can be acquired. The Navesink Highlands, in northern Monmouth County, N.J., highest point along the Atlantic coast, has been on many lists of proposed parks over the years, including the first *Regional Plan of New York and Its Environs,* published by Regional Plan Association in 1929. Some of it has just been bought for high-rise apartments.

Buying land to preserve it in its natural state, which involves nothing more than a transfer of title and an exchange of money, does not consume any of the economy's resources. No irreplaceable minerals are taken out of the earth; no energy is consumed; no manpower is diverted from other work. From the viewpoint of the national economy, a costless "transfer payment" occurs; but from the human viewpoint, a priceless investment in the future is made.

A rough estimate of what it would cost for the whole nation to buy an adequate inventory of public land if we could pay for it right now in cash would be $100 billion. That would include in this area a 10,000-square-mile park system along the Appalachian Mountains from Maine to North Carolina, all the wetlands that should be preserved, all the remaining open oceanfront, and small parks in city and old suburban locations that have too little open space.

If we phased a $100 billion bond issue for this purpose over the next decade or so as land was identified and purchased, with repayment scheduled over a 50-year period, repayment would be $6–6.5 billion a year nationwide. (For comparison, the federal budget is now over $220 billion.) On the average, over the 50-year period, the cost of "buying back America" would be about $25 a person per year.*

But, in fact, $25 a year is more than it would cost the typical taxpayer.

First, a great deal of the cost can be recovered by renting back the land to the present owner, to do with as he chooses as long as he preserves it in its present state. If he is farming it, it can remain a farm, perhaps indefinitely.

Second, we can get some of the money from people who benefit most from the land purchase, such as those who own nearby vacant land *not* bought by the government. If part

---

* We do not have in mind a regular bond issue, which on this scale might badly tilt the money market. Recommended instead would be some method of paying the landowner with bonds directly or paying in installments tied to his continued use of the land as long as it is not needed for public recreation. Perhaps direct sales to the public, analogous to a war bond campaign, might be used.

of the proposed public open space purchased were the Marlborough orchards north of Newburgh, N.Y., the value of land near the orchards would be increased. It might be reasonable, then, for the government to attach to the "buy back America" bond issue some tax apparatus for harvesting the extra land value conferred on private land nearby.

Against Buying It All Immediately. Despite these advantages and despite even a money saving over the long run, there are arguments against a "buy back America" bond issue.

First, is open space worth all this attention right now?

Second, should we trust the planners of today to decide how much and lay out all the open space needed for half a century? Shouldn't it be bought piece by piece after it is clear to the general public that each piece of land is worth acquiring.

Third, should one generation make such an important decision for the next generations?

CHOICE NINE: Should public open space be purchased:
A. From annual appropriations and small bond issues, choosing land to be purchased every year?
B. From a large long-term bond issue, purchasing all the open space desired for the next 50 years?
C. No opinion

Open Space for Inner-City Residents

Whether large amounts or small are spent on parks and recreation, there remains a question of where to spend the money. And since people living in the older cities near the Region's center, particularly in New York City, Newark, and Hudson County, need outdoor recreation sites far more than others in the Region, it is most important to decide how to best serve their needs, however we raise the money.

One Alternative: Enlarge Parkland in Cities. One way would be to concentrate on turning every possible open space in the dense inner communities into outdoor recreation areas, including sitting parks. There are a number of potential sites, but they are in demand for housing or industrial parks. Recently the Glen Oaks golf course in Queens was sold for housing. Three 32-story apartment buildings are to be built on it. Yet Queens is below accepted standards of outdoor recreation space for its population. The Tri-State Regional Planning Commission observed that if Queens were to meet accepted standards of open space it would need 32,000 acres more parkland. (Or, under the straited circumstances, 1,400 more acres.) The golf course could have helped, but use of it was changed from outdoor recreation to housing because the city could not afford to buy it for a park when the owner had to sell, and city people needed housing.

But if the city were perceived as part of the whole New York Urban Region, the decision might have been different. Then it might have been seen that the vacant land outside the city would be far more suitable for housing, while a green oasis in eastern Queens would be the Region's best park buy.

Similarly, use of the Harlem River banks in the Bronx for parkland was proposed as another recommendation of the First Regional Plan in 1929. New York State at last agreed to make a park there. Before the plans got far it was decided to put high-rise housing in the park. Now the plan calls for something that is less like a park than like a landscaped housing development. That part of the Bronx is already far more densely populated than its access to jobs and services warrants. In regional terms there would be little question that the Bronx needs all the parkland it can get—16,400 more acres, if it were to achieve the recommended standards, and a minimum of 500 acres more, according to Tri-State.

Use for industry of the Gowanus Canal and Newtown Creek areas in Brooklyn is being proposed. From the regional viewpoint they might better be used for parks (after they are cleaned up).

The Palisades across from Manhattan in Hudson and Bergen counties are being carved up for housing, though they are the most striking natural landmark in the inner core of the Region. Hudson County needs more parks, according to Tri-State—5,600 more acres to reach usual urban standards, 2,700 at least. Essex, including Newark, needs 6,400 more acres to meet usual urban standards and should have 1,100 more, Tri-State says. If, with relocation taken care of outside city boundaries, neighborhoods cleared of slums were changed in substantial part to parks, perhaps a good share of the needed open space could be achieved.

This first alternative, enlarging outdoor recreation space for city residents, would not change the cities into suburblike neighborhoods, but the city neighborhoods might be interspersed with green spaces and dotted with playgrounds and swimming pools. Children would have some relationship to nature—to trees, birds, and even small wild animals within walking distance of their homes.

What is requisite is a regional view both of open space and

of housing. It requires finding space for more city residents to live *outside* the older cities and priority for park funds to be spent *in* the older cities, whether bought year by year or through a large bond issue.

Parks in the city cost more than parks outside. Recent accounts of the New York City Parks Department show the price of small parks around the city: $110,000 for a Brooklyn park covering two thirds of an acre, with basketball courts, checkers tables, etc.; $223,000 for a Queens park of just under an acre, with handball and volleyball courts and a comfort station; $580,000 for a 4.5-acre Queens playground with Little League ball fields—nearly $1 million spent to buy and develop less than six acres. Just the land for four small parks purchased in the Bronx and Brooklyn in 1968–69 cost an average of about $300,000 an acre.

Second Alternative: Easy-to-Reach Outlying Parks. That same $300,000 spent on an acre of land in New York City could have bought a 1,000-acre natural park in, say, the Hudson Highlands of Putnam County. Furthermore, maintaining larger parks is cheaper than keeping up scattered small parks having the same total area. Much of the money for improving outdoor recreation in the cities would probably be spent on maintenance.

An alternative might be considered: large parks outside dense city neighborhoods with fast, convenient, and subsidized transportation to them. For example, there is some consideration of siting state parks in Westchester County on commuter rail lines where a weekend train stop could be located. In outer Bergen County and Morris, Somerset, Nassau, and Suffolk, similar train- or bus-served parks could be established for inner-city residents. Even to parks as close as Breezy Point, Great Kills, Sandy Hook, and Jamaica Bay now combined into the Gateway National Recreation Area, transportation is expensive; so subsidized transportation for families might be a worthwhile expenditure.

Let us assume that an equal amount could be spent (1) primarily to provide large parks at the end of subsidized rail or bus service far from crowded city neighborhoods, or (2) primarily to buy more city parks and maintain all city parks much better than they are maintained now. We recognize that the alternatives would result in quite different recreation experiences—they are not exactly two ways to achieve the same goal. We also recognize that some money might be spent on each. But which kind of expenditure should be emphasized right now?

CHOICE TEN: Which policy should be emphasized to improve recreation for city residents? (Check one.)
A. Buy more city parks and maintain them better
B. Provide large parks outside cities with subsidized rail, bus, or boat service to them
C. No opinion

IV. TOWN MEETING ON POVERTY

We know that cities are in trouble, that poverty continues in the midst of wealth, that unemployment is high, that malnutrition is widespread, that injustice exists, that tensions endure. In sum, we know that our society is not functioning the way it is supposed to.
—*The National Urban Coalition* (1971)

It may seem obvious that the first need of the poor is money, but the obvious is worth stating here because it is too often forgotten in the discussion of comprehensive antipoverty programs . . . Most of the poor cannot alter their status. To them, incentives are meaningless.
—*Bruno Stein, "On Relief"* (1971)

The Effects of Poverty on the Urban Region

In the 1960s America began to comprehend that increase in national income does not automatically ensure a rising income for everybody and that an underprivileged minority is left outside the mainstream by technological and social barriers created by society as a whole. Our high-technological economy simply does not have jobs enough for those with few skills, nor does it pay amply for low-skilled jobs. Moreover, of that minority in chronic distress large numbers are poor because they are unable to work due to old age, disabilities, or taking care of children. In the urban economy, support of them has long been a public responsibility.

Poverty has many meanings and many dimensions: there is poverty of the spirit and there is emotional poverty, both of which cut across all income groups; but in this discussion, we shall limit ourselves to poverty as a shortage of money, the major medium of exchange for which goods and services are obtained in our society.

Poverty is rarely looked upon as a *regional* problem. It either evokes concern because of the plight of individual human beings in distress or it is talked about as a federal problem, since most long-term solutions involve action by the federal government. Our approach in this town meeting starts from a different viewpoint—that of the interest of "our town," the 20-million Urban Region in New York, New Jersey, and Connecticut. It was built as a machine for facilitating interaction among people on a huge scale, but its smooth functioning is being disrupted by poverty more than by anything else. Where to live and where not to live, what street to walk on and what street not to walk on, what school is good and what school is bad, where to take a job and where not to take a job, whether to take the subway or to pay for a cab, and a whole host of everyday decisions like that are no longer taken on their own merits, but looking over the shoulder at poverty in fear. More generally, our unwillingness to deal with poverty directly—by reallocating money in our society—is costing us dearly in economic terms: it drives us to avoid regulating, say, traffic congestion or pollution by means of prices, so as to avoid hurting the poor, but the resulting waste of resources helps nobody. Our prize invention—the market mechanism—cannot do its job right, if wealth is too unequally distributed. So, from a regional perspective, we can see much clearer how poverty hurts the majority and not merely the poor.

And the concentration of poverty in the Region is proceeding: New York City, as an example, holds a greater share of the nation's poor today than it did 20 years ago.

Let us look at some of the ways in which poverty is distorting the shape of the Urban Region.

The exodus of the middle class from the central cities is the most familiar one. It started simply as a search for better housing on more land. But it has been grossly exacerbated by the pressure of poverty, by neighborhood conditions and crime attributed to poverty, by declines in public services, and by tensions in race relations which stemmed to a large degree from the difficulties faced by blacks and Puerto Ricans in breaking out of poverty.

As secondhand housing in the Region's cities was vacated by the middle class, it was taken over by the poor, coming in from rural areas, for whom it was an improvement over what they had before. We had not equipped the central cities to handle this influx of the poor. In the absence of sufficient compensation from higher levels of government, the cities' declining resources are drained by partial efforts to provide income support and social services for the poor. Meanwhile traditional functions of city government—needed by everybody—deteriorate: the upkeep of parks, the repair of streets, investment in public transit, the collection of refuse, the operation of schools, libraries, and museums, health services, police and fire protection.

Consequently, a general degradation of the urban environment has set in: deteriorating transit increases automobile traffic jams, deteriorating housing conditions force longer and longer journeys to work, and declining school performance causes more and more parents to choose housing in school districts where the children presumably can learn more and where discipline is less a problem.

Businesses follow residences in the flight to the open country-side, where hundreds of acres are paved over for parking, and a totally auto-oriented "spread city" is created. Because of "defensive zoning," housing cannot cluster around these new places of employment. Large lot sizes and low densities are enforced partly as a defense against the possibility of poor people's moving in too, but also partly because the "image" of dense urban development is identified with poverty.

Of course, the fear of poverty and race tension are not the only forces causing suburban sprawl. But when alternatives are proposed—when planners say, Don't build office buildings, colleges, and hospitals on isolated campus sites, put them into present downtowns or into new high-rise centers; don't build just on one-acre lots, build some attached town houses on small lots; don't scatter your garden apartments at random, put them in developments large enough to support public bus service, so sorely deficient in the suburbs—when alternatives of this kind are proposed, the arguments against them usually hinge on issues of crime, poverty, and race.

The argument is not necessarily irrational. The public or private developer will often say that his budget is not set up to meet the extra costs of operating in or near a poor area and that he is not prepared to wage a one-man war against poverty at his own expense. But society as a whole pays in other ways —more natural landscape is destroyed, more automobile travel is created, greater distances have to be traversed, and the resulting dispersed settlement, while gaining some amenities of the countryside, loses the ingredients of intensive interaction, variety, spontaneity, and sense of place that made cities great. One goal is achieved in this new world: in vast areas of the Region very few poor people can be seen.

Apart from the ecological and social costs, there are immediate economic costs as well. The downtown office buildings, which have to stay close together because of linkages among themselves, are having increasing difficulty recruiting trained white-collar workers who have moved to faraway suburbs.

The factories, which have tended to leave the central cities for suburban areas to get more land and easy truck access, have often left behind thousands of blue-collar workers who would like to move nearer suburban plants but are prevented from doing so by zoning barriers which have pushed the cost of housing far above middle-income levels, let alone that which lower-income workers could afford.

For those who commute from suburbs to city jobs, or from city to suburban jobs, the cost is high and the trip time-consuming. The cost is high to the Region at large too, because more highways must be built to transport people to work.

On paper, a planner's solution would be easy: build more higher-income housing in the central city, build more lower-income housing in the suburbs, and build more expressways in the city to ease truck access to those manufacturing plants that could stay in the city and generate blue-collar jobs where the blue-collar workers live. In reality, the second plank in the program has been opposed by the well-to-do, who fear an influx of the poor, and the first and third planks are often opposed by the poor, because we seem unwilling to compensate them adequately for relocation, to provide replacement housing, and because our past failure to do so evokes no trust among the poor.

Thus, poverty not only degrades the environment of central cities; it also stalls the large-scale public projects which could rebuild them. This deadlock jeopardizes the operation of the cities' office economy—the major economic growth sector of our large metropolitan area.

The Effects of the Region's Growth Pattern on the Poor

While imposing extra costs on everybody, the new regional development pattern in many ways restricts, rather than expands, opportunities for the poor. There are about 2,700 square miles of urbanized land in the New York Region; in more than 2,000 of these square miles, almost no poor families can now afford housing, and most of the future population and employment growth will occur in these outer areas if current trends continue. New jobs, new services, new shopping facilities will be placed increasingly in areas where the less affluent cannot reach them.

The relatively few new factory jobs projected to locate in the Region in the future will go to places 40 to 80 miles from Manhattan. In New York City, Regional Plan Association projects a *loss* of more than 130,000 factory jobs by 1985. Employment in various service jobs, suitable for low-skilled workers, will grow in the city but not enough to offset the factory losses.

Meanwhile the jobs staying in the Region's center and growing in number are white-collar jobs. About one third of them are projected to locate in New York City. This could mean opportunity for black and Puerto Rican young people. However, if the educational advancement of the city's residents progresses at past rates, there will not be enough skilled white-collar workers to fill these office jobs. Regional Plan Association projections suggest that by 1985 there could be close to 300,000 new white-collar jobs in New York City, most of which would have to be filled by commuters—unless, of course, the upgrading of skills among the city's lower-income population is much accelerated.

Because of the shift toward a white-collar economy, higher education will be the ticket to more and more jobs in the future. But higher education is too often being located beyond the physical reach of most lower-income families. Most new higher education facilities since World War II have been put outside the Region's cities. Nearly all of these are very difficult to reach except by car.

Services and shopping have followed a similar pattern. Doctors and dentists have followed the higher-income population to the suburbs; there are twice as many physicians per capita in Westchester County as there are in the Bronx or Brooklyn, just for instance. Shopping in many older downtowns is declining, since the people with the most money to spend prefer driving to outlying new shopping centers. Thus, many parts of old cities are left with stores that specialize in selling to people with the lowest incomes. This kind of store frequently offers inferior merchandise at inflated prices.

Wide separation of lower-income families from the rest of the population has separated schoolchildren by income too. This has often meant less money for lower-income children's schools, also loss of whatever benefit could have been derived from their attending school with children of families with more education. As ghettos widen, the opportunity to choose an integrated education for those who want it declines.

Finally, one of the most serious handicaps of lower-income families, caused by the way the Region is developing, is that they are exposed disproportionately to danger from antisocial elements. As one black resident of Bedford-Stuyvesant wrote to the *New York Times:* "I want to see my son grow up into a happy, successful, and honorable person. The odds are now definitely against that happening. So many of my friends, neighbors, and relatives are getting mugged, stabbed, assaulted, and robbed that I know it is just a matter of days or merely hours before my turn will come. . . ." The writer is an ex-Marine sergeant.

It is clear that the effort of so many to run away from poverty is not creating a desirable or efficient Region. It is clear that in addition to the barriers against advancement imposed on the poor by their low income, further barriers are created by their growing geographic separation. We seem to want to perpetuate the condition we are running away from. Yet infinitely worse than the ecological and economic losses caused by the flight from poverty is the human destruction associated with poverty. This human destruction is closely linked to the emotionally charged issues of crime and racial discrimination.

Poverty and Crime

The high incidence of crime in poverty areas is documented by police statistics. In 1970 there were per 100,000 residents 197 murders in central Harlem, between 30 and 60 murders in the South Bronx and in central Brooklyn, 37 murders in Newark, and 26 in Trenton, compared to 1 murder in high-income Nassau County, 2.5 in middle-income Suffolk County, and generally between 1 and 5 in middle-income neighborhoods of Queens, outer Brooklyn, and the outer Bronx. Murder is, of course, a relatively rare event; besides, some 70 percent of all murders nationwide are committed by relatives or acquaintances. Still, the statistics are a telling index of violence and social disorganization. The general tendency in crimes of violence such as murder, aggravated assault, and robbery is to rise steeply with declining income: the rates for the latter two crimes are typically 10, or 20, or 30 times higher in poverty areas than in surrounding neighborhoods. In contrast, less violent crimes against property, such as burglary, theft, or auto theft, are much less discernibly related to poverty, in part because there is less property to steal in low-income areas.

It would be too simplistic to say that economic hardship "causes" crime; after all, there are criminals among the well-to-do, and in the nation as a whole, crime seems to be rising alongside rising affluence. Nevertheless, several chains of reasoning do indicate that crime would be relieved if poverty were relieved.

1. Poverty does block the usual channels for an individual's advancement in society, and therefore does tend to channel energies into less acceptable pursuits. The denial of access to the resources of society—which lack of money signifies—can,

like any denial, generate a variety of responses, from violent self-assertion to passivity and despair, and frustrated self-destruction, as for example addiction. In fact, addiction has sometimes been called the only alternative to riot. Unemployment rates among blacks and Puerto Rican teen-agers average 30 percent in ghetto areas, tapering off only slightly as the youth enter their early twenties; and crime rates are highest precisely among this segment of the population which is most likely to be unemployed. Summer jobs started by the Neighborhood Youth Corps in 1965 have helped to channel the energy of youth but remain grossly inadequate in number. Jobs, better education, and social services, as well as greater family security and a vested interest in one's own future, all require money, both from the government and in the family.

2. Poverty aggravates the effects of emotional disturbance in the individual. It is present among all social classes. But its effects can be cushioned with money. A middle-class alcoholic, for example, will destroy himself gradually in the privacy of his own home, without becoming a public nuisance in the process. An affluent neurotic has the means to hire a psychiatrist and at least bring his problems under control, instead of acting them out on others.

The vast majority of heroin addicts are poor people living in slum neighborhoods: New York has about 150,000 of them —about half of the known addicts in the country. The average addict is reported to need about $45 a day to buy drugs, or some $300 a week in addition to what he needs for food, clothing, shelter, etc. How is an addict to feed this appetite except through theft, prostitution, or selling drugs to other victims? Small wonder that *half* of the city's arrests are for drug-related crimes. And since very few addicts can kick their habit on their own, the only hope lies in enlisting outside help. To date, however, society seems to prefer spending money on rehabilitating human bodies rather than human minds. Only 32,000 of New York's 150,000 addicts are in treatment, about a fifth of the city's addicts. According to New York's Addiction Services Agency, there are another 20,000 addicts on waiting lists to get into a treatment program called "Methadone maintenance," in which the synthetic drug Methadone is given to addicts as a substitute for heroin. According to some reports, about two thirds of those who take Methadone find they can resume a normal life, holding a job or going to school.

3. The people who suffer most from crime are poor people who have no choice but to live in slums where the addicts live. Not only can poor families not afford to move away, but the children of the poor grow up in the destructive atmosphere of

the ghetto. Association with and exposure to those with criminal records, aggravated by the harsh conditions of slum life, tend to perpetuate antisocial behavior. Furthermore, because of the isolation in the ghetto, few examples of people who "made it" in legal economic pursuits can be seen. Giving people afflicted with poverty the means to alter their condition can help them gain control over their lives and channel their energy toward constructive ends.

How society decides to deal with those individuals who persist in destructive behavior is a subject beyond the scope of a discussion on poverty. What can and should be pointed out is that the actual number of offenders is small compared to the number of offenses. Nationwide, of all the offenders arrested on criminal charges in 1970, 68 percent are known to have been arrested before, an average of six times each; of the individuals arrested in 1965 and released to the community (on probation, parole, or because of acquittal or dismissal of charges), 63 percent were arrested again within four years. Thus, it can be said that pretty much the same hard core of people engage in crime. It is a tiny fraction of the poor, who are its first victims.

Poverty and Race

Discrimination barriers due to race and ethnic origin have traditionally aggravated problems of poverty. In 1968, 58 percent of black and Puerto Rican families in New York City had incomes less than $5,000 a year, compared to 19 percent of other families. Meanwhile only 7 percent of black and Puerto Rican families had income above $10,000 a year, compared to 32 percent of all others. Looked at another way, 55 percent of all the city's families with income below $5,000 were black or Puerto Rican. The figures for cities and suburbs in the Region outside New York City also show that black and Puerto Rican residents are bearing the burden of poverty out of all proportion to their number.

This is true particularly of the young. Nationwide, 30 percent of blacks under 22 years of age living in cities are counted as "below the poverty level" by the U.S. Census, whereas only 12 percent of the whites in the same age group are so counted. In this definition the whites include Puerto Ricans.

Complete 1970 data for the whole Region were not available as of this writing, but in the New Jersey sector of the Region the income gap between blacks and whites actually widened between 1960 and 1970; the blacks' gains in income for that period were $600 to $1,800 less than the average gains in income, so that black family income by 1970 trailed the general average by $2,300 to $4,200 in New Jersey.

Discrimination continues to persist. Only a tiny fraction of construction workers are from minority races, and according to the federally financed Urban Institute, a massive number of blacks hold jobs which would pay far more money if they were held by whites. A study by the Institute found that if blacks were paid as much as whites for the same work, their income would rise by *27 percent.* If blacks got equal pay and also had their fair share of the job classifications, black income would rise 45 percent.

In New York City, during the 1960–70 decade, there was a significant advance of the minorities, at least with regard to occupation. The net out-migration of some 235,000 white workers from the city to the suburbs between 1960 and 1968 was balanced by the entry into the work force of an equal number of blacks and Puerto Ricans, the majority of whom filled white-collar positions, including 33,000 professional or managerial jobs and 96,000 clerical or sales jobs. Still, in the long run this rate of entry is not enough to fill the white-collar jobs likely to emerge in the city. And in the short run, high rates of unemployment in the less-skilled occupations persist, especially among the young. Some 170,000 employable persons in New York City are permanently without work because they lack skills. Thus, even when racial barriers are lowered, barriers caused by a deprived background due to poverty will still handicap the minorities.

Money may not be the answer to everything, but in our culture a person without money is excluded from the way of life of the majority. This is not to say this way of life is a model to be emulated by all or that in an open society a variety of life-styles is not desirable. It is to say that access to a way of life should be voluntary, without the inequality and lack of choice that poverty imposes. Relieving poverty will go a long way toward relieving racial tension.

What Is Poverty? Or Who Gets How Much?

Before we proceed to discuss various ways of relieving poverty, we must first decide precisely what it is that we are talking about. There are various ways of defining poverty.

The Census Bureau developed the most widely quoted definition of poverty by using figures based on an economy food plan designed for "emergency or temporary use when funds are low." For households of three or more, the "poverty line" is three times the cost of the 1963 economy food plan, adjusted for cost-of-living increases. In 1972, that figure is about $4,200 for a family of four, or slightly more than $2,000 for a single person in the New York Region.

Anyone living below the "poverty line" can be defined as "hard-core" poor, living at less than the subsistence level. In New York City, 1.2 million people (or 15 percent of the population) lived at that level in 1970, and in the Region outside the city, 0.8 million (or 7 percent).

A similar fixed standard but a more liberal one is used by the U.S. Bureau of Labor Statistics for what it calls a "lower level of living budget." That, in 1970 prices, was roughly $2,700 for an individual and $7,300 for a family of four. With that as a yardstick, 2.3 million residents of New York City, or almost one third of its population, had less than an adequate standard of living, and the number of poor outside the city in the Region, largely in such older cities as Newark, Paterson, and Bridgeport, was 1.8 million. Altogether, 4.1 million people, or one fifth of the Region's population, lived below the BLS "lower level of living" budget.

Nationwide, the proportion of individuals living below the Census "hard-core" poverty level declined from 22.4 percent in 1959 to 12.2 percent in 1969. If that decline should continue, poverty would disappear from the United States by the beginning of the next decade. But will it?

Historically, definitions of poverty have changed with changing standards of living. Things that used to be luxuries become necessities: telephones, television sets, automobiles; and frequently they are indeed essential to full participation in society. A fixed minimum subsistence standard makes no allowance for this. One could, of course, adjust it upward once in a while to include more goods, but that would excite endless disputes as to what a low-income family "really" needs and underscore the arbitrariness of fixing a standard to begin with.

One can argue that any fixed standard is an inappropriate measure of poverty, since poverty itself is a relative thing. The equivalent of a $4,000 income level is considered an average income in Europe. It is affluence or even wealth in Africa or Asia. But it is well below what is considered a decent but modest scale in a city like New York. In fact, a family of four living in the New York Region with a $6,000 income feels more poor than affluent. In other words, people perceive themselves as being poor by comparing themselves to others, not by multiplying their minimum food budget by three. Therefore, instead of trying to define how much a family "really" needs (needs expand so easily!), one can look at how much it actually gets, compared to everyone else. Professor Bruno Stein of New York University put it this way: "As the pie [of the economy] grows bigger . . . all the slices tend to grow, although not necessarily at an even rate. It is the relative size of the slice that counts, because this is what people perceive."

To measure the size of the slices, it is convenient to divide the population into, let us say, five groups equal in size: the lower fifth, the lower-middle fifth, and so on, up to the upper fifth. Then we can see how much of the total money income each fifth gets. This is done in Table 4 for the U.S., the Region, and New York City, based on figures from the 1970 census.

Table 4. Share of All Income (Before Taxes)
Received by Families and Unrelated Individuals, 1969

Income Group	U.S.	Region	N.Y.C.	Income Range in 1969
Lowest fifth	2.8%	3.1%	2.9%	Under $ 3,000
Lower-middle fifth	9.4	9.8	9.4	$ 3,000–$ 6,500
Middle fifth	16.8	16.4	15.9	$ 6,500–$10,000
Upper-middle fifth	24.8	23.5	23.7	$10,000–$15,000
Highest fifth	46.2	47.2	48.1	Over $15,000
Top 5%	(18.5)*	20.4	20.7	Over $27,500
Top 1%	(5.4)*	7.3	7.4	Over $50,000

SOURCE: 1970 Census of Population, General Social and Economic Characteristics.

* Estimates by Regional Plan Association.

It is evident that in the New York Region the lowest fifth of all households gets only about 3 percent of all income, whereas the highest fifth gets 47 percent. In New York City the distribution of income is somewhat more unequal, with the lowest fifth getting less than 3 percent and the highest fifth getting virtually half of all money income. In all cases, the highest fifth is *more than fifteen times* richer than the lowest fifth.

If the income of the poor and the lower-middle class—or the bottom 40 percent of the population—is added together, those in the top fifth still get 3½ times as much. In fact, the top 5 percent of all households earn substantially more than the bottom 40 percent combined, as evident from the 1970 census figures shown in Table 4.

Census income figures tend to be somewhat under-reported, and other sources (such as shown in Table 7 later on) give figures that can differ by a percentage point here or there, but the overall picture of a high degree of income inequality remains unchanged. Nor is it changed much if the numbers are corrected for after-tax income. As we show later in Table 8, the combined incidence of local, state, and federal taxes is not at all as progressive as most people think, so that the share of income paid in taxes rises only mildly with rising income. Therefore, the shares of income after taxes received by each fifth of the population are not greatly different from those in Table 4. A study by Letitia Upton and Nancy Lyons of the Cambridge Institute indicated that in 1962, the income share of families in the top fifth of the population declined only from 45.5 percent before taxes to 43.7 percent after taxes, while the bottom three fifths increased their income share only from 31.8 percent before to 33.2 percent after taxes.

These shares of income have remained fairly stable in recent times. There was a redistribution of income following the Depression in the 1930s and during World War II, but more recently there has only been a slight shift from the highest group to the upper-middle group. The poorest fifth of all families and unrelated individuals has stayed within 3 to 4 percent of all income for more than two decades and seems to be losing out now. What this means is that all the antipoverty and welfare programs of the past decade have not even enabled the poor to keep up with the growth of the economy; in fact, their position with regard to other groups has apparently worsened.

This is not to argue for absolute equality of income. A society in which everybody has the same income is just about unthinkable, because abilities are unequal, because society perceives the need for some people more than for others, because when some resources are scarce, not everybody can have them. Some inequality creates incentives for performance and management, and helps the accumulation of capital for investment —both essential to the economic growth from which all classes benefit.

But the rejection of complete equality does not mean that the present distribution of income has to be accepted. One can argue whether the present distribution of income reflects the best balance between the stimulation of the economy and the broadest possible satisfaction of human needs. Do the highest-income 5 percent of all households really need more than the lowest-income 40 percent to keep the economy going? Should the contrast between the lowest fifth and the highest fifth be fifteenfold, or, say, eightfold, or fivefold? One can argue that cutting the income of the highest fifth by 10 percent would more than double the income of the lowest fifth.

Outlining Possible Solutions

What can be done to solve the problem of poverty? "Nothing," say some, quoting the Bible to prove their point:

"The poor ye shall always have with you." Those with this point of view argue that no matter what sort of income distribution might exist, there would always be a "bottom 20 percent," people who would feel deprived when they compared their income with others around them.

But there is a contrary argument, namely, that if the contrast between the extremes of the income distribution is reduced, finding oneself in the "bottom 20 percent" will be much less onerous.

Ever since President Lyndon Johnson declared an "unconditional war on poverty" in 1964, literally dozens of programs have been introduced and experimented with. Some, such as the Job Corps, were begun in a blaze of publicity and have since died. Others, such as the Office of Economic Opportunity community action agencies, did not wipe out poverty, but they did help create a self-awareness among low-income groups and a new leadership, essential for advancement. Some programs did achieve unpublicized success: for example, federally financed college scholarships provided an incentive for many poor blacks and Puerto Ricans to finish high school and go on to college. The proportion of young adults (aged 20 to 29) with at least a high school education rose 55 percent among blacks in the 60s and only 25 percent among whites. Of course, the whites started from a higher base and still have a much higher percentage of young adults with a high school diploma (81 versus 62 percent), but the blacks are catching up. The proportion of the nation's population living below the officially defined "poverty" line was cut virtually in half during the 60s (largely, of course, due to the overall rise in incomes), and the share of the federal budget devoted to various income maintenance schemes (ranging from the various pension plans to Medicare, welfare, and food stamp programs) did rise dramatically: from 27.7 percent of all federal expenditures in 1960 to 33.8 percent in 1970 and nearly 40 percent in 1973. Still, as we pointed out above, the poor seem to be getting poorer, if you look at the *share* of the nation's money income they receive.

The question really is not what can be done. It is: Where do we go from here? Many of the programs begun in the 60s, ranging from manpower training, to aid for education, to help for minority businesses, will undoubtedly continue. Some may be modified or cut back, depending on circumstances. There will probably be an emphasis on greater efficiency, on evaluating the effectiveness of each program in reaching its objectives.

But the major emerging issue seems to be this: Do we continue to emphasize programs which attack poverty indirectly—by providing education, training, community leadership, loans to small businesses, and youth programs—or do we say that poverty equals the shortage of money among some groups of the population and that a direct way to cure that is by redistributing the apportionment of money in our society?

The practice of federal intervention in the income distribution pattern achieved by the private market in the U.S. is by no means new—the progressive income tax dates back to 1918, and federal minimum wage standards and Social Security payments to 1938. The question is merely this: Should these kinds of tools be used to a greater degree than previously to achieve a more nearly equitable distribution of income, to reduce the contrast between the rich and the poor?

In this vein, the rest of the discussion will touch upon education (mostly in terms of money allocations) and will deal with three major ways of income redistribution. These choices are summarized in four steps:

1. Improving educational opportunities
2. Improving employment opportunities
3. Boosting low incomes
4. Reforming taxes

The emphasis (excepting the question of school integration) is on the distribution of money, simply to keep the discussion within manageable limits. Some issues related to poverty are further discussed in the town meetings on housing and the shape of the Region, but a host of issues are frankly left out: how to improve the *performance* of schools and teachers, how to improve the effectiveness of training programs, how to increase the political power of the poor, how to deal with crime, how to deal with racism and remaining discrimination, as well as the all-embracing psychological and ethical issue—how to increase the amount of responsibility and mutual understanding in our society.

Part A: Improving Educational Opportunities

The Need to Read and Write

Knowledgeable experts estimate that about 20 percent of the children in the United States fail to read and write at the level required for available employment. In some poverty areas this figure reaches 75 percent. More than 9 million children now enrolled in public schools eventually will enter the labor market as functional illiterates unless public education is vastly improved. The data for performance skills in mathematics, also essential for participation in the American economy, are similar.

A generation ago, a person with a third- or fourth-grade education could get a job. As recently as 1963, 17 percent of the labor force was unskilled. But the U.S. Secretary of Labor estimates that by 1976 only 5 percent of the nation's jobs will be unskilled.

What will happen to the functionally illiterate in a society which demands more and more education? One answer can be found by looking at the reading abilities of people who end up in prison. A recent survey of the New Jersey prison system revealed that the *average* reading skill of inmates was between the second and fourth grades. The average inmate was functionally illiterate—that is, unable to read a newspaper or a job application.

Over the long haul, perhaps no step to wipe out poverty is more important than teaching everyone sufficient skills in reading, writing, and arithmetic. Of course, school education is not a panacea. Recent studies, such as *Inequality* by sociologist Christopher Jencks, cast doubt on how much difference formal schooling can make on determining a person's lifetime earnings. The fact remains that a minimum level of scholastic competence is essential for advancement in our society.

Unfortunately, it is easier to state the problem than to suggest a remedy. Limited experiments have demonstrated that even the most disadvantaged child can be taught. But there is a dis-incentive to change in most public school systems which outweighs the incentive to change and to increase performance. Over the years, delicate and complex relationships have developed among school boards, administrators, parents, and teacher unions, all of which aim at minimizing friction and maintaining stability, even if it is at the expense of teaching performance. Without pretending to cover the full spectrum of educational issues, three of them can be singled out.

School Integration

School segregation by race and evidently by income has been increasing sharply in the Region. Between 1968 and 1970 alone the percentage of minority students attending public schools in which minorities account for more than 90 percent of the enrollment increased from 45.5 to 49.2 percent in New York State. In New York City, 23 percent of the schools were moderately segregated and 66 percent were totally segregated in 1969, according to the U.S. Department of Health, Education and Welfare. The growing segregation of residential areas has contributed to this.

The massive Coleman Report in the mid-1960s, involving hundreds of thousands of students, indicated that minority students tended to perform better if the majority of students were middle-class whites. This early evidence has been confirmed by the U.S. Senate Select Committee on Equal Educational Opportunity which recently completed two years of study and hearings on the issue. It found that most available evidence suggests disadvantaged children—be they Appalachian whites, Chicanos, Negroes, or Indians—are all likely to do better in school if they are educated with middle-class children.

In Berkeley, black youngsters had been gaining only 0.5 year in reading performance for every year in school, thus slipping farther and farther behind. But when they were transferred out of segregated schools to integrated schools, they gained 0.8 year in reading ability for every year in school. While still below the average, this was significantly better. Similar evidence was cited in Hartford's Project Concern and in Hoke County, N.C., where the achievement of black students was more than 50 percent better after a year of busing to integrated schools. A Harvard professor named David Armor, in an investigation of five northern cities, however, found no evidence of scholastic improvement as a result of busing. The evidence that integrated education improves scholastic performance of disadvantaged children is contradictory, then, but on the whole it leans in the direction of integration.

The Senate study found that the performance of middle-class children did not drop in integrated classes, as long as the majority of the students were from middle-class homes. One might add that there is likely to be a psychic benefit to both middle-class and minority children from exposure to differences, from not being frozen within a static environment.

Beyond that, there is a moral issue. As the *New York Times* editorialized: "We believe that the integrated school, even if it produced no educational gains, must be the goal of a free and integrated society." Black opinion has been divided on the issue. The National Black Political Convention at Gary, Indiana, in 1972 initially opposed busing to integrate schools, because it found a greater value in strengthening ghetto schools. But it later reversed its position, saying that busing was one device for giving blacks a better education. The NAACP has been strongly committed to busing as a way of "building a single society" and avoiding the attempt to keep "black children contained in segregated educational compounds."

It will be recalled that our town meeting on housing posed choices which looked toward reducing the growing segregation of the Region by building more subsidized housing in middle-class residential areas. This may be a "natural" way to get integrated schools, preferable to busing students from one district to another. However, despite the passage of Open Housing laws, segregation of residential areas is growing in our Region.

The existence of a massive stock of fairly low-cost second-hand housing in the older parts of the Region, which cannot be duplicated soon by subsidized construction programs on any scale, is a physical fact encouraging large-scale segregation. Scatter-site low-income housing construction to increase integration has run into local opposition. But, even if programs to build subsidized housing away from ghetto areas were much expanded, the number of minority students integrated in middle-class schools this way would be very small.

There are, of course, many areas in the Region—mostly along the fringe of hard-core ghettos—where the resident population is fairly mixed now; this does not mean, however, that the schools in these areas are integrated. In Jamaica, Queens, for example, one can find predominantly white and predominantly black schools within walking distance of each other. The Fleischmann Commission found this to be a typical pattern in New York State—probably the result of heightened white defenses in areas where minority population is expanding. Still, by changing school attendance boundaries and enforcing racial balance in the schools of racially mixed residential areas, a noticeable degree of desegregation can be had in the Region. Schools can be desegregated within walking distance or within a very short bus ride of the children's homes.

It is likely that at least some of the opposition to busing children for the purpose of integrating schools stems from the huge scale at which segregation occurs in the Region. If, in a racially mixed area, there are two schools within view of each other and one of them is 90 percent black and the other 90 percent white, a clear case of discrimination is at hand, of the kind outlawed by the Supreme Court in 1954 in the *Brown vs. Board of Education* decision, which found that "separate educational facilities are inherently unequal." However, if the two schools are a long trip apart and one is located in a large all-black area where other schools are also 90 percent black, the other in an all-white area where other schools are also 90 percent white, it is more difficult to speak of "separate" facilities within each area and more difficult to integrate the schools between areas. If their children have to travel too far to a better school, black parents often fear their isolation in an inhospitable environment, and object to loss of control over "their" school. Similarly, in addition to whatever bigotry is present, white parents will object more to the dangers of a distant ghetto area.

Another source of opposition is the percentage of disadvantaged children in the classroom—the higher the percentage, the greater the opposition. An investigation for the Fleischmann Commission showed that in spite of huge racial imbalances in different parts of New York City it is physically possible to integrate the entire city school system by means of busing. But admittedly some of the busing would have to be over long distances, such as from Brooklyn to Staten Island. Just what the appropriate geographic area is, within which integration should occur, has never really been specified by the courts or by anyone else. Even a relatively short limit on busing—such as five miles—could integrate such areas as Bedford-Stuyvesant and Forest Hills, parts of Harlem and parts of Bergen County, parts of the central Bronx and southern Westchester County, South Jamaica, and parts of Nassau County. But, far short of complete integration even across state or county lines, much greater racial balance in the schools of the Region can be achieved by busing within counties, over presently customary distances.

CHOICE ONE. Should the public schools become more integrated, and if so, how? (Check as many as desired.)
A. No
B. House more low-income families in middle-income neighborhoods
C. Change school attendance boundaries for more integration within walking distance
D. Use buses to achieve more integration over wider areas
E. No opinion.

Spending More on Disadvantaged Children

Next to school integration is another issue involving equal opportunity in education: How much is spent on each child?

Traditionally, public education in America has been financed primarily by local property taxes. This has given rise to large inequities due to the wide differences in local tax bases. Englewood Cliffs, N.J., has $145,000 worth of assessed property for every child to be educated in the school district. Newark has only $19,000 of property value behind each of the students in its public schools. The consequence is that Englewood Cliffs can tax itself relatively lightly and can spend more per pupil than Newark, which must tax itself more heavily in order to spend less.

The New Jersey Tax Policy Committee (the Sears Committee) confirmed this disparity by saying that residents in the low-income bracket pay an effective property tax rate which is *five times* as high as those in the high bracket, and have poorer schools.

It is not the poor only who suffer from inequities in the property tax. So do middle-class families unlucky enough to live in a school district which has no industry within its borders. On the other hand, there are a number of tax-haven communities which have few children to educate and much local industry to tax. The difference in taxes between communities can range up to 300 percent. For example, the owner of a house worth $30,000 in Ridgefield, N.J., paid about $336 in 1971 for property taxes, while the same kind of house in River Vale, only a few miles away, is being taxed over $1,200 —a difference of more than 250 percent.

The Sears Committee, appointed by Governor William T. Cahill, recommended that public education be financed by *statewide taxes* rather than by local property taxes. Governor Cahill accepted the recommendation, but it was defeated in the legislature. A similar recommendation for a statewide tax for schools was made by the New York State Commission on the Quality, Cost and Financing of Elementary and Secondary Education (the Fleischmann Commission).

It will be recalled that one choice offered in our housing program was that school costs be borne by a statewide tax rather than by local property taxes. However, the argument there was that property taxes inhibit housing construction for all but the top fifth of all households. The additional argument here is on grounds of equity in financing education.

The present system of financing public education has been found to be unconstitutional by the Supreme Courts of California and New Jersey, because, as California's court put it, the present system "makes the quality of a child's education a function of the wealth of his parents and neighbors." Generally, the wealthier school districts spend more per child, the poorer districts spend less; in addition, there are differences according to how much each district is willing to tax itself. These also tend to work against children from poorer families.

Should children from better home backgrounds have the

additional advantage of having more money spent on them in public schools?

Some say yes—traditionally, those who have more have gotten more in our society, and there is no sense trying to change that. Others read "equal opportunity" literally, and say that in public schools each child should receive the same public investment. A third line of reasoning is that this too will tend to favor middle-class children who enter school better prepared academically, coming as they do from homes where intellectual skills are encouraged. To give disadvantaged children a truly equal start in life, *more* should be spent on them, according to this line of thought, to compensate for the lack of intellectual preparation in the home.

The idea of compensatory education is by no means new. The Elementary and Secondary Education Act of 1965, the first major federal aid to public schools, targeted $1 billion annually on improving the education of children from poor homes. Over the years, that figure has risen to $1.5 billion, about $150 million of which has been spent annually in the Region, or between $200 and $300 per pupil per year, over and above regular outlays.

The effect of the program on improving the ability of disadvantaged children to read and write has been disappointing to many. As measured by objective national tests, the reading and math performance of students in the older cities of the Region has, in fact, been slipping farther and farther behind national norms. In New York City 54 percent of the students were behind national reading levels in 1965. By 1971, 66 percent or two thirds of the students were below grade level in reading performance. Unquestionably, much of this slippage is due to the fact that large numbers of middle-class students have moved out of the cities and been replaced by newly arrived, disadvantaged students.

But there is the more important issue of exactly how the money for compensatory education is spent.

The federal law gave state departments of education the right to set standards and determine what local school districts had to do to receive federal aid. Many state departments of education avoided getting into battles with local school districts on standards by simply rubber-stamping local applications for aid. The result was that some of the federal money was spent on equipment of dubious value, much of it went simply into paying higher teacher salaries, and generally the funds were spread thin over many students instead of being focused on those who were most in need of extra help. California, on the other hand, was willing to set firm standards, requiring that all the money be spent on disadvantaged students, that most of it be focused on improving math and reading skills, and that periodic testing be done to measure impact. For daring to tell local school boards what to do, California's state department of education had to fight many thorny battles, but the result is that the entire state school system has been able to show marked improvement in reading and math performance—a claim no other state can make. And there have been enough examples in individual classrooms, schools, and school districts to show that disadvantaged children are able to learn much more if the effort is focused on them.

In this Region, the State of Connecticut has actually vetoed a number of local applications for federal aid and has been reducing the number of students served to maximize results. The approach has been effective and the 50,000 students served last year gained 1.1 years in reading for 1 year in school.

Thus, one way of trying to improve the educational opportunities of poor children is for state departments of education to tie school funds more specifically to the performance of the children in each school. The Fleischmann Commission in New York State has come out with similar recommendations. The price of all such schemes is, of course, greater central control over local school matters, an idea that is resisted by many.

CHOICE TWO. How much money should be spent to educate children whose reading and math scores lag seriously behind national norms? (Check one.)
A. The *same* as is spent on other children
B. *More than* is spent on other children
C. *Less than* is spent on other children
D. No opinion.

Preschool Education and Day Care

Children from poorer homes, homes where there is little reading or other intellectual stimulation, begin school behind their classmates. Psychologists tell us that about half of an individual's full intellectual development occurs during the first five years of life—before most children are placed in a planned learning environment. And, by age three, poor children already lag behind children from more affluent homes. Therefore, the argument goes, preschool care might reduce the handicaps of children from poor families and be of benefit to middle-class children as well.

This has been the rationale for the Head Start program,

begun in 1965. However, this and related programs are very limited in scope, reaching only about 5 percent of the nation's 11 million pre-kindergarten youngsters. They have demonstrated that intensive experimental programs can raise the test scores of disadvantaged children dramatically but that the gains tend to fade when the children grow older. And it remains unclear whether children eventually end up with a better education if they start very early. Many people feel that at the ages between two and four, the home is better for a child than any kind of institutional environment, even for a few hours a day. Nationwide about 80 percent of five-year-olds attend kindergarten, and pre-kindergarten programs are attended by 23 percent of four-year-olds, 9 percent of three-year-olds, almost none of the two-year-olds.

Alongside the argument for early childhood development goes the argument for providing day care so that mothers have a genuine choice between staying at home and going to work. This would enable many families among the working poor to have second wage earners, and would help many female welfare recipients who are heads of families. A study conducted by Dr. Lawrence Podell in 1966 reported that 70 percent of all welfare mothers stated they preferred working to staying at home, and would work if day care were available for their children. Their background suggests they meant it, since 80 percent had worked previously, one third for 10 years or more. Moreover, many of them had some white-collar work experience and could obtain white-collar jobs, of which there is a continuing increase.

But day-care facilities are extremely limited. In 1970 in New York City, only 32,700 children were enrolled in public and private day-care programs; in addition, the Department of Social Services reimbursed in-home babysitter costs for about 7,000 welfare mothers who were employed or attending training programs. Altogether, these services covered about 6.5 percent of the city's preschool children. The situation is similar in other cities of the Region. Regional Plan Association estimates that day-care services for an additional 85,000 children could free 50,000 mothers in low-income families for white-collar jobs. That could reduce poverty in New York City by as much as one sixth.

A program of this kind would not be cheaper than keeping unmarried mothers on welfare, for the costs of quality day care are high. Day care focused on child development may cost $2,500 or more per child, while care of the babysitting variety would cost $1,000 or less. Clearly, a free nationwide program covering all of the nation's 11 million pre-kinder-garten children would be prohibitively expensive, as well as wasteful. Besides, trained pre-kindergarten teachers simply would not be available in these numbers—only 4,000 to 5,000 of them are graduated each year. But national pre-kinder-garten enrollment might be doubled from 1.3 million to 2.6 million, according to the National Urban Coalition, if 80,000 early education teachers and 160,000 paraprofessionals were trained. And an additional half million children could be given day care. The costs of a limited program, doubling or tripling the present small enrollment, could be kept within bounds if it were free only to low-income families, with partial subsidies on a sliding scale as incomes go up.

CHOICE THREE. Should preschool education and day care for children of working mothers be more widely available, with the charge varying from nothing to full cost, depending on income?

YES   NO   NO OPINION

Part B: Improving Employment Opportunities

Unemployment and National Economic Policy

Having considered some ways of equalizing opportunity in education, we now can turn to direct attacks on poverty.

The single most powerful cause of poverty is unemployment. Unemployment, in turn, is largely influenced by national economic policy. The purpose of national economic policy is to achieve a growing economy with high employment and stable prices. However, throughout the postwar era, attempts to reach this goal have been frustrated by the fact that high levels of employment meant rising inflation. This was most recently demonstrated in the late 60s, when unemployment reached a long-time low of 3.5 percent of the labor force but inflation increased prices 5 to 6 percent a year.

To understand the role management of the economy can play in the reduction of poverty we must distinguish between two types of unemployment.

There is unemployment which is widespread, generally af-fecting most segments of the labor force, and which is caused by depressed economic activity and insufficient demand for goods and services. It results from cutbacks in the number of people employed to produce these goods and services, and is generally known as *cyclical unemployment* because the ups and downs of the economy go more or less in cycles.

The second type of unemployment persists even when cyclical unemployment is at a low point and the economy is in high gear. This type of unemployment results when some workers are unable to meet certain requirements to fill available jobs—such requisites as education, skills, geographic location. It is called *structural unemployment* in the sense that it is due not to a lack of jobs in the national economy as a whole but to barriers in the local labor market where the unemployed are looking for jobs.

The traditional monetary and fiscal tools government uses to manage the economy can affect only cyclical unemployment. The *monetary tools* are controls over the amount of money in circulation and over the availability of credit. The *fiscal tools* are policies on taxes and on government spending—whether, for example, to run a deficit or a surplus in the federal budget. When economic activity is sluggish and the demand for consumer goods is low, unemployment is high by virtue of the reduced need to produce more goods for people to buy. To stimulate the economy the government may make money and credit more easily available through a reduction in interest rates, a tax cut, or deficit spending. In theory, more money in circulation will increase the purchasing power of the population, create more demand for goods and services, and thus increase employment. But as the economy recovers to a point where vacant jobs go unfilled because of the shortage of qualified workers, the increased demand for goods becomes more difficult to meet and prices begin to go up: hence inflation. If it appears that inflation is getting out of hand, the government may cut back the supply of money and credit and in effect try to buy greater price stability at the price of more unemployment.

A situation like this arose at the end of the 60s, when the supply of money was deliberately throttled, economic growth was slowed down, and so eventually was inflation, but unemployment increased, as did the number of persons in poverty.

There is this apparent trade-off between employment and inflation: the lower the unemployment, the higher goes price inflation; the more stable the prices, the higher goes the unemployment rate. This trade-off cannot be portrayed by an exact curve, because additional factors, aside from unemployment, influence inflation. For example, as automatic cost escalation clauses are written into more and more contracts, inflation tends to become endemic and more of it is needed to attain a given level of employment. On the other hand, deliberate wage-price controls can reduce inflationary pressures.

Much depends on the characteristics of an economy, and on the behavior of its work force: How effectively do workers, when they are in great demand, press for higher wages? Some countries have had virtually full employment with a modest inflation rate, whereas others, including the United States today, seem to require a relatively high inflation rate to come close to full employment. The experience in the U.S. over the postwar decades is shown in Table 5 and in the graph in Figure 6.

Table 5. Unemployment and Inflation in the U.S. since World War II

Year	Percent of the Work Force Unemployed	Percent Increase in Consumer Prices During the Year
1948	3.8	7.8
1949	5.9	−1.0
1950	5.3	1.0
1951	3.3	7.9
1952	3.0	2.2
1953	2.9	0.8
1954	5.5	0.5
1955	4.4	−0.4
1956	4.1	1.5
1957	4.3	3.6
1958	6.8	2.7
1959	5.5	0.8
1960	5.5	1.6
1961	6.7	1.0
1962	5.5	1.1
1963	5.7	1.2
1964	5.2	1.3
1965	4.5	1.7
1966	3.8	2.9
1967	3.8	2.9
1968	3.6	4.2
1969	3.5	5.4
1970	4.9	5.9
1971	5.9	4.3
1972 (August)	5.6	3.6

SOURCE: U.S. Bureau of Labor Statistics.

Figure 6

U. S. UNEMPLOYMENT VERSUS INFLATION 1946-1972

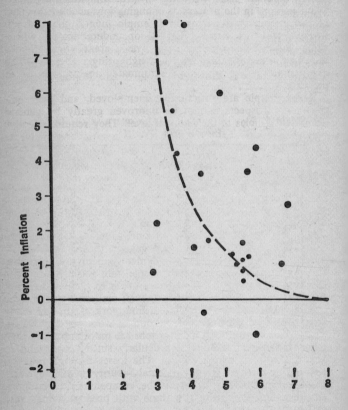

NOTE: The curve shown is patterned after the "Phillips curve"—a relationship between inflation and unemployment—adjusted to fit data for the period shown.

But why is it that even with high inflation rates and so-called full employment we can bring the unemployment rate only down to 3.5 percent, which, after all, means that there still are nearly 3 million workers in the nation without jobs? Why so much residual unemployment while employers have positions that go unfilled? Here we come to structural unemployment. While persons in the process of changing jobs account for part of the unemployed during "full employment," the rest are workers who are either unskilled or undereducated, whose skills have become obsolete, who live in areas where all jobs are filled while openings exist in neighboring places to which they cannot get, or who are discriminated against because of their age, sex, or race.

These people are structurally unemployed, and their employment prospects cannot be improved greatly by general economic policies at the national level. They require selective measures geared to their particular circumstances, such as adult education and manpower training programs and better information about and access to jobs outside their immediate area.

Conversely, however, *education and job training cannot create jobs that do not exist.* We shall deal with these issues in greater detail shortly; meanwhile, let us return to the trade-off between unemployment and inflation.

While inflation does affect everyone, generally the losers are those who lend money and the gainers those who borrow money. On the whole, high employment policies and moderate rates of inflation tend to help people with less than average incomes. Conversely, the sacrifices made to combat inflation are most heavily borne by workers with modest income: some become poor because they cannot find work at all, and many others are forced by the competition to work for low wages. To workers with modest income, jobs are more important than losses because of inflation, particularly since wages tend to keep up with inflationary costs. The losses through inflation suffered by the aged living on Social Security or other government pensions tend to be, or can be, compensated by congressional action. It is primarily those with private savings who suffer.

As Table 5 and Figure 6 show, the relationship between inflation and unemployment is not an exact one, but the overall direction—less unemployment tends to mean more inflation—seems clear. Very roughly, one can suggest that heating up the economy to provide 1 million jobs might increase the inflation rate by about 2 percentage points under current conditions.

CHOICE FOUR. In the fall of 1972, the inflation rate was 3.6 percent, and there were 4.5 million unemployed in the nation. Assuming that a 2 percent higher inflation rate would reduce the number of unemployed by 1 million, would you be willing to accept it?

YES   NO   NO OPINION

Relieving Structural Unemployment

The Region—the 31 counties in southern New York, northern New Jersey, and western Connecticut—has roughly one tenth of the nation's work force, about 8 million out of 80 million workers. The unemployment rate in the Region is only slightly higher than in the nation. When, in the fall of 1972, there were roughly 4.5 million unemployed in the nation, there were some 475,000 unemployed in the Region. Of that number, about one third, or 150,000, could be considered cyclically unemployed, and would find jobs if national economic policy were to put the economy in higher gear.

However, in 1968 nobody was out of a job because of the cyclical ups and downs in the demand for goods and services; the private economy was performing as best it could, at "full employment." In New York City and the Region there were no white-collar unemployed that year, except for those who happened to be in the process of changing jobs. Nevertheless, in New York City 75,000 lower-skilled blue-collar workers were without jobs, and only 20,000 job openings were available to them. In suburban counties, 55,000 lower-skilled blue-collar workers were without jobs, and only 40,000 job openings were available. In addition, New York City had some 170,000 potentially employable people with low skills who had given up looking for work and were not officially counted among the unemployed. In sum, regionwide there were some 300,000 unemployed lower-skilled blue-collar workers, for whom only 95,000 job openings were available, according to a Regional Plan study for the City of New York.

A. Job Placement and Transportation

Why didn't the 300,000 at least grab at those openings which were available? The major reason is that a great many of the openings were at or near the minimum wage level, which was $1.60 in 1968, and $1.85 in 1972. At that level, only a self-supporting single individual can live above a "lower level of living budget" ($1.85 an hour represents $3,800 a year). For a two- or three-person family, minimum legal wages from one worker produce only marginal incentive for employment, compared to a welfare allowance. For a family of four, there is little incentive when the 1971 welfare allowance was about $4,000 in New York, New Jersey, and Connecticut.

However, more than half of the lower-skilled blue-collar openings available in the Region in 1968 did pay adequate wages; interestingly, these openings were most of them in the less accessible parts of the city or the less accessible parts of the suburbs. *Lack of knowledge* and *difficulty of access* might have prevented the unemployed from taking these jobs.

Information about job openings is still mostly by word of mouth, and the employment offices, both state and private, deal mainly with individual employers. Computerized "job bank" files, instantly listing all available openings, have now been put into operation in several counties of the Region, but they are, of course, only as good as the jobs reported to them.

And while a worker in, say, New York City could, with some effort, find out what jobs are available in, say, Nassau County, that would be of little help to him unless he had an automobile. The blue-collar jobs accessible by public transit tend to pay the lowest wage rates. Reduced railroad fares in the reverse direction—from the city into the suburbs—would, according to Regional Plan calculations, help at most 2,000 city workers find new jobs during full employment. Special bus routes to outlying plants, experimented with in various cities, were generally expensive—from $500 to $1,250 per worker per year. At these rates, it would be more efficient to subsidize auto ownership for selected low-income workers, perhaps under the aegis of job training and placement programs. Indeed, Regional Plan has found that blue-collar workers who drive to work, even when they don't own a car but drive with someone else, do have considerably higher wages.

Reverse-commuting rail subsidies, some auto subsidies for low-income workers, and greatly improved job information and placement would help to fill some 10,000 lower-skilled blue-collar jobs in New York City (or half the city's job openings at that level in a peak employment year like 1968) and some 20,000 outside the city (again, half of what might be available in a full employment period). That would help reduce poverty in the Region, under the most optimistic assumptions, by some 5 percent. Bringing housing closer to existing jobs would have about the same effect on unemployment, though it would have much larger additional benefits by reducing travel costs and improving the living environment of low-income workers now employed.

The conclusion is clear: improved job placement, improved transportation for low-income workers, and housing closer to jobs are all necessary, but the problem is a regionwide surplus of lower-skilled blue-collar workers.

B. Training Programs

The main reason for persistent unemployment in New York City and the Region, even in times of prosperity, is that most of the unemployed lack the skills this specialized economy demands. In the Region, 55 percent of all jobs are in white-collar occupations, while the overwhelming majority of the unemployed are blue-collar workers. In three poverty areas surveyed by Regional Plan Association, 64 percent of the unemployed never finished high school, while 70 percent of those who were employed were high school graduates. The case for manpower training and education seems clear.

Another possibility lies in improving the preparation given by high schools for the world of work. Only 10 percent of today's high school students receive any vocational training, and many of them are learning vocations for which there is little demand. The federal government spends $11.7 billion on job training after school but only $300 million on the unskilled who are still in school. Students are told not to drop out, but many of those who listen receive diplomas that have been called passports to nowhere.

In sum, improvement and expansion of work training programs are clearly needed, but the issues are rather technical, not easily summarized in a broad choice having to do with changes in public policy. The same holds true for the earlier issues of job placement and transportation. A choice on moving housing closer to jobs has been included in our town meeting on housing.

C. Public Service Jobs

Whatever is done in the fields outlined above will help reduce structural unemployment in the Region over time, but holds out no early relief for the roughly 300,000 people who are permanently out of work in the Region. If all of them had jobs now, paying, say, $3 an hour, poverty in the Region would be cut in half.

Yet, even as they have to remain idle, there are thousands of jobs that need to be done, which only government can pay for: nonprofessional aides in hospitals and schools, workers on neighborhood improvement, park and street maintenance workers, construction workers on low-income housing. Hence arises the argument that government should be the employer of "last resort," employing all those willing and able to work who cannot find jobs in the private sector.

The proof that the private sector cannot provide the jobs is apparent. The 300,000 or so hard-core structurally unemployed in the Region were out of work in 1968 and 1969, when unemployment nationwide was down to 3.5 percent, the lowest it had been in 20 years.

There seem to be limits to what the usual fiscal and monetary tools of government, which regulate the private economy, can do for the hard-core unemployed. There are three additional reasons why overheating the private economy with fiscal and monetary tools may not be the best course of action:

1. While moderate rates of inflation generally do not hurt people with below-average income and our economic system has adjusted to live with continuing inflation, trying to absorb into the private economy all those whom the private sector needs least, namely the hard-core unemployed, could encourage inflationary pressures so high that they might disrupt the economy, its credit system, its international relationships, and so on.

2. Because of differences between various regions of the country, economic expansion may in some areas pull new workers into the labor force who never thought of working before, while the unemployed may still remain unemployed in other areas, unaffected by the boom in particular industries.

3. The products for which the private market will create a demand during a boom may not be the most socially desirable ones. What are likely to increase are sales of, let us say, snow-mobiles and motorboats instead of park maintenance and health services. In other words, overall stimulation of the private economy may not be a medication sufficiently accurate to cure the kind of special unemployment problems that plague large cities. While traditional full-employment policies are a necessary condition for dealing with poverty, they are not enough; hence the need for public service jobs.

The largest public job programs in U.S. history were the WPA (Works Progress Administration), the PWA (Public Works Administration), and the CCC (Civilian Conservation Corps) during the Depression, which at their height put 4 million people to work. While there was some waste, work of value was accomplished. The building program alone produced 116,000 buildings, 78,000 bridges, 651,000 miles of roads, and improvements at 800 airports and at innumerable national, state, and local parks. The early network of parkways (Grand Central, Belt, and Henry Hudson) and river crossings (Midtown Tunnel, Triborough Bridge) in the Region, built by Robert Moses largely following RPA's First Regional Plan, would not have been possible without PWA financing.

In the Employment Act of 1946 Congress affirmed the responsibility of the federal government for "creating conditions under which there will be afforded useful employment for those able, willing, and seeking work," but the notion of public job creation did not surface again until 1965, when the National Commission on Technology, Automation, and Economic Progress identified the need for more than 5 million additional public employees simply to bring the quality of public services up to minimum standards.

The first concrete step in this direction was the Emergency Employment Act of 1971, which set up a Public Employment Program of 150,000 jobs nationwide. New York City's quota was 3,000, about 1 percent of the city's unemployed. Of the first 1,600 people hired under the program, 650 were former city employees laid off due to budget cuts.

The major argument against large-scale public service employment is one of cost. If all of the 5 million jobs identified by the National Commission on Technology and Automation were to be filled at public agency wage rates characteristic of large cities—about $9,000 a year—the nationwide cost would be $45 billion, compared to the 1973 adjusted budget of $257 billion for the federal government as a whole. However, a program at one fifth the scale would still have a tangible impact, and the pay could be lower, close to the legal minimum, so as not to threaten existing wage rates. On that basis, the National Urban Coalition estimates that 1 million jobs could be created for a cost of $4.5 billion. For the Region, that would mean about 100,000 jobs paid at $2.50 an hour which would provide work for roughly one third of the structurally unemployed.

New York University Dean Dick Netzer points out: "To permit essential services to go unprovided, while there are unemployed persons capable of providing such services, is to be completely bemused by a money illusion. That is, governments may say they cannot afford the *money* cost of such services. But to society as a whole, the *resource* costs are very small," because the resource—the unemployed people—is idle anyway.

The other arguments against large-scale public service employment have mostly to do with efficiency and morale, which deteriorate if there is permanent overstaffing of government jobs. Low-prestige "make-work" jobs reduce self-respect and productivity. Between 1967 and 1971 the number of New York City municipal employees grew by 66,000, to reach 414-000, yet many people complain that city services are worse rather than better. What would happen if 250,000 new public service jobs were added to this, which is what a 5-million-job national public employment effort would imply? To some people, this would be a nightmare of boondoggling and inefficiency. One can retort that for the people involved it would still be much better than idleness and unemployment and that efficiency would depend a great deal on how the program was organized and run.

CHOICE FIVE. Should the government provide jobs for the unemployed? (Check one.)
A. No
B. Yes, for some of the unemployed
C. Yes, and guarantee a job for all who want to work
D. No opinion

Part C: Improving Income

Raising the Incomes of the Working Poor

Having examined various ways of reducing unemployment, we have now found that no single approach is sufficient, that several ways must be pursued, and even when accomplished will solve only part of the poverty problem. That is because we have yet to deal with two other major sources of poverty: (1) the low wages of the working poor (who typically have large families—two thirds are in families of four or more), and (2) inadequate support payments to those who cannot work because they are too young, too old, incapacitated, or caring for children too young to go to nursery school—in other words, most of the present welfare cases.

Let us start with the working poor.

As we have shown earlier, about one fifth of the Region's population, some 4.1 million people, live below the Bureau of Labor Statistics "lower level budget," less than about $2,700 for a single individual, and $7,300 for a family of four. Most of their income is earned from work: about 60 percent is earned, while 30 percent comes from welfare and 10 percent from Social Security. In New York the City Planning Commission estimates. there are 1 million workers who work full time and earn less than $80 a week ($4,160 a year), and 1.5 million who earn less than $100 a week ($5,200 annually). This represents about one quarter of the city's workers. Should they, if they have a family to support, live below the poverty level? And if not, what can be done?

The simple answer seems to be: raise the minimum wage. Employers will pass on the increased cost of doing business to their customers, and thus everybody will pay for a redistribution of income, without government interference. For example, a minimum wage of $2.50 an hour would give a low-skilled worker an income of $5,200 a year, enough to keep a family of four above the hard-core poverty level. A minimum wage of $3.50 an hour would result in an annual income of about $7,000, just about the "lower level of living budget" for a family of four.

The difficulty with this is twofold. As employers pass on the higher cost of wages to their customers, their product goes up in price, the demand for it is reduced, and marginal businesses dependent on low-wage labor fold, increasing unemployment. Moreover, to keep their costs down, the remaining employers substitute more machines for labor or simply lay off workers who are not essential, again increasing unemployment. The extension of minimum wage provisions to agricultural workers in recent years did throw out of jobs a good many farm workers in the Deep South. While a moderate increase in the minimum wage would be helpful, increases that would seriously alter the condition of the working poor could be effective only if there were public service jobs for those laid off.

Another proposal is to help the working poor with child allowances. The argument is as follows:

Present minimum wages are enough to support a single individual. But they are not enough to support a family with children. So why not pay a cash grant in the form of monthly payments for each child and give it to everybody, to avoid the stigma of a means test and welfare-type payments. Those who are better off and do not need the assistance would pay most of it back to the government in taxes.

The problem here is that to really help the working poor, the child allowance would have to be large—at least $1,000 a year per child: thus, huge sums of money would be shifted around, and most families would be returning most of the payments to the government in taxes—not a very efficient procedure. Moreover, income would tend to be redistributed from childless people to people with children and from small families to large families. While child allowances are customary in several Western countries, they are quite small and make little difference in the family budget.

To avoid the pitfalls in both approaches—excessive interference with the private market, and paying out monies which are then taken back by the government in taxes, Milton Friedman of the University of Chicago, a conservative economist, introduced in 1962 the concept of the "negative income tax," sometimes called a cash assistance grant. Under this concept, people above a certain income level (an income level that would be different for each family size) would continue to pay federal income taxes (though they would have to be higher than now), while people below that income level would receive cash (negative taxes), the lower their income and the larger their family, the more money.

To maintain the incentive to earn more, the "negative tax payments" would be set up so that as a family's income rises the payments would be reduced by an amount less than the added earnings, so that the higher its own earnings are, the better off is the family.

A criticism of this approach is that by paying subsidies to workers with low wages the government would indirectly be helping the employers who pay low wages; in effect, it would be subsidizing the production of marginal goods and services which would not be produced if we had to pay the full cost of a high minimum wage.

So the issue is: If we are subsidizing anyhow, why not subsidize work in the public sector by creating public service jobs and thus buy, let us say, clean beaches instead of artificial flowers?

Of course, such a policy of raising minimum wages in the private sector to high level and creating public service jobs for all those laid off would involve a large shift of resources from the private sector to the public sector. Regardless of which path is chosen, the income supplements or the public service jobs would have to be paid from tax monies.

CHOICE SIX. What should be done to raise the incomes of the working poor? (Check one or two.)

A. Nothing

B. Raise minimum wages and provide public service jobs for everyone laid off as a result

C. Support low wages with federal cash supplements varying with family size ("negative income tax")

D. No opinion

Guaranteeing a Minimum Income

Having reviewed the possibilities of raising the income of the working poor, we can turn now to those who cannot work. The New Deal legislation of 1935, greatly expanded since, introduced a number of federal programs to support the income of those who cannot earn. The major ones are the old age, survivors, disability and hospital insurance (OASDHI), or Social Security for short, which in essence guarantees a minimum income to retired workers, their survivors, to the disabled; and the unemployment compensation program, administered by the states under federal guidelines, which provides temporary payments to workers who are laid off.

Part of the original Social Security legislation was federal grants to share in the cost of state welfare programs; the latter were viewed as an interim measure, to help those unable to work until such time as everybody in need was adequately covered by Social Security; among these programs was aid to families with dependent children (AFDC). In 1950–55 it aided nationwide about 2.2 million people, until suddenly the number of recipients began to grow, more than doubling between 1965 and 1970 and reaching more than 11 million in 1972. New York City has experienced a similar though somewhat slower rise from 500,000 welfare recipients in 1965 to 1,265,000 in 1972, and the State of New Jersey an even steeper one, from 174,000 in 1966 to 461,000 in 1971. Though the "welfare problem" is obviously concentrated in large cities, it is not limited to them, as the following figures for selected New Jersey counties show:

Table 6. Percent of the Population on Welfare in Selected New Jersey Counties

County	October 1966	October 1971
Essex (including Newark)	6.4%	13.5%
Mercer (including Trenton)	3.0	7.5
Monmouth	2.1	7.0
Union	1.3	3.5
Morris	0.6	1.3

There are many reasons for the increase: the recession of 1970, which increased welfare rolls nationwide by 22 percent; the gradual disappearance of low-skilled jobs, both in agriculture in the South and in the cities in the North; and changing attitudes: people in need begin to perceive some kind of a minimum income as a right and claim it. Another influence has been the increased size of payments to recipients. New York, New Jersey, and Connecticut now give a family of four about $4,000 to live on—not a large sum, but many jobs pay minimum wages which amount to less money than welfare for large families.

The rise in welfare rolls has aroused critics who maintain that it is due to fraudulent applications or to "chiselers" who are shirking work. Welfare agencies reply that only a very small percentage of the applications are fraudulent. Controversies are raging but are virtually impossible to resolve, because of the way the program of aid to dependent children is set up. If the statute says that an indigent unmarried mother with a small child is entitled to public assistance, it is, in practice, impossible to prove or disprove that she had it deliberately to get on welfare or that she does in fact live with a man who may or may not work.

It is on this aspect that rational criticism of the present welfare system is focused: it is demeaning, and it does tend to break up families: in most jurisdictions, there are no benefits to families who are poor but are headed by a working male. A third point of criticism is that the system discourages work. Until 1967 welfare benefits were reduced by $1 for every dollar earned. Amendments to the public assistance law in 1967 allowed recipients to keep $30 a month plus 33 cents of each dollar earned, but this is a small work incentive, particularly as working recipients have to pay the Social Security tax and may lose medical and other benefits. The fourth point of criticism is that benefits vary widely from state to state, from an average of $54 a month in Mississippi to $294 in Hawaii.

This has led to a number of proposals that would replace the present AFDC system by one that would:

• Guarantee each family with children a minimum income (nationally more or less uniform), determined by family size.

• Reduce this benefit by substantially less than $1 for each dollar earned, to make sure that there is an incentive to seek employment.

The question of guaranteeing a minimum income for those who cannot work and the question of providing income supplements to the working poor cannot be separated. For if a free income is available for those who cannot work, their number is inevitably going to rise, by legitimate or illegitimate means. Only if enough of the "guaranteed income" can be kept in addition to the money earned is there a real incentive to work and to strive for higher wages.

Opponents of guaranteed income schemes hold that people

getting income support should be required to work, on grounds that no one should feel that the government "owes me a living." But in fact most people presently on welfare simply cannot work even if they wanted to.

According to the Human Resources Administration in New York City, of the 1.25 million welfare recipients, 650,000 are under age 18, 110,000 are disabled, 75,000 are over age 65, and 243,000 are mothers of children abandoned by a male wage earner. Only 28,000 recipients are in families in which an able-bodied adult is unemployed. Some 160,000 are in families with a wage earner working full time and earning less than the welfare level; the income of these families is supplemented to meet the welfare minimum.

There is dispute whether mothers with school-age children should be required to work. The New York and Connecticut legislatures recently passed laws requiring all able-bodied recipients to register for work. The results were that in 1971 out of 1.7 million recipients in New York State, only 38,400 were rated "employable," and 23,000 people were removed from welfare rolls for refusal to accept training or employment. About 7,500 were assigned to job training. But only 4 percent of the 38,400 "employable" got jobs that lasted any length of time; and only 1 percent had earnings high enough to get off relief.

Another criticism is that anyone with a guaranteed income would lose the incentive to work. To test this thesis, the U.S. Office of Economic Opportunity contracted with a private firm in New Jersey (Mathematica, Inc.) to conduct an experiment involving 1,200 poor families. They were given different levels of guaranteed income, ranging from $1,800 to $4,600 for a family of four. It is still too early to tell what effect these various rates will have. But on the whole, in the three years the experiment has been running, "There was no precipitous withdrawal from the labor force by families who receive income maintenance payments." The number of hours worked per family did decline somewhat among the families receiving income support—by about 12 percent—mostly because some wives stopped working, presumably to care for children. However, male heads of the supported families were apparently able to find better jobs, because of the security that the support payments provided. The decline of the income earned from work was insignificant, but total income of the poor families involved was significantly improved by the income supplements provided.

In summary, if there is to be a uniform income support program providing a basic minimum to those unable to work, as well as supplements to the earned income of the working poor, two questions arise:

1. What should be the minimum payment?
2. How high should the income supplements go?

Some explanation of the relationship between the guaranteed basic minimum and the income supplements is needed.

Let us assume, just as an example, that a guaranteed annual income were set near the present poverty level, at $4,000 for a family of four, and that anyone earning slightly less than that could keep it. In this case, some low-income workers' income would virtually double overnight, while present welfare recipients would remain where they are now, at least in the Region. Moreover, anyone earning, say, $6,000 a year would have every incentive to reduce his income from work below $4,000, so as to get the guarantee payment. A way has to be devised to scale down the supplemental payment as income rises, so that a person earning even a little money would have an incentive to earn more and would still get some supplements as long as his income is fairly low. Let us assume the *rate of reduction* in the supplemental payments is 50 cents for every dollar earned. Then, with a guaranteed minimum of $4,000, the income picture for families of four in different income groups would look as follows:

Earned Income	Income Supplement (50% reduction rate)	Total Income
none	$4,000	$4,000
1,000	3,500	4,500
2,000	3,000	5,000
3,000	2,500	5,500
4,000	2,000	6,000
5,000	1,500	6,500
6,000	1,000	7,000
7,000	500	7,500
8,000	none	8,000

It is evident that if the basic payment for a family without income were set near the present poverty level and the rate of reduction were sufficiently low to encourage earnings—50 percent in this case—income subsidies would extend all the way up to an income of $8,000 a year. If we should decide not to subsidize families of four in that income range, the rate of reduction could be increased to 67 cents for every dollar earned. In this case, only incomes up to $5,970 would be supplemented. That would keep costs down but provide little work incentive, particularly if Social Security and other payroll taxes were to be withheld from the remaining 33 cents, as is the case now. Conversely, a lower rate of reduction, say 33 cents for every dollar earned, would extend income subsidies all the way up to an income of $12,000.

Thus we see that a low rate of reduction in income supplements, which encourages one to earn more, inevitably intrudes into the middle range of incomes; on the other hand, a high rate of reduction does confine the income supplements to the lower income range but proceeds to discourage earnings and encourage withdrawals from the labor force.

A similar dilemma confronts the basic payment: if the payment is high enough to keep above the poverty line a family which is unable to work—say, $6,500 for a family of four—then, with a 50 percent reduction rate, income subsidies extend all the way to an income of $13,000. On the other hand, if those with incomes above $7,000 are not to be subsidized, then the basic income guarantee, $3,500, cannot pull the nonworking family above the poverty line.

These considerations have led to a number of proposals for a guaranteed minimum income, set at different levels and geared to income supplements with different rates of reduction. Three of them are illustrated below.

1. $2,500 minimum income for a family of four, with a 67 cents per dollar reduction for every dollar earned up to an income of $3,600 and strict work requirements for the recipients. This plan was approved by the House of Representatives, with Administration support, in 1971, but failed to pass the Senate. The proposed minimum is lower than the welfare payments now in force in all but five southern states. Without federal incentives for additional payments, the proposal could have resulted in a *reduction* of benefits in many states, particularly those of the Region (New York actually did cut welfare benefits by 10 percent in 1971, even though about 44 percent of its welfare burden is currently borne by the federal government). The added cost of the proposal was estimated at around $5 billion annually.

2. $4,200 minimum income for a family of four, rising to $4,700 by 1976, with a 50 cent reduction for every dollar earned, supplementing incomes up to $9,400 for a family of four. This proposal by the National Urban Coalition is aimed at eliminating poverty, as officially defined. It would help welfare recipients in the Region only moderately, but would improve the position of low-income working families in the

Region, and would shift the income support from state and local to the federal government. The cost, if the program were restricted primarily to families (without unrelated individuals), would be on the order of $28 billion, on top of the $16 billion the federal government now spends on welfare. (The total federal budget, $257 billion in fiscal 1973, includes $102 billion for income support payments of all kinds—for government pensions, veterans, Social Security, Medicare, unemployment compensation, subsidies to farmers, and so on.)

3. $6,500 minimum income for a family of four ($2,250 for a single person), with a 66.6 cent reduction for every dollar earned, supplementing incomes up to $9,750 for a family of four. The minimum level is derived from the Bureau of Labor Statistics lower level of income budget, set at around $7,200 in 1972, established as necessary for the "maintenance of health and social wellbeing, the nurture of children, and participation in community activities." This proposal, advocated by the National Welfare Rights Organization, is estimated by it to cost about $60 billion over and above what is currently spent on welfare.

In Table 7 and Figure 7, we compare the effect of four hypothetical income support plans, with basic guarantees of $2,400, $4,200, $5,000, and $6,500 for a family of four. In order to make the programs comparable, we assume these sums are reduced by 50 cents for every dollar earned. Thus, the charts describe not any of the three proposals outlined above but four strictly hypothetical options. Also, we assume the options cover all households, that is both families and unrelated individuals (the cost can be cut a lot by not covering unrelated individuals).

What do we learn from these calculations? A $2,400 guaranteed minimum income, with supplements extending up to an income of $4,800 for a family of four (Option A), would redistribute about 1 percent of all money income from the top fifth of all income recipients to the bottom fifth. It would cost about a 7 percent increase in the federal personal income tax (which earned about $90 billion in 1970), should we choose to pay for the plan this way.

A $4,200 guaranteed minimum income for a family of four, with supplements extending up to $8,400 (Option B), would redistribute about 5 percent of all money income from the top two fifths to the bottom two fifths. It would cost the equivalent of a 38 percent increase in the personal income tax.

A $5,000 guaranteed minimum income for a family of four, with supplements up to $10,000 (Option C), would redistrib-

Figure 7

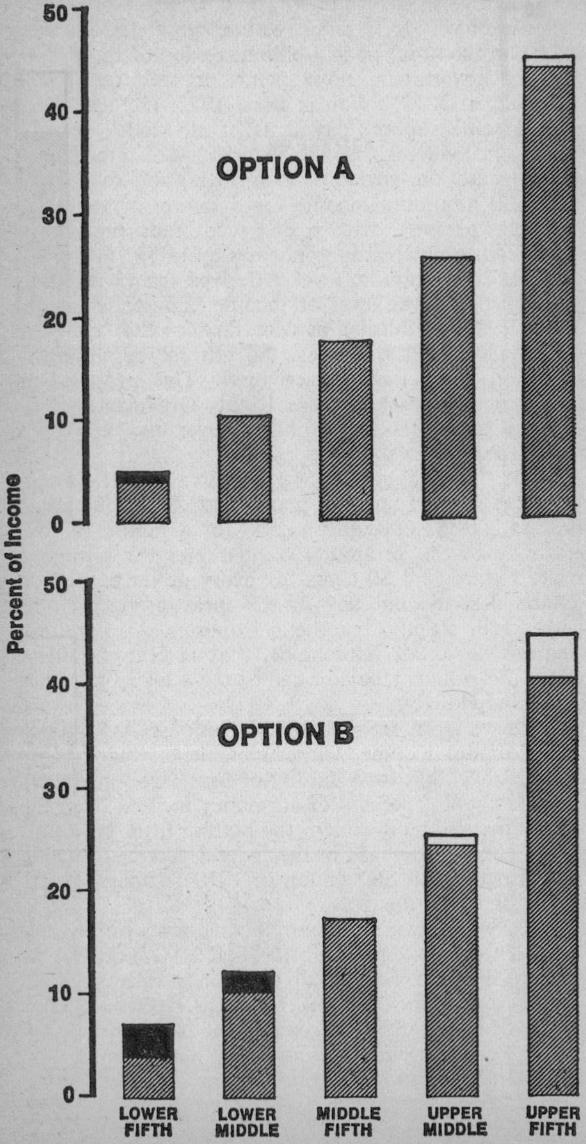

OPTION A
OPTION B
Percent of Income
0
10
20
30
40
50
LOWER FIFTH
LOWER MIDDLE
MIDDLE FIFTH
UPPER MIDDLE
UPPER FIFTH

THE EFFECT OF FOUR ILLUSTRATIVE INCOME SUPPORT PLANS ON THE DISTRIBUTION OF INCOME

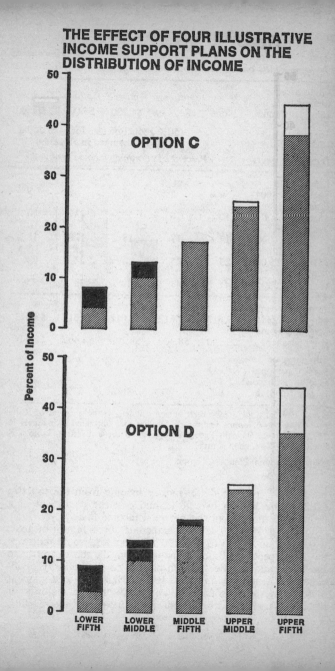

Table 7. Estimated Effect of Four Hypothetical Guaranteed Income Plans on the Distribution of Income, in 1970 Dollars

Guaranteed income for a family of four	None	Option A $2,400	Option B $4,200	Option C $5,000	Option D $6,500
		(50% reduction rate for each dollar earned assumed in all cases)			
Income brackets	*Percent of all money income received*				
Lowest fifth (below $3,300)	4%	5%	7%	8%	9%
Lower middle ($3,300–6,700)	10	10	12	13	14
Middle fifth ($6,700–10,000)	17	17	17	17	18
Upper middle ($10,000–15,000)	25	25	24	24	24
Upper fifth (over $15,000)	44	43	40	38	35
Average income per household	$9,612	$9,612	$9,612	$9,612	$9,612
Median income per household	$8,350	$8,300	$8,200	$8,400	$8,800
Surcharge on present personal income tax needed to pay for plan	0%	7%	38%	62%	96%

Note: The existing income distribution (under "None") based on *Current Population Report,* income of families and unrelated individuals in 1970. Slight variation in figures compared to those given in Table 4 is due to the difference in sources.

SOURCE: Regional Plan Association.

ute about 7 percent of all money income from the top two fifths to the bottom two fifths, and cost the equivalent of a 62 percent increase in the personal income tax.

Lastly, a $6,500 guaranteed income for a family of four, with supplements up to $13,000 (Option D), would redistribute 10 percent of all money income from the top two fifths to the lower and middle three fifths, i.e., to the *majority* of income recipients. It would cost the equivalent of a 96 percent increase in the personal income tax. While the majority of the population would be benefited, the income of the top fifth would be cut by roughly 20 percent.

CHOICE SEVEN. Should the government guarantee a minimum income for everybody in need, and if so, what should be the guarantee for a family of four?
A. $2,400 with supplements up to an income of $ 4,800
B. $4,200 with supplements up to an income of $ 8,400
C. $5,000 with supplements up to an income of $10,000
D. $6,500 with supplements up to an income of $13,000
E. None

Reforming Taxes

Obviously, most of the choices offered above to solve the problem of poverty will involve taking money from some people and giving it to others. It is not enough merely to suggest how many billion this or that proposal would involve. One must also indicate what the options are for paying the bill.

Taxing Higher Income Families More

A reduction of the gap between the most and the least affluent was found desirable by American lawmakers when the principle of the progressive income tax was established. However, exemptions, deductions, and various tax preferences or loopholes make federal taxes much less progressive in reality than they look on paper. A tax study by Joseph Pechman and Benjamin Okner of the Brookings Institution found that if the federal income tax rates were applied without loopholes, an extra $77 billion would be raised, principally from families in the higher income brackets, which would be enough to increase the federal budget by about one third and do more than just wipe out poverty.

Still, even with its present loopholes, many of which have a reasonable purpose, such as encouraging home ownership or accumulating capital for investment, the federal personal income tax is more progressive than other taxes. State and local taxes, particularly property and sales taxes, tend to be regressive, i.e., they take a larger percentage bite out of the lower-income person's money. The end result is that when all taxes are put together, the various income groups pay a fairly similar share of their income in taxes, as shown on page 180.

It is evident that, if it were not for the federal personal income tax, our tax system would actually be regressive. The groups with income below $10,000 a year (in 1968 terms)

Table 8. *Share of All Income Paid in Taxes,*
by Income Group, in 1968

Income Level	All Taxes (Federal, State, Local) as Percent of Income	Federal Personal Income Tax as a Percent of Income
Under $2,000	25.6%	0.6%
$2,000 to $4,000	24.7	2.5
$4,000 to $6,000	27.9	4.7
$6,000 to $8,000	30.1	6.5
$8,000 to $10,000	29.9	7.6
$10,000 to $15,000	30.9	9.1
$15,000 to $$25,000	31.1	10.3
$25,000 and over	38.5	16.0
All income groups	31.6	9.5

SOURCE: Roger A. Herriot and Herman P. Miller, U.S. Bureau of the Census.

are bearing a heavier burden of other taxes than the groups between $10,000 and $25,000. This is particularly the case in states such as New Jersey and Connecticut, which do not have a state income tax on individuals. The local sales and property taxes in force there are highly regressive, with the lowest income group paying close to one fifth of its meager income in state-local taxes, as Table 9 indicates. In addition to being regressive, the property tax, from which 57 percent of local and state government revenue in New Jersey is derived, is what economists call inelastic—that is, it does not automatically respond to rising income—hence New Jersey's perennial

Table 9. *Incidence of State-Local Taxes in New Jersey,*
by Income Group

Income	Percent of Income Paid in State-Local Taxes	Percent of Taxpayers	Percent of All Money Income
Under $3,000	19.1	5.5	1.0
$3,000–$5,000	15.2	7.3	2.4
$5,000–$7,500	13.7	17.8	9.9
$7,500–$10,000	12.1	21.0	15.8
$10,000–$15,000	11.3	28.6	29.8
$15,000–$25,000	9.9	16.8	26.5
$25,000 & over	5.4	3.1	14.7

SOURCE: New Jersey Tax Policy Committee, Summary Report, 1972.

tax crisis. A progressive income tax, by contrast, tends to raise revenues at a rate slightly faster than the rate of rise in income.

The average tax rate on all income in the table shown above is 10.3 percent. This means that if all state and local taxes in New Jersey were to be replaced by an income tax, even a nonprogressive one, but one merely charging everybody 10.3 percent of his income, all taxpayers with income of less than $15,000 in 1970 would benefit—80 percent of all taxpayers. Only the top 20 percent would suffer by having their effective taxes raised. The middle-income group would experience small reductions in taxes—1 to 3.4 percent—while those with incomes below $5,000 would have their taxes cut by one quarter to one half.

If a progressive rate were established, the benefits to the lower half of the middle class would be substantially larger. However, despite the fact that a shift from property and sales taxes to income taxes would be clearly to the benefit of the overwhelming majority of New Jersey residents, state income tax proposals were defeated twice in the legislature in recent years.

There may be two explanations why sales taxes and other regressive taxes retain their uncanny popularity. One is, of course, that the well-to-do have more political clout in state and local legislative bodies; the other one may be that sales taxes are paid in small increments, in contrast to income taxes, which are seen in bigger chunks on the paycheck and are thus more noticeable.

The various schemes we've discussed for improving education, employment, and income will obviously require money, which will mean higher taxes for some; existing federal programs have shown themselves impervious to significant budget cuts. The National Urban Coalition proposed cuts totaling nearly $25 billion (of which $20 billion was in the defense budget) in order to pay for programs to provide a million public service jobs, a guaranteed income of $4,708, expanded day care, etc. But it still went on to suggest the need for a general tax increase in these words:

> We estimate that a rise of about 10 percent in individual and corporate income taxes will be needed *assuming that the expenditure cuts suggested above are made.* For every recommended dollar reduction *not* achieved, taxes will have to be increased correspondingly. . . .

If we are serious about solving our problems, we must be willing to tax ourselves more to do so. Currently, governments in other Western nations command a higher proportion of their Gross National Product for taxes than does the United States.

The tax load totals 42 to 37 percent of the Gross National Product in the Netherlands, England, France, West Germany, Austria, and Denmark, and goes as high as 48 percent in Sweden, which provides a wide array of social services. Compared to that, the United States rate is only 31.5 percent now.

Arthur M. Okun in *The Political Economy of Prosperity* says this on increasing federal taxes:

> If the nation were willing to return to the average tax rates that prevailed from 1954 to 1961, we could have roughly $25 billion a year more to spend on social programs than with the tax rates now in prospect for the early 1970s.

With a trillion-dollar Gross National Product, 1 percent of GNP is $10 billion, so that if we decided to tax ourselves as heavily as Western Europe, we could have roughly $100 billion more in government revenues each year.

If programs necessary to reduce poverty and to achieve a somewhat more equal distribution of income are to be implemented, this additional tax burden would have to be borne by the more affluent segments of the population.

But even if none of the programs were to be implemented, a redistribution of the existing tax burden in the United States would in itself be of great benefit to lower income groups, as illustrated by our New Jersey example.

Thus to the question: Should those who earn more be taxed more than they are today? The two basic ways of doing that, as suggested by the above discussion, are (1) making federal taxes rise more steeply with rising income, primarily by eliminating various tax preferences or loopholes that favor mostly the well-to-do, and (2) shifting state and local taxes away from sales and property taxes, which fall more heavily on the poor, toward income taxes, which fall more heavily on the better off.

The counterargument to all income redistribution schemes, including shifts in the tax load, has traditionally been that if those better off are taxed too much, they will lose their entrepreneurial incentives and, perhaps more importantly, money will be diverted from investment to consumption. Without enough money for risk capital and investment, the growth of the economy will slow down, the "goose that laid the golden eggs" will be killed, and everybody will suffer. Nobody really knows where this breaking point is. And the persistence of a large low-income population is not doing much for the growth of the economy.

The experience of West European countries indicates that the United States is still very far from the point where higher taxes on the upper income portion of the population would hurt the economy as a whole. Of course, if far-reaching income redistribution schemes are to be considered for implementation, detailed studies of the changed flow of money and the changed allocation of resources would have to be carried out, to estimate their impact on all of society.

CHOICE EIGHT. Do you favor or oppose any of the following tax policies?
A. Making people with higher incomes pay more federal income tax

     FAVOR   OPPOSE   NO OPINION

B. At the state and local level, relying less on sales and property taxes, and more on income taxes

     FAVOR   OPPOSE   NO OPINION

V. TOWN MEETING ON CITIES AND SUBURBS

A lovable city is the key to a living city.
—*Paolo Soleri* (1969)

The great cities of the world . . . provide the settings where the new ideas of the period are tested first . . . much more human welfare and cultural activity is generated here per unit of resources than anywhere else in society.
—*Richard L. Meier* (1970)

The overriding urban problem of the coming decade may well be the general inability of large city governments to make ends meet . . . a basic decision must soon be made about the nation's interest in preserving . . . the long-run viability of the older central cities.
—*The Brookings Institution* (1972)

The issue is not whether Congress can solve the problem of the cities, but whether Congress is willing to take action to enable our society to go from an urban society to what might be called a regional metropolitan society. It is already too late to save the cities as we have known them. Will Congress wait until it is too late to save our society?
—*Congressman Herman Badillo* (1972)

Summing Up

We have now suggested alternative policies for choice in housing, environment, transportation, and poverty. And a theme emerges from all four discussions.

1. If we want more moderately priced housing for more families in the Region, we must shift our emphasis from the most expensive housing types—single-family houses on large lots or elevator towers—toward more detached houses on small lots, attached town houses, and low-rise apartments.

2. If we want to preserve more of our natural environment, to have a cleaner distinction between the natural and the man-

made, we should also build more compactly, on less land. Less obviously, more compact urban development will also save energy.

3. If we want less reliance on the private auto, and more reliance on public transportation, we also need to build more compactly on less land. Travel demand by all modes of transportation would be reduced this way.

4. A major centrifugal force, blocking compact urban development, is the growth of poverty in our central cities. If, instead of trying to run away from poverty, we turned our energies toward reducing the contrast between rich and poor, toward curing the social problems associated with poverty, an ecologically more responsible urban pattern would also be easier to attain.

In this fifth discussion we shall try to weave these four strands together, and a fifth one: the location of economic and cultural activities in the Region. Do we rechannel some of the energy of prospective urban growth from the fringes of the Region back into its central cities? Or do we continue the long-term trend toward dispersal and decentralization?

There is another basic theme running through our sets of choices which may be even more significant than density. It is our willingness to live together interdependently rather than trying to escape public problems and privatize ourselves. More nice parks versus larger backyards; public transportation versus the auto; downtowns versus privately owned shopping centers and independent shops and offices along highways. Poverty and racial conflict are an important cause of this privatizing thrust, but they are not at all the only one. The cause may be deep in America's tradition, but it manifests itself strongly now because much of the public machinery has been shaken by conflicts in our society.

The Forces of Dispersal

Until about the time of World War II, cities in the Region were the centers of life around them. The urban jobs and services were there; the major shopping was there. People generally got together there. Not just in Manhattan; in Newark and Paterson, Hackensack and Trenton, Bridgeport and New Haven, Poughkeepsie and Newburgh, downtown Brooklyn, Fordham Road, Jamaica. But since World War II, offices and colleges have increasingly chosen broad campuses in rural surroundings; shopping has gone to highwayside plazas; hotels have closed in downtown areas, while motels open along the roads. Urban life is losing its focus.

The reasons were often enough stated and restated, and bear repeating only briefly. Their roots go far into our history.

1. Our cities were thrown together in a big rush in an era when quick profit and fast growth were paramount. The Region increased its population *tenfold* between 1850 and 1950. Under these conditions, few really desirable urban environments, with a sense of beauty and permanence, were created. The speculative semifireproof apartment in the Queens of 1950, with its fire escapes, creaking floors, and assorted kitchen smells in the corridor was, after all, not that great an improvement on the new-law tenement in the Bronx of 1910. Both offered street asphalt as a playground for children. Both could be viewed as a disposable environment in a society accustomed to pulling up stakes.

2. With all its social and visual ugliness, amply documented by contemporary planners, our Region of cities was held tightly together by fixed transit links—the ferries, the railroads, the subways and elevateds, and the trolley car lines, later replaced with buses. Only within walking distance of these movement channels was urban development feasible. Suddenly, in the 1920s, a million and a half private automobiles became widely available, and another million and a half by 1950. Their effect was held back by the Depression and World War II, but when they were unleashed, they discovered hundreds upon hundreds of square miles of buildable land, farther in distance, but actually closer in time to your job, to your shopping, to your relatives, than an arduous trip by public transit.

3. The well-publicized Anglo-Saxon dream of "one's home, one's castle" came into play, as 1,375,000 detached one-family houses dotted the landscape in the post-World War II era. Compared to Jersey City or the Bronx, to Brooklyn or Paterson, the pattern had lots of lawn and plenty of trees, testifying perhaps to the proposition that in a country where 96.7 percent of the land is still more or less in a natural state, there may not be the need to confine the entire human population to 3.3 percent of the land. Few thought about how to redesign and rebuild the cities, for the land values there were inflated by the expectations of growth according to past trends. In this economic setting, federal subsidies to deflate land values in urban renewal areas could only be a drop in the bucket. With an amortized housing stock and high densities, even low rents were initially producing a "fair" return on the land.

4. As the middle class abandoned the heritage of the Industrial Revolution for greener pastures, another heritage— that of slavery and colonialism—announced its presence, as

some 2 million blacks and Puerto Ricans were glad to exchange the rural poverty of the South for the uncertain chance of an urban job in the Region, even taking advantage —for a time—of hand-me-down urban environments. The urban ghetto and the suburban large-lot pattern became self-reinforcing. Today, most of the poor and most of the blacks are confined to about 100 square miles in old cities of the Region—large and small—while the rest of the population lives in the surrounding 2,600 square miles of urbanized land. With larger suburban lot sizes, nearly 50 square miles—more than twice the area of Manhattan—are converted to urban use each year, but not for the use of everybody. "Two societies, separate and unequal."

5. "Decentralization" has been written on the banner of most urban planners in the twentieth century, and it was the goal of our own first Regional Plan prepared between 1922 and 1931. The planners of the 20s did not foresee that spontaneous dispersal of urban activities would exceed their ambitions by far. They did not foresee that Manhattan's population would drop by *one third* between 1920 and 1970, or that distant Suffolk County would have six times the population they projected. They did foresee more of a Queens type of development (the 1924 forecast for the population of Queens in 1965 was right on the nose—1.9 million). Figure 8 illustrates the extent of urban spread in the Region between 1935 and 1962, when built-up land expanded from an estimated 600 square miles to 1,740 square miles, more than 2½ times within the study area of the First Regional Plan, while population grew by less than two fifths.

A decline in average urban densities is by no means peculiar to the Region—it has been going on in virtually all metropolitan areas of North America and Western Europe since the early part of this century, and sometimes even earlier. The exact pattern has varied from place to place, but its major cause has been the same—declining transportation costs compared to the income of the population. With greater ability to travel, one could afford to use more land.

Cities have been called machines for communication. This was true in ancient Mesopotamia, where writing was invented in the first cities some 6,000 years ago. This was true in ancient Greece, where culture flourished in cities. This was true in the Middle Ages, where the accumulation of knowledge, wealth, and political power that created the modern world gathered force due to communication in cities. And it is true today, when the business of shuffling papers and computer tapes in gleaming office towers is, after all, communication, essential

BUILT-UP LAND IN THE
NEW YORK REGION

Figure 8

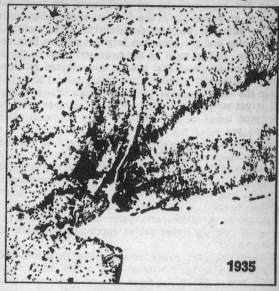

1935

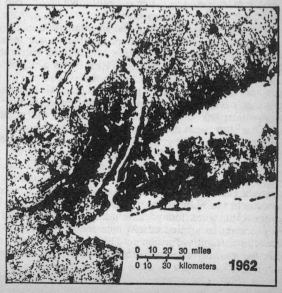

0 10 20 30 miles

0 10   30 kilometers   1962

to the management of our complex society. Complexity, specialization, dependence on others mean that people have to be in direct or indirect contact with large numbers of other people. Electronic communication aids notwithstanding, being in contact ultimately means being in personal contact, as well as delivering goods. Both are made easier by people's proximity to each other, and this is what urban areas provide.

How you measure proximity—which means the efficiency of the city as a machine for communication—is a separate subject. Saving time is important to us, because our lives are finite. How many contacts we can make in a unit of time is a good measure of the performance of an urban area.

This is important for the decision-maker, who needs to get in contact with many different people before he makes, or implements, a decision. This is important for a manufacturer or a salesman, who wants to reach the maximum number of customers in a short time. And it is important for the man in the street, who does not want to waste a lot of time running from store to store comparison-shopping, who wants a broad choice of jobs and other social opportunities, again without wasting time.

Opportunities for urban contacts—be they business contacts, jobs, stores, or whatever—are pretty much related to the distribution of population and employment in the area, that is, urban density, and to the speed within which one can move in the area, that is, transportation.

Let us take an abstract example. In Manhattan in 1850, the population density was 100,000 people per square mile. The average speed of movement within Manhattan, which was on foot, was three miles per hour. In 10 minutes a person could cover half a mile. Within a half a mile squared, he could encounter 25,000 people. There were 25,000 opportunities for contact within 10 minutes of travel time. In our outer suburbs in 1970, say northern Westchester, the population density is 100 times lower—about 1,000 people per square mile. But the speed, by auto, is 10 times greater—about 30 miles per hour. In 10 minutes a person can cover five miles. Within a square of five-by-five miles, he can still encounter 25,000 people. Thus, the "effective density" of opportunities for contact within a unit of travel time was, rather incredibly, the same in the Manhattan of 1850 and in the northern Westchester County of today: a tenfold increase in circulation speed bought us a hundredfold increase in space, without reducing opportunities for contact. This is the arithmetic underlying the growth of spread urban development, the basis for the argument that it is no more difficult to transact business in Los Angeles than it is in New York.

Now, this is not to say that in all cases the suburbs are just as efficient for providing urban opportunities as the downtown areas. In many cases they are not. Obviously, the density of employment (rather than population) in Manhattan is much higher today than in 1850, and the speed of internal movement also greater than three miles per hour. So, as a machine for communication, as a decision-making switchboard, the Manhattan central business district offers roughly 20 times the opportunities of a suburban, auto-oriented environment. And a middle-sized central business district, such as that of Newark, offers about twice the opportunities—as measured simply by the number of workers reached within 10 minutes of travel time—than, shall we say, the scattered employment cluster of central Nassau County. However, compared to small downtown areas, such as those of Paterson, New Haven, or Stamford, as they exist today, the suburban pattern can easily be superior. Theoretical calculations of this type are visibly supported by the evidence of office construction—it has been vigorous in Manhattan in the past decade, there was some in the larger downtowns of the Region, but the smaller downtowns have lost out to dispersed suburban development—unless deliberate steps were created to improve their access and their environment.

Broadly applied, the concept of population density or employment density multiplied by the speed of travel is, of course, an oversimplified one. Population and employment are not homogeneous, and a production plant wins little from being accessible to white-collar executives living in an area, just as a large population of poor may win little from being accessible to executive offices in its area. We shall come back to this problem shortly.

Meanwhile, let us look at what kind of population pattern the forces of dispersal have produced.

Resulting Shifts Within the Region

To look at the structure of the Region, it is useful to divide it into four rings of development: the *Core*, the *Inner Ring*, the *Intermediate Ring*, and the *Outer Ring*. The *Core* comprises the City of New York without Staten Island (which is suburban in character), plus Hudson County and the City of Newark in New Jersey, altogether some 300 square miles which were rather fully built up by 1950, with an average population density of 36,000 people for every square mile of developed land (i.e., subtracting parks and vacant parcels). The *Inner Ring* comprises the bona-fide suburbs—Nassau, southern Westchester, Bergen, southern Passaic, western Essex (without Newark), and Union counties, plus Staten Island, altogether about 1,000 square miles, which are getting to be rather fully built up, but at an average density of about 7,600 people for every square mile of developed land. The *Intermediate Ring* of about 4,000 square miles extends east to include the larger part of Suffolk County on Long Island, communities along the shorefront of Connecticut including the metropolitan area of New Haven, north to include northern Westchester and Rockland, and west into New Jersey to include Morris, Somerset, Middlesex, Monmouth, and Mercer counties with the City of Trenton. This ring is fairly independent from the Region's Core, focused mostly on its own employment; the developed land density is about 3,500 people per square mile. The *Outer Ring* is largely rural, with 7,500 square miles in northwestern Connecticut, in the mid-Hudson Valley up to the Catskills, in New Jersey counties along the Delaware, as well as Ocean and eastern Suffolk counties. Population changes over the past two decades in these rings are shown in Table 10.

Table 10. Population in the Region by Ring of Development, 1950, 1960, 1970

| | Population (thousands) | | | Annual Rate of Growth | |
	1950	1960	1970	50–60	60–70
Core	8,786.6	8,575.9	8,591.8	−0.2%	0%
Inner Ring	3,104.1	4,342.8	4,800.0	3.4	1.0
Intermediate Ring	2,427.6	3,612.4	4,886.8	4.1	3.1
Outer Ring	828.6	1,093.3	1,473.2	2.8	3.0
Region Total	15,146.9	17,624.3	19,751.8	1.5	1.1

SOURCE: U.S. Census.

It is evident that population growth, which stopped first in the Core, is now slowing down sharply in the Inner Ring as well, but picking up in the Outer Ring. Meanwhile, the Intermediate Ring is still growing fastest both in percentage terms and in absolute numbers: it absorbed 2.4 million people in two decades, more than half of the Region's growth.

Now, one might say to all of that, obviously the structure of the Region is changing—so what? Obviously population grows on vacant land, and not by rebuilding to higher densities, and obviously it tends to spread out, as long as so much land is available around the Region. Even if the high ecological costs of spread development were brushed aside, the high costs do translate themselves into economic costs to some extent, and thereby determine what kind of people settle on newly developed land.

Income comparisons over time are tricky, because both overall rise in real incomes and inflation have to be taken into account. Very roughly, we can divide all families in the Region into *low, middle,* and *high* income as follows: *low* is assumed as less than $4,000 a year in 1949, and less than $6,000 in 1969 (Census income data refer to the year preceding the Census); *middle* is assumed at $4,000 to $10,000 in 1949 and $6,000 to $12,000 in 1969; *high* is assumed above $10,000 in 1949 and above $12,000 in 1969. Table 11 shows the distribution of families in these income groups by ring of development for the two years.

Table 11. Families in Each Income Group by Ring of Development, 1949 and 1969

| | Low | | Middle | | High | | All Families | |
	1949	1969	1949	1969	1949	1969	1949	1969
Core	62%	62%	55%	46%	50%	35%	59%	44%
Inner Ring	16	15	26	22	33	31	21	25
Intermediate Ring	16	16	15	24	14	27	15	24
Outer Ring	6	7	4	8	3	7	5	7
Region Total	100	100	100	100	100	100	100	100
Number of families (in thousands)	2,245	994	1,526	1,797	222	2,275	3,993	5,066

SOURCE: Regional Plan Association based on U.S. Census.

It is evident that while the *low*-income group (in this particular definition) shrank more than in half over the two decades because of rising real incomes, its distribution among the various rings of development remained the same. Nearly two thirds of this group used to, and still do live in the Core. The *middle*-income group, which grew moderately in absolute numbers, declined in the Core and grew in the outer counties roughly in the same proportion as the population as a whole (all families). The dramatic shift was confined to the high-income group: not only did it multiply tenfold in the Region, but two thirds of its growth went outside the Core. That is, two out of three families who entered the *high*-income bracket (as here defined) during the period 1949–69, either lived in, or moved to, one of the rings outside the Core. As shown in the table, the proportion of the high-income group living in the Core shrank from one half to nearly one third, while the proportion living in the Intermediate and Outer rings doubled to one third. The proportion of the high-income group living in Manhattan (not shown in Table 11) shrank from 17 percent to 6 percent during the 20-year period. Thus, the outward movement was not just an outward movement of people, but an outward movement of wealth.

Equally dramatic, on the other hand, were the shifts in racial and ethnic composition. During the two decades, 2.5 million nonwhites* and Puerto Ricans were added to the 1.4 million who lived in the Region in 1950, raising the Region's minority population from 9.2 to 19.8 percent of the total. Three quarters of this increment settled in the Core, raising its minority population from 12.5 to 34.6 percent. Only one quarter settled in the counties of the other three rings of development, raising their minority population from 4.6 to 8.4 percent.

Against this background, what happened to jobs, the economic engine of the Region? Detailed 1970 Census figures are not available as of this writing, but Table 12 shows, in rounded figures, the change in the Region's job composition between 1950 and 1970.

Table 12. *Jobs in the Region, 1950 and 1970, by Type*

	(*in millions*)	
	1950	1970
White-collar jobs in office buildings	1.1	1.9
Other white-collar jobs (schools, retail, etc.)	2.1	2.9
Blue-collar jobs (factories, construction, & transport)	2.6	2.7
Service jobs (maintenance, personal services, etc.)	0.9	1.1
Total	6.7	8.6

SOURCE: Regional Plan Association.

* A Census term referring primarily to blacks, but also including Orientals.

It is evident that jobs in office buildings have been growing fastest. Other white-collar jobs have also grown fast, and service jobs have increased somewhat, but their overall number is small. Blue-collar jobs have barely increased at all, partly because of the rapid advances of automation in manufacturing, partly because new manufacturing plants increasingly prefer sites elsewhere in the nation, outside the New York Region, if not established especially to serve it.

As one would expect, most of this job growth occurred outside the Core, in the growing rings of development. But the experience of New York City is instructive. Over the period 1959–67, it gained 225,000 white-collar jobs and 54,000 service jobs, but lost 33,000 blue-collar jobs. Projections indicate the loss of another 130,000 blue-collar jobs from New York City by 1985, while service jobs there could grow by about 70,000, and white-collar jobs conceivably might grow by as much as 420,000, of which about three quarters would locate in the Manhattan central business district.

Of all the different employment types, office jobs are by far the most concentrated (about 50 percent of them in the Region are located in the Manhattan central business district, and another 22 percent in the remainder of the Core). Production-oriented jobs are more dispersed (22 percent in the central business district and about 28 percent in the rest of the Core) and are continuing their decline in the central area, even as office jobs continue to increase. As factories move out of the Core, they generally manage to find a more or less adequate local labor supply, but the workers they leave behind all too often become unemployed. In the "full employment" year of 1968, the unemployment rate among low-skilled blue-collar workers in New York City was 9 percent, while in the suburban counties it was 3 percent. And, while the Core area has a surplus of unskilled blue-collar workers, for whom there are no jobs anywhere in the Region, it has a shortage of skilled white-collar workers, a factor which has contributed to the movement of offices closer to the suburban labor pool.

The conflict shown here at the regional level is repeated, in microcosm, in the smaller sub-regions of Bridgeport, of Stamford, Trenton, or Paterson: factories move from the old cities following technological necessity, but blue-collar workers cannot move after them because of zoning-induced housing shortages; following their locational logic, offices would be centrally located, but all too often prefer the white-collar environment of low-density areas to the troubles of cities. The Region is being turned inside out, and cross-commuting is mounting.

Now, it is clear that some outward spread of population with continuing growth is irreversible. It is rather unthinkable to imagine putting, say, an additional 5 million people on top of the 8 million who now live in the Core. Clearly, most of them will have to settle on undeveloped land, mostly in the suburban rings. But the question remains: How far out, and how will this growth be organized? Will it increase opportunities and reduce the need to travel—or will it reinforce segregation and maximize travel?

The location of employment and economic activity is a most powerful force determining these issues. It is what gives the Region its structure, what determines how it works, how we travel, what it feels like, and where we live. This will be the focus of this fifth town meeting.

Options for the Future

It is sometimes argued that the trends toward dispersal are so powerful that to try to fight them, not to speak of reversing them, is futile. But, upon closer inspection, it turns out that not all cards are stacked in favor of endless spread. Spread, just like growth, may have some built-in limits, and the trick is to discern them in time, instead of blindly following past trends. The energy of urban growth over the last quarter of this century could be harnessed to *solve* rather than exacerbate existing problems.

Shown in Table 13 are some of the major nonresidential building blocks of the Region likely to be needed over the next 30 years, the components of this growth. The assumption is that population grows by 5 million with an average of two children per family, as discussed in the town meeting on environment. Of course, these numbers will change, if the added population is only 2 million, or if it should be as much as 8 million. But the amazing thing is that many of them will change rather mildly, not at all in proportion to the prospective population increment. The reason is, as we said in the previous discussion of growth, that the majority of the prospective workers in office buildings, workers in factories, shoppers in department stores, or college students needing the projected space over the next 30 years have already been born. Thus, only elementary and high school enrollment can respond forcefully to future changes in the birthrate. And, of course, the growth prospects after the end of the century will be affected by it dramatically. But not those of the immediate decades ahead.

Table 13. Probable Need for Selected Regional Activities,
1970–2000

	Total in 1970	Added 1970–2000
Population in the Region	20 million	+ 5 million
Total employment	8.6 million	+ 3.2 million
Jobs in office buildings	1.9 million	+ 1.5 million
Jobs in factories	2.0 million	− 0.2 million
Other jobs	4.7 million	+ 1.9 million
Square feet of office floor space	505 million	+430 million
Square feet of department store space	37 million	+ 20 million
College enrollment	0.7 million	+ 0.8 million
High school enrollment	1.3 million	+ 0.2 million
Elementary school enrollment	3.3 million	−0.2 million

SOURCE: Regional Plan Association.

One thing is immediately clear from Table 13. As a result of the "baby bust" there will be few requirements for additional elementary schools, traditionally a heavy local expense. Of course, outer counties of the Region, like Suffolk or Ocean or Dutchess, will need many new elementary schools. But in large parts of the Region, developed in the post-World War II period, many school buildings will have empty classrooms, as overall need declines. That, along with smaller family size, and a greater proportion of elderly people, will undoubtedly reduce pressures for further spread.

There will be a need for new high schools—partly because of a rise in the high-school age group, but also because of more years in school. High schools are less tied to local residential neighborhoods than elementary schools, and could be built as a part of local multipurpose community centers, thus encouraging some concentration of activity.

The college age group is projected to increase by roughly 15 percent under the 5 million growth assumption. Today a slowdown in the past, precipitous growth of college enrollments is prominent in the public mind. Changes in the labor market, financial difficulties of many universities, and some disenchantment with traditional teaching methods have all contributed to this. We are not saying here that the "colleges" of 1999 will be exact replicas of those of 1972. But the general shift of our society away from goods-handling and toward the handling of information or knowledge is probably the most dominant long-term trend of the time, which makes increased participation in various forms of higher education rather inevitable, despite short-term fluctuations. Past rates of expansion suggest more than a doubling of college-age enrollment in various institutions of higher learning by the year 2000.

Jobs in factories will actually *decline* by about 10 percent, while jobs in office buildings will *increase by about 75 percent.* Total employment will grow by more than one third. The trend away from a manufacturing economy and toward a white-collar economy will, if anything, accelerate. The continuing white-collar revolution will mean that by the end of the century, close to two thirds of all employment in the Region will be in white-collar positions, not just in office buildings, but in sales, services, educational, medical, community, and other organizations. A greater proportion of the population will be working, meaning more income, reflected in part in the rising requirements for department store floor space shown in Table 13.

Office buildings, department stores, colleges—this is the stuff urban downtowns are made of, essential parts of the urban "communication machine"—will grow. Other facilities, of course, are associated with them—hospitals, clinics, libraries, meeting halls, movie theaters, specialty shops, restaurants, and so on. For the sake of simplicity, we have singled out only the major "anchor" facilities that symbolize the vitality of an urban center. They will all grow.

By contrast, those facilities that cannot possibly be concentrated in an urban center, such as elementary schools, which need to be in residential areas, or factories and warehouses, which require lots of space, are not expected to grow much. The decline in factory employment does not mean that factory floor space will not increase—more space is needed for automated plants—or that the pressure for out-movement from older cities will not continue. But the importance of manufacturing and goods-handling activities generally in the total economy will decline.

The need to house small families and elderly couples and individuals will grow. Both need rather compact living environments, so children can meet other children, so older people have places to walk to. By contrast, the need to house large families with many children—a major cause for the single-family house on a large lot—will decline.

Income, of course, will soar, and this is the big imponderable: Where will we spend it? To buy more second homes in Vermont and fly there by helicopter, to rip up the land with snowmobiles? Or to make the urban parts of the Region attractive and lovable?

We have a choice. Do we take the building blocks of possible vital cities and scatter them randomly around the countryside, along highways and campus sites, and let our former cities decline and thin out?

Or do we take this vital new economy and channel it deliberately into the old cities, to give them once again a meaning and a purpose, and to open the door into the new economy for those who are now locked out of it?

The first alternative can be called—keep building spread city.
The second one—build a region of strong urban centers.

Part A: Are Centers Necessary?

The Fate of Existing Downtown Centers

In looking for possibilities to recentralize the Region, to build more compactly on less land, the option of reinforcing the old, somewhat worn-out magnets of established downtowns in the Region is an obvious one. In almost every county of the Region there is at least one city that over the years served as downtown for country residents as well as city—long before it was surrounded by suburbia or embedded in New York City: in Brooklyn, downtown Brooklyn; in Queens, Jamaica; in the Bronx, Fordham Road; in Nassau County, Hempstead; in Westchester, White Plains and the three cities along the New York City border, Yonkers, Mount Vernon, and New Rochelle; in Fairfield County, Stamford, Norwalk, Bridgeport, Danbury; in south-central Connecticut, New Haven; in Dutchess, Poughkeepsie; in Orange, Newburgh and Middletown; in Bergen, Hackensack; in Passaic, Paterson and Passaic; in Morris, Morristown; in Union, Elizabeth; in Middlesex, New Brunswick; in Monmouth, Long Branch and Asbury Park; in Mercer, Trenton.

Manhattan and Newark are different; they have always served far more than their immediate surroundings. They are regional centers. What we are talking about here are places that would be called metropolitan centers if they were outside the New York Urban Region. In fact, some *are* called that in the Census. Paterson, Jersey City, Bridgeport, New Haven, Trenton, Waterbury, Stamford, Norwalk, Meriden, all are recognized as central cities of Standard Metropolitan Statistical Areas in the U.S. Census.

But these cities, with partial exceptions, no longer serve as metropolitan centers in the Region. Most people living around them do not go there and do not identify with them. In fact, when observers speak of the whole Region, they usually lump these cities into "the suburbs." Their share of the low-income and black and Puerto Rican population has risen as their influence in the surrounding area has declined. There is little attraction to live in the old cities when less is going on there, yet the housing is old and more crowded than outside the cities. So, in large measure, those who cannot go elsewhere live there. And because these downtowns become surrounded by low-income and low-skilled residents, the attractiveness to new office, health, and educational jobs and services declines.

Yet some of these cities have a lot going for them. They could become metropolitan centers again, providing a wide area around them with jobs and urban services. Should they? First we have to decide:

Do we need urban centers outside Manhattan anymore, or are they obsolete?

If we don't need urban centers or if we prefer to build them outside the older cities, what should happen to the older cities and how can their residents be guaranteed a share in the new jobs and services opening up outside?

We will focus on urban centers outside Manhattan in this discussion because Manhattan is unique in many ways. Regional Plan Association's *Office Industry* study has shown that there is economic potential for the total number of workers in Manhattan's central business district to grow anywhere from 7 to 20 percent over the rest of the century. Transportation improvements contemplated or actually under way will be able to serve that growth, if it occurs. But any growth greater than that is primarily circumscribed by the fact that the number of workers living within an easy distance of Manhattan is not likely to get much greater. So, there is not a great deal of leeway for different policy. By contrast, policy changes channeling suburban office growth into local downtowns, easily accessible to growing suburban labor markets, could possibly make some of these downtowns two, four, or eight times bigger than they are now. Compared to their present size, the possibilities for change are huge.

Some Say We Do Not Need Metropolitan Centers. They really are obsolete. People prefer to drive, so activities should be along major highways and not too close together, because that makes traffic jams. If people drive in every direction in the rush hours, all lanes on the highways are used just about equally. Contrarily, if jobs are clustered in a downtown, the lanes going in are jammed in the morning and the lanes going out are jammed in the evening. Highway capacity is wasted. People don't need to see each other face-to-face much anymore. Closed-circuit television will soon replace the business conference. Most of the things going on downtown were to-gether not because they had much relationship to each other but only because they had to tap in on the same public trans-portation system. Now that public transportation isn't neces-sary, the offices can go off on one campus, the shopping center by itself, the college and the hospital on their own. This way, no coordination is needed. No layers of government red tape as in urban renewal in an old city, no new authority shepherd-ing everything into a tight fit to build a new downtown.

Besides downtowns attract crime, demonstrators, and dis-rupters. Even shopping centers have been having trouble with kids gathering there, drunks and drug addicts lying on benches. The more we can decentralize and the less chance there is for people to get together, the better.

Some Say Yes. For a time, we did think that downtowns were no longer needed—that everyone soon would be able to get around by car so public transportation would not be neces-sary and that there was no particular value to bringing all these facilities together. But we now find this untrue. Everyone can-not get around by car, and requiring a car discriminates against poor families and the disabled as well as disconcerting the old and the young. Traffic where everyone must move by car is not easily handled, particularly because there is no coordina-tion of job sites with each other and with highways. As we observed in the town meeting on transportation, people seem to prefer their cars only when they provide superior service. This may not be the case when jobs are clustered in urban centers rather than scattered.

Nor are the links really meaningless between the activities that used to go on downtown—between one department store and another, between one office building and another, and among the different kinds of activities—the library, the offices, higher education, the stores and museums, and theaters and restaurants.

Many department stores have come to recognize that. The early "regional" shopping centers started with a single depart-ment store and a few specialty shops in the 1950s. Now, shop-ping centers have three and four department stores, hundreds of specialty shops, restaurants, movie theaters, a few have legitimate theaters, banks, and even some office buildings. Ex-plaining why Alexander's moved recently to Roosevelt Field, alongside Macy's and Gimbel's, the department store's presi-dent said: "We probably won't build a freestanding [i.e., by itself] store again. Shopping today is almost a leisure activity, a spectator sport. The center is the downtown of today and tomorrow." People "like to walk about a shopping center and compare prices."

Corporations recognize the links among offices, too. Even most of the corporate headquarters that have moved out of Manhattan (and that is still a very small minority of the major corporations in the Region) retain strong links with Manhattan. Nearly all the recent move-outs have kept their headquarters near Manhattan, with frequent limousine service testifying to remaining connections. The real proof of the importance of connections among offices and their services is that (1) despite all the aggravation of getting to and surviving in Manhattan, the bulk of the Region's major corporate headquarters remain there, and (2) generally around the country, the places that are gaining the most office space are the downtowns of large urban regions, serving sectors of the country like San Francisco, Houston, or Atlanta, which offer enough links to make downtowns worth the trouble. Over the rest of the century, as the number of office jobs in the Region grows, a number of the older downtowns in the Region could become large enough metropolitan centers serving sectors of the Region, to provide attractive links for office enterprises, too.

As to links between offices and other activities: developers of office parks are talking about adding retailing for the convenience of employees, another example of trying to get some of downtown back together again. That was the reason why Uris Buildings Corporation put a shopping concourse into the Blue Hill office development in Rockland County.

The connections between higher education are particularly important. Colleges can provide professional-managerial short courses for office workers and upgrade subprofessional skills like those in hospital-health work; offices and other downtown employers provide part-time jobs for college students; faculty consults with downtown enterprises; students have a live laboratory of urban affairs, business, health services, and the arts to study; students use the library, and others in the downtown may use the university library; students and faculty help to support the arts; others coming downtown help to support student artistic presentations. These relationships are much more likely to happen if higher education is part of a downtown. As college education moves farther from strict classroom activity to the campus-without-walls concept in which students learn from the whole community, it would seem even more sensible to locate whatever college activities *are* brought together in an official college facility downtown.

Planners have long observed that people tend to do things if the opportunity is right on their way that they would not do if it required a separate trip. Every activity in spread city requires a separate trip. In a downtown, there they all are. A few years ago, for example, a survey found that the great majority of people going to museums in New York and Newark combined that visit with some other activity.

Apartments for households without children also are well placed in downtowns. Where better to live, if you don't need much space, than near jobs, near transportation in every direction (if you're too old to drive well or don't want to own a car), where things happen, where the swingers are (if you're young).

So downtowns still offer advantages. Most people do not seem ready to abandon their human contact or the unplanned meetings and human panorama of a place to which people come for many purposes.

But Are Downtowns Worth the Trouble? Shopping centers, privately built, well supported by the retailers, and new, are attractive. That is demonstrated. Can we trust local governments to design and maintain really attractive downtowns, whether brand-new or urban-renewed? Can a large downtown —large enough to support good public transportation, office services, cultural activities—be built without congestion and overpowering architecture? People don't want to be jammed into crowds anymore.

Some cities have demonstrated that their downtowns can be attractive and spacious, though large. The Minneapolis mall is one example; Montreal's plazas, Toronto's mixture of plazas, walk-throughs, high buildings and low. Even a very large downtown like Midtown Manhattan doesn't have to be crowded, Regional Plan Association's recent study of pedestrian needs related to building bulk proves. Downtowns, in short, can be uncongested and green. The choice is between bringing some space and green to the downtown or scattering downtown around the countryside.

There are several arguments why old city downtowns could be efficient locations for new urban activity.

1. Transportation. They have the best public transportation in their vicinity, bus service to them and train service to Manhattan. Many of these city downtowns also have or soon will have the best highway access in their areas (e.g., Paterson, White Plains, Bridgeport, New Haven, Trenton, Newburgh).

2. A great deal already there. Despite declines in the importance of most of these downtowns, nearly all still have the most office jobs and retail trade in their area, as well as the main library and largest hospital. Having this start is important, because links to other activities are one of the main attractions:

the more there, the more desirable to be there. Many are county seats; county government seems likely to become more important in New Jersey and New York.

3. Housing support. More people live close to these old downtowns than near any potential sites on vacant land. That provides built-in support for public transportation and the jobs and activities there. A large percentage of people walk to work in these downtowns (e.g., about one in seven in White Plains).

4. Under-used land and utilities. Most of these downtowns do have land in and adjacent that is not being used to full advantage, given the location and the transportation and utilities available.

There are, needless to say, barriers.

1. Relocation. Introducing large new buildings into a downtown scaled to more intimate size will require some demolition and disruption, not just for building sites, but for highways, sewers, power, and telephone conduits. While areas selected for demolition should have little historic or economic value, demolition does mean relocation, of people and businesses, a prospect that has never been popular. For this reason, urban renewal has been slow, fraught with delays and uncertainties for the developer. If urban centers are to compete with isolated roadside sites and campuses, business people have to have a fast construction schedule and be able to count on it.

2. You can't start fresh in an old downtown. Renewing them gradually would not always provide a grand new design, exciting enough to woo investment away from independent locations.

3. The human equation. But all of this is academic at the moment. Corporations are not considering most of the older cities as office or department store sites. The states are reluctant to put colleges in them. Hospital boards are reluctant to enlarge or replace hospitals there despite all the advantages of a central site. The reason is fear, crime rates, racial antagonism. Office growth has been strong in recent years in White Plains, which has a much smaller poverty problem and a much better image than most of the other older downtowns.

While fear and preference for avoiding slums and racial friction are probably among the main obstacles to putting more enterprises into older downtowns, there are others.

Why locate offices precisely where the people with white-collar skills don't live? Few enterprises want the chance of opening an office in the midst of low-skilled residents, leaving their competitors to locate their offices where white-collar workers do live. This is particularly true for recruitment of women, who tend to work much closer to home than men.

And why go to old cities that have crushing fiscal difficulties —very high taxes and poor services?

Why indeed? If these city downtowns do not become metropolitan centers, what will become of them? What will become of the people living there? Factories need more space, so they have moved out of city centers. And unskilled factory jobs are declining in the Region, anyhow. Not much future there. To support the economy of the future in the Region, white-collar skills will have to be acquired by many more people. If office jobs concentrate in the older cities, would there be more chance that the school systems there would be alerted to prepare youngsters for those jobs, that training programs for adults would be instituted, and that those needing new skills would be drawn into the programs?

Contrarily, if the dynamic part of the economy locates outside the world of city residents—hard to reach and not really known to them—they will be further delayed in getting a fair economic share. This will also be the case if the best shopping, medical care, libraries, and museums move out of their easy reach. If everything the white, middle-class suburbanite needs is outside the cities, the hope of one society is pushed back further.

This possibility is not imaginary—it is already happening. Shortly after World War II, Paterson State College moved out of Paterson. Now, Paterson General Hospital is moving its main activity out of Paterson and would have moved the whole institution out had the move not been challenged in court. The Passaic County Technical High School has been moved out of Paterson. Stern's department store moved out (though a local department store has taken its place).

Morris County Library, the best one in the county, moved out of Morristown. Morris County Community College is inaccessible by public transportation. So is the Morris County TB clinic. The list could go on and on.

But would larger centers in old cities really achieve better conditions for city people and racial and economic integration? Newark is an example of a place where some downtown offices have grown but the condition of Newark's residents remains far below that of the rest of the Region. Merely bringing people together does not create one society.

True. But there is some evidence that Newark residents are better off, not worse off, for having strong office activities in downtown Newark. Take Prudential's national headquarters, for example—the city's largest office employer. Even though just over 80 percent of Prudential's employees live outside the city, nearly 1,500 do live in Newark (about 1 percent of the city's employed labor force). Many probably would not continue with the company if it were located on an isolated campus outside the city. Of these 1,500 Newark residents, a third are black and over 10 percent have Spanish surnames. Prudential paid $7.7 million in taxes to the city in 1970, the corporation and its employees contributed $600,000 to the United Community Fund, its officers headed the Community Fund campaign, the United Hospital Fund Drive, which raised $14 million to modernize the city's hospitals, and other civic activities. Prudential has built 270 units of middle-income cooperative housing, completed in 1970, and has invested $100 million in city real estate since mid-1967, "investments primarily designed to help the city," according to a company spokesman.

Nonetheless, a case has been made that the black residents of Newark would be better off without the white-dominated downtown. Imamu Amiri Baraka (LeRoi Jones), poet, playwright, and political leader, has belittled the contribution of white business and implied that black Newarkers would be better off without it. He argues that the 75 percent of Newark residents who are black and Puerto Rican "get hold of less than 1 percent of this economic power. The rest of it is carried out to the suburbs by whites who feel no responsibility or commitment to live in Newark at all." The chairman of Prudential has replied that the money Prudential handles in Newark is not generated in the city but comes in the form of premiums and returns on investment mainly from outside of Newark. If the company left Newark it would not be leaving the money to local residents but would be taking all of it out, including that now paid Newark residents, that spent by suburban employees in stores and restaurants and such, and that contributed to the city in taxes. Still, the symbol of those towers high over unrebuilt slums seems galling, all those suburban whites fearfully entering the city and as quickly as possible leaving it.

But even if the way of downtown metropolitan centers is hard, consider the alternatives. We take it that it is unthinkable to allow the rapid out-movement of many jobs and services from the older cities without some well-planned arrangement for something to take their place for the people who will still live in those cities. That something could be transportation aid to allow city families to reach suburban sites where no regular public transportation now goes. (Enough aid to provide and run two automobiles per family probably would be more economical than special bus service.) Information would have to be readily available on jobs and other opportunities scattered outside the city. Even so, if black and Puerto Rican city-dwellers are forced to come out to the new white world on their perimeter, will integration work any better than if white suburbanites have to enter the city world, partially dominated by blacks and Puerto Ricans?

That's one alternative. Another might be intensive aid to city residents to establish their own businesses and institutions, largely separate from those of the surrounding area. Given the persistent inequality of opportunities black people have faced in the white business world, this alternative undoubtedly looks attractive to many in the minority community. But about half the new businesses set up throughout the country every year fail within a year, so heavy reliance on small firms to provide the jobs and services the cities need would be shaky. Furthermore, the talent may be there to meet the cities' needs, but the experience and resources usually associated with business and institutional success may not.

And even if the necessary skills could be brought together, can the two societies—mainly lower-income black and Puerto Rican in the cities and mainly white and affluent in the suburbs—live side-by-side isolated? The majority in the Region has refused to let many blacks and Puerto Ricans live in their communities—not because they don't want to live with them, they say, but simply because they can't afford the school taxes if lower-income families with children move in. In the cities, white middle-income neighborhoods have opposed public housing—not because they don't want to live with blacks and Puerto Ricans, they say, but simply because they are afraid that lower-income families harbor criminals. Having rejected blacks and Puerto Ricans as neighbors, they have generally defeated school busing that would have enabled their children to attend school with nearby communities where blacks and Puerto Ricans have been allowed to live—not because they don't want their children to go to school with blacks and Puerto Ricans, they say, but simply because they favor neighborhood schools. So here we are, with what might be considered a last proposal for some relationship of the white majority with the black and Puerto Rican minority of the Region: to work together in offices and stores, to share shopping, health facilities, and higher education, and to exchange perceptions of the world through cultural and sports events. Should we say no to this, too?

Can Older City Centers Be Rebuilt? Even if both blacks and whites are willing to work together in city centers as the least difficult alternative, can it be done under the present rules of the game? The answer is yes, on a small scale, though we will need new rules of the game to do it on a large scale.

White Plains and Stamford both have active downtown renewal programs. White Plains has a commitment from a major developer for two additional office towers and two motel towers with connecting shopping arcades and underground parking. New county buildings are being completed, and new apartments have been finished within walking distance of downtown in the past few years. Without government aid, White Plains has added one department store, doubled another in size, and added a large new hotel, a new movie theater, two new office towers, and dozens of restaurants and specialty shops.

Stamford is the first smaller downtown in the Region to attract a major national corporate headquarters, General Telephone and Electronics from Manhattan. GTE considered a suburban campus but narrowed its choice to a new building in New York City or in a smaller urban location, and chose an urban renewal site in the heart of Stamford. Two other office buildings and a number of downtown apartment buildings also are being added in Stamford.

Bridgeport and New Haven have new office buildings and shopping centers in their downtowns, and Trenton is embarked on the Trenton Mall—a shopping and office complex of advanced design—aided by the guarantee from the State of New Jersey that it will lease office space in the development.

Paterson's leadership—black, Puerto Rican, and others, with the white mayor and black Model Cities director in the forefront—have come together several times to plan the steps needed to make Paterson a metropolitan center. Paterson's first office building in half a century is under construction, a loop road around the downtown renewal area is partially completed, and an expressway design that would have hurt the historic preservation district and the waterfront has been stopped. Alternative ways of giving downtown more access are under study.

New York City has accepted the principle of metropolitan centers in downtown Brooklyn, Jamaica, and Fordham Road and is shaping planning policies to encourage them. In Jamaica, Queens, a new downtown is emerging from old junk yards, complete with a new subway, a new university, new office buildings, new government buildings, possibly new arts and medical facilities later. To quote Dr. Canute Bernard, former chairman of the South Jamaica Steering Committee: "What we have here is a model of cooperation between blacks and whites, between business and the people of the community working together to build a community in which we all have a stake. We are willing to lay our lives down for what we are building here, a forward-looking process which takes the ethnic sting out of relations between people of all colors who sit down together and forge a unity."

CHOICE ONE: What should be done with the Region's older cities (outside Manhattan)? (Check one.)
A. Rebuild them as major centers of economic activity and housing
B. Subsidize them as residential areas for minorities
C. Abandon them over time
D. No opinion

New Centers on Vacant Land

The existing downtowns of the Region could, if we change the rules under which development proceeds, absorb a large part of future economic activity in the Region. But, if the Region were to add 6 million people over the next three decades, much of this growth would be out of reach of existing centers, particularly on Long Island and in southern New Jersey. Suffolk County, with 1.1 million people and growing toward 2 million, has no downtown in sight, and Ocean County, the fastest growing in the Region, will repeat a similar experience if present trends continue.

If we look for ways to curb dispersal and spread in roadside commercial strips, at highway interchanges, in isolated shopping centers, and on individual campus sites, should we not be thinking of new multipurpose centers, new downtowns on vacant land in the suburbs? Couldn't we even dream a little of huge bulldozers scraping up some day the roadside commercial chaos along a Route 9, Route 17, or Route 22, into shiny new centers, and returning the roadsides to greenery and open space?

New sites do have advantages, compared to rebuilding present downtowns.

1. No relocation is involved, progress can be faster and simpler.
2. There is greater freedom in design and construction when you start from scratch, more opportunity to use the latest technology.
3. There are no social problems to deal with.

But organizing the suburban growth in new multipurpose

centers does have its own problems, which don't immediately meet the eye.

A Downtown Needs a Town Around It. Computer models of different employment and residence patterns done by Regional Plan Association indicate that a large, dense center of employment embedded in a flat, even spread of residences, such as we have in the suburbs, is actually less efficient from a transportation viewpoint (just to take one consideration) than a dispersed employment pattern. It requires no less travel, but needs many more highway lanes. Only if an appreciable part of the residences (such as one third) are clustered around the downtown at higher density do we get transportation advantages from the center: a big reduction in the need for highway lanes, greatly increased use of public transportation, and less travel altogether.

So, Why Not New Towns? The ideal of a new town is that of a relatively self-contained community where most services —jobs, shopping, medical care, education—that the residents need are available locally (reinforcing, among other things, identification with a place and a community spirit). However, with advancing technology the market area of typical facilities, such as hospitals or department stores, tends to get bigger and bigger, which means the minimum workable size of a community is also getting bigger. The British have upped the desirable size of their new towns several times. A population of at least 300,000 is needed to support a shopping center with some diversity of merchandise. Hospitals are increasingly planned as complexes offering a wide spectrum of services and facilities for in-patients and out-patients, with increasingly sophisticated technology. Populations of 300,000 to 500,000 are needed to support such a full range of specialists and equipment. Central libraries will increasingly be sources of all kinds of information available by computer. Again, for the widest possible range of services, the bigger the population the better. We have shown earlier that metropolitan areas in the 1 to 2.5 million range seem to be the most viable in North America today, based on their rates of growth.

If urban activities are to be clustered, rather than dispersed, and surrounded tightly by housing of diverse types, density, and income level, and if these urban clusters are to be relatively few, because of the large tributary population a diverse center needs—then one quickly runs out of sites that would have the necessary tributary population even in the year 2000, and even with the 5 million population growth, which may not materialize. Mitchell Field in Nassau County comes to mind—

still a largely empty tract surrounded by a population of 1.5 million; perhaps two or three other sites in Suffolk and in such areas of New Jersey as Monmouth, Ocean, or Morris counties. For true metropolitan centers, the old central cities of the Region still remain the best bet. They have a large tributary population to start with, and merely have to expand it.

But What About Smaller Centers? All right, so our opportunities for truly new metropolitan communities are limited. But what about smaller developments, such as Columbia, Maryland, a new city for 110,000 people which is developing a large downtown center? (Reston, Virginia, with 80,000 people projected, is predominantly a residential community, and not really a regional center.) Two points of caution here. The urban center of Columbia feeds on a much larger tributary population, located as it is within a half hour of the suburbs of both Washington and Baltimore. Moreover, while the center itself does not take much land (no downtown area in North America, except for Manhattan and Washington, D.C., occupies more than one square mile, to allow for walking within it), the entire new town of Columbia occupies 22.5 square miles.

Assembling a site of this size near the Region would be extremely difficult, because scattered suburban development, cutting up land in bits and pieces, now extends from the core of the Region 40 to 50 miles out. Besides, some opportunities that might exist could be competitive with present downtowns and affect them adversely. It was in order not to compete for office space with Newark, Paterson, and Jersey City that the Hackensack Meadowlands Commission cut down sharply its proposals for a big new urban center in the Meadowlands.

Beyond a distance of 40 to 50 miles, the present tributary population for a new center will be too small, as a rule, to support a cluster of office buildings, department stores, and other activities. They would have to wait for the population of the new city and its surrounding area to build up—a slow process. Even when finished, the tributary population of an outlying center will be smaller, and facilities in the center less competitive, than those closer in. Significantly, most of the new suburban office buildings have located roughly within 25 miles of Manhattan, which is where they have sufficient access to the opportunities they need; beyond that distance, access thins out. The possible market for office space in centers is shown in Figure 9.

In sum, to really capitalize on the advantages of clustering, a new center on vacant land would have to be large. Centers

Figure 9

URBAN CENTERS IN THE NEW YORK, NEW JERSEY, CONNECTICUT REGION: POSSIBLE SIZE AND LOCATION

NOTE: The outlined square represents Manhattan in relation to other centers. The area of the squares is proportional to potential space in office buildings after 2000.

work better than scattered highwayside offices and stores only when there is a lot going on within walking distance. Then good public transportation can be supported and many more people can meet with each other within a short travel time than could do so in the spread-city world where a car is needed for each trip. Because cars can travel long distances rapidly in low-density areas, enough population can be gathered together in spread city to support a movie theater, a good restaurant. Unless a center can provide considerably more choice and variety than the auto world outside, there is no great advantage to coming there during the day or living there in an apartment. Despite the progress White Plains has made in apartment growth and attracting other activities, single people complained in a recent news report that there is no place in Westchester lively enough for singles to want to live.

Both American and European experience since the automobile has dominated urban life testify to the need for large downtowns if they are to offer significant advantages over spread city—downtowns perhaps as large as Minneapolis or Milwaukee. The arts particularly require a large market area for support—at least half a million people for a repertory theater or major museum, much more for a first-class symphony and even more for a resident opera company.

Nevertheless, isn't there any way to reconcile our limited opportunity for big new downtowns in the suburbs and yet gain some advantages of a multipurpose center? Yes. It can be done by regulation rather than competition. If zoning kept most of the large offices and stores out of other sites so they could only go to the centers, we could get small centers. Then, by limiting the parking space and instituting really good bus service, more people would use buses than would have made the choice normally to reach such a small center. Centers close to each other might coordinate arts activities—just as an example—so people living in adjacent communities would join to support offerings in several centers, perhaps dividing what is offered so one center gets a theater, another a concert hall, a third a museum.

Positive government and business policies supporting metropolitan centers could make *large* centers attractive enough *to compete* with a spread city for business and apartments, and large centers would naturally support good public transportation. Smaller centers probably would be successful only if large facilities *were required* to locate there and automobile use was *restricted* in favor of good public transportation.

There still would be advantages even to smaller multipurpose centers:

1. Linkages between various activities—on foot: walks from office to store to restaurant, as an example.

2. Opportunities for more vitality and spontaneous meetings or activities.

3. Some opportunity for public transportation.

4. Less land consumption (garages instead of parking lots, as an example).

5. Opportunities for more exciting architectural design.

6. Opportunities for more community identification (espe-

cially if the center includes such facilities as a high school auditorium and other places where people congregate).

CHOICE TWO: What should be the dominant pattern for economic and cultural activities in the suburbs? (Check one)
A. Grouped in tight clusters, where walking is encouraged.
B. Grouped in loose clusters, or dispersed, with most movement by auto
C. No opinion

Part B: Policies for Particular Activities

Having gained some idea of what general direction we want to pursue, let us look at the issue from the viewpoint of specific activities that will make up the centers—or the spread city —of the future. Naturally, we cannot deal with all of them, so we single out three major region-shaping activities—office buildings, colleges, and large retail stores, and then discuss their relationship to housing.

Where to Build Offices

Half the office space in the Region today is located in Manhattan; about 13 percent is located in 15 smaller downtowns in the Region outside Manhattan; and the remaining 37 percent is either in still smaller urban clusters or dispersed throughout built-up areas or on suburban campus-type tracts. In the past decade, Manhattan has captured roughly half of the new construction, but the smaller downtowns have captured much less than their past share—about 9 percent. The rest went to dispersed sites. The shift toward dispersed sites was greater, if one considers employment. This is so because much of the office construction in Manhattan and in smaller centers is for replacement, or for expanding space per worker, while construction in places where there were no offices before is strictly for new employment. The office exodus to the suburbs may not look large in absolute numbers, but it is growing, especially since about 1967, a period when twelve major company headquarters moved. Moreover, in the tug-of-war between Manhattan and suburban campus sites, it is the smaller centers of the Region that are losing out.

What does an office need to locate at a particular site?

First, it needs a labor market of sufficient quality, and access to the labor market by transportation.

Second, it needs linkages to other partners in the business, competitors, contractors, and auxiliary enterprises, ranging from blueprint services to restaurants.

Third, the space itself has to be suitable (say, all in one building) and available at a reasonable price.

Fourth, the environment must be suitable, preferably in the way of prestige, but at least with regard to safety in the street and such.

Fifth, access to the rest of the world—mostly by airplane— is also important.

The traditional complaints of offices that move out from Manhattan largely follow this list. Manhattan has the biggest labor market in the Region, but it is supposedly deteriorating in quality. Public transportation had also deteriorated for a while, resulting in frequent lateness of employees and time loss. The linkages of Manhattan—the business services, the access to specialized firms, the restaurants (where so much business is transacted over lunch), the shopping, and the theaters—are the best, but they also tend to distract employees on occasion. The need for traveling to Manhattan for business meetings may not be such a big burden. Space in the suburbs is generally somewhat cheaper, and it is easy to add on to a building, as need arises. The environment with lots of trees visible through the plate glass is more pleasant, and no crime problem exists.

Those who did move to the suburbs, and are not too happy, will add a list of "buts" to this list. Sure, there is a labor market of nonworking housewives in the suburbs, who will not make the trip to Manhattan, but will travel to a nearby office building. But that market is rather limited and tends to be absorbed by the first offices locating in an area. Lower-paid workers, who have no car, cannot get to the isolated office building; nor are apartments available at tolerable rents. Car pools are unreliable; when one driver can't make it, the others get messed up. A special company bus costs money, and other workers complain: Why aren't their travel expenses paid? The trip to work is usually easier for the company president—many new offices have located near where the chief executive lives— but not always for others. Data provided by one company with a suburban campus-type office building in northern New Jersey indicate that the average trip to work of their employees— measured as the crow flies—is more than ten miles, compared to less than nine miles for the average trip to Manhattan. Work trips to smaller downtowns in the Region are typically shorter still—about six miles on the average. (Measured in time, the ten-mile auto trip will be shorter than a nine-mile transit trip.)

Other aspects: local business services—consultants, photostat places, and such are inferior and poorly accessible on outlying sites; it is difficult to get some top talent to come out to the country from Manhattan; in the absence of stimulation from their colleagues in other companies, executives get stale: "You see the same people, eat with the same people, talk about the same things, and end up reinforcing your own ideas." There is no opportunity for chance meetings, every trip has to be planned. There is only one company cafeteria to eat in, the clerical staff is more productive, but is bored, and in the absence of shopping and other city attractions the company must provide sports facilities, beauty shop, and what not, in addition to the subsidized cafeteria. Grounds have to be kept up and all of these extras may easily add $1.40 per square foot to building cost, making it not much different from the $10 in the city. It was reported that of seven corporations that moved from Manhattan recently, six had slipped in their Fortune 500 ranking of top industrial corporations, one as much as 12 notches.

Not listed in this sketch of private costs are the costs to society at large. Is it more important to employ a young black trainee, who lives in the city and cannot get out to the campus site, or a suburban housewife who wants to supplement the family income? What about all the new highways that spread suburban office development makes necessary? Rough calculations indicate that 1 million square feet of a suburban office building require about eight lane-miles of expressway (i.e., one lane eight miles long) in addition to local roads. In Manhattan, it requires roughly one track-mile of subways. And in a small downtown, where much of the access is by bus, about two lane-miles of expressway are required. Added to this must be the extra cost of providing utilities to an isolated site—telephone conduits and such—for which the public pays, too, even if indirectly. And what about the ecological costs in land consumption? A million square feet of office space on an open site needs about a 25-acre parking lot, and the whole site is typically 80 acres. In a small downtown, a million square feet, in a 25-story building with ample landscaping and an appropriate parking garage, can be accommodated easily on six acres. In Manhattan, with virtually no parking, a million square feet needs only one acre of land, assuming a 50-story building, half of the site in a landscaped plaza.

If only *half* the office space projected for the Region under the assumption of a 5 million population increase were to be located on suburban campus sites at prevailing densities, it would cut a swath half a mile wide and 54 miles long, the distance from the Battery to beyond Princeton. The same space located in Manhattan would take up only 200 acres, about 3.5 percent of the area south of 60th Street. But, if we were to take one third of the projected office space and divide it— evenly, just for the sake of illustration—among 15 smaller downtowns, each would get some 32,000 jobs, for which it would need some 60 acres of land, half of it left to greenery and plazas, and one third—true—devoted to parking structures.

Needless to say, the exact prescription would be different for each city. This is merely to sketch the rough dimensions of the possible renaissance of "satellite cities" in the Region. One should note that relative decentralization of new office growth in the Region is fairly inevitable. The labor market of Manhattan is likely to grow, due to improved access by subway and railroad, and possibly due to small population increases in the area surrounding it, but only moderately; the major increases in population are likely—no matter what policies are pursued —to occur outside the center of the Region, and offices located in satellite downtowns can attract this labor market just as well as those on dispersed campus sites—in fact, better, because access by public transportation, and not just by auto, is possible to these downtowns. Some of them, to be sure, will need added access by expressway. But, in addition to the labor market, the smaller downtowns will offer—albeit in a much smaller degree than Manhattan—the external linkages to shops and services and restaurants and libraries and schools that an isolated site cannot provide. As we have seen, these links are important to both management and workers. And the downtown locations will provide opportunities in the growing new economy for lower-income people who are inevitably excluded by transportation and distance from the campus sites. The vice-president of a major company that considered moving out of Newark, but decided against it, put it this way:

> Let me tell you—Newark is not going down the drain. Business needs a central place to function properly. When you move out, you don't solve problems—you just move them.

On the subject of minority hiring practices, another executive had this to say:

The New York City Administration exerts tremendous pressure on businesses—more so than does the federal government. This is sometimes seen as negative, forcing us to hire people who are not really qualified . . . I feel, however . . . that the metropolitan area in general is definitely the best place to recruit high-caliber people, minority or otherwise. Generally, the city's interference is healthy and needed.

On the subject of employee morale at outlying campus sites, here are two conflicting opinions:

Here our employees . . . are in closer touch with one another. They arrive on the job in a better frame of mind, for they haven't had to fight traffic . . . they have a more friendly, family-like spirit here than they had in New York.

We used to run into each other in a vertical way. Secretaries would see presidents in elevators . . . This facility was all laid out horizontally. In addition, we now have an executive dining room and an employee cafeteria. It took precisely one year for the officers and executives—all housed in the same posh wing—to forget everyone's name.

And two Manhattan-based executives disagreed as to the effect of location on "company loyalty."

I think those firms which have moved attract the sort of people who identify with a particular company . . . they probably capitalize on this by providing a more homey atmosphere . . .

Suburban professionals rationalize not changing jobs by saying they have a loyalty to their company. Practically speaking it's just a lack of opportunity.

Examples can be continued. But perhaps the following summary is not too unfair: an office building may need only to be near a city, but it takes office buildings to build a city.

CHOICE THREE: Where should office buildings predominantly be located?

	MOST	SOME	NONE
A. In old city downtowns			
B. In new downtowns on vacant land			
C. Along highways and on campus sites			
D. No opinion			

Where to Build Colleges

As is evident from Table 13, colleges will expand at an even faster rate than office buildings over the coming three decades, partly because of an echo to the baby boom of the 50s and early 60s, partly a result of a greater proportion of young people entering college. And, over the postwar years, higher educational institutions in the Region have already expanded spectacularly: numerous new campuses were opened.

The locational needs of a college or university are obviously different in many ways from those of an office building; a college needs much more land and is likely to be placed at the edge of a downtown area, rather than within it. But there are similarities: both are "people-intensive" uses, giving vitality to an area, and both tend to be more highly diversified the closer they are to a center. Two thirds of the Region's enrollment in four-year and graduate programs is to be found in colleges and universities that are adjacent to urban centers, and only one third in more or less suburban or isolated institutions. Thus, urban linkages have an important impact on universities as well. Because of the increasing attendance of college by evening students, the growing involvement of the university in urban affairs, the magnetism of scientific and technical schools for research laboratories and industrial firms, and the attractiveness of living near the amenities and the cultural life of universities, the location of new campuses can have a powerful seeding effect on the locations of related activities and on the Region's shape.

Of course, there are, among educators, two schools of thought about where an ideal university should be. Some subscribe to the theory of isolation from the world, a secluded monastery in a rustic setting, where one can concentrate on learning without the distractions of the world. Others emphasize the responsibilities of an urban university, which is an integral part of the community it serves. In a pluralistic world, there is most likely a place for both, but the question is, where should the emphasis be? Even assuming that the existing 200 institutions of higher learning in the Region expand their enrollment by two thirds—and many are not about to do that as a matter of policy or because of financial pressures—we would need about 30 new college campuses of 10,000 students each by the end of the century, if there are 5 million more people in the Region by 2000. That is, about one new campus each year.

Some of the practical considerations of locating a new college can be illustrated by the case of Ramapo College in northern New Jersey. It was to serve primarily the population of older urban and suburban communities north of the Hackensack Meadowlands, and was originally proposed to be located on a large, open tract in suburban Saddle River. Regional Plan proposed an alternate location in the City of Hackensack, much closer to the future students, adjacent to an existing downtown, which it could help revitalize. The college board objected that the site was too expensive and too small. Regional Plan showed that:

1. The added cost of auto travel all the way north to Saddle River would come to $125 per student per year, or $624,000 annually for the entire college. To relieve the students of this cost, as much as $6.6 million additional investment in land was justified.

2. The proposed 68-acre site in Hackensack could accommodate 7,000 students at a density of about 100 students per acre, compared to the densities of some urban schools, such as: Queens College—470 per acre; University of Illinois—190 per acre; Illinois Institute of Technology—155 per acre; Georgia State—160 per acre; Staten Island Community College—140 per acre, and so on. All of these campuses have a spacious, uncongested appearance. Thus, 68 acres would by no means be too small.

3. There is frequent local bus service in downtown Hackensack, which would not only be helpful to students and reduce the need for parking at the college, but would also be very helpful to its many lower-income employees.

Eventually, Saddle River objected to having the college for fear urban students would disturb its suburban tranquility, and the mayor of Hackensack objected because the site proposed by Regional Plan was used for oil storage tanks. The tanks removed, the city would lose taxes, since the college would be tax-exempt. The college was eventually located on a more than

300-acre site in Mahwah, six miles north of Saddle River and 15 miles north of Hackensack, 15 miles away from the students for whom it was intended.

Not all city-suburban college location controversies have ended with the college going to the country. The New Jersey College of Medicine and Dentistry was located in Newark, not in suburban Madison; York College was located in downtown Jamaica, Queens, where it forms a bridge between the business district and the black community of South Jamaica, not on the shore of Long Island Sound, where it might have had a view of the water, but where all students would have been forced to drive. And Passaic County Community College has been located in Paterson. On the other hand, SUNY at Purchase may be the epitome of an isolated suburban location: accessible only by auto, and isolated from downtown White Plains (which could have used its auditoriums off hours), it preferred instead to locate a music school under an airport runway. There is no adequate performing arts center in Westchester County, yet an auditorium at Purchase could not serve that function because it would be physically impossible to fill a 2,000-person hall by car over the narrow two-lane road leading to it.

Similar stories, perhaps less dramatic, can be told about other outlying locations in the Region. For example, the branch of a state university a few miles from a downtown, but accessible only by auto, where some local students hitch a ride or walk three miles to school, and where only one out of 1,200 students is black. Sure enough, proper placement policies can enable minority students to go to outlying colleges—the State University of New York at Stony Brook has about 10 percent blacks in the freshman class, and so does the University of Connecticut at Storrs. And, sure enough, auto use can be high even in urban schools. But there still remain questions of spontaneity, choice, and convenience, access to part-time students or part-time employees or part-time jobs, as well as to city life in general.

At Stony Brook, with 12,000 students 50 miles away from Manhattan, one faculty member said: "The students are aware of New York City as a force—on weekends, people just vanish." And about one third of the faculty still live in New York City. In casual interviews, several staff members expressed the opinion that the school was located too far east on Long Island.

Again, examples and opinion can be continued. Perhaps not every college needs a downtown. But should every downtown have a college within walking distance?

CHOICE FOUR: Where should new universities and colleges in the Region be located?

	MOST	SOME	NONE
A. Near urban centers			
B. Away from urban centers			
C. No opinion			

Where to Build Retail Centers

Retailing is the most intensive of all building uses. Every square foot of retail floor space attracts roughly 20 times more trips on foot than an office building, and roughly 50 times more than a residence. The proportions are similar, though less dramatic, for trips by mechanical means, for the pedestrians have to get there in the first place. Because retailing amounts to a very small fraction of all land use in a city (about 3 percent, typically), and because the use is so intensive, it has traditionally exemplified the center, the "$100 percent" location, representing the age-old function of the city as the marketplace.

Retailing occurs at two rather different levels—the day-to-day shopping for groceries and convenience goods, which occurs in the local neighborhood, and the department store and specialty store shopping, which is a more unique event and requires more effort. In this discussion, we will focus on the latter, on shopping that requires large facilities and long trips, and influences the shape of the Region.

The location of large retail stores is, much more rigidly than that of office buildings, not to speak of colleges, tied to the market—in this case, the surrounding population and its buying power. The opportunities within a short travel time we have mentioned earlier, represent, in this case, dollars of purchasing power within a given travel time. When the single most accessible location, because of the convergence of transit lines, was downtown, all major retailing was located downtown.

But, as city streets became choked with automobile congestion, while on highways outside the city travel was still fast, the point arrived when the population beyond the immediate vicinity of a downtown could actually be better served from a non-downtown location; that is, a market area large enough to support, say, a major department store, could be found outside the city, and people would find it quicker to travel to the suburban store. This was the birth of the shopping center in the early post-World War II period.

Access to the shopping center was shorter and more con-

venient (provided one had an auto), but the selection of merchandise was generally poorer, because the tributary area was
smaller than in a downtown. Also, the links by which retail
and other downtown activities reinforce themselves were missing: there were no office buildings, providing noontime customers, no movie theaters or restaurants for the evening. Aside
from perhaps another department store and strings of specialty
shops between the two, the place was strictly a one-function
place: shopping. If one wanted to do other things, one had to
drive elsewhere.

This sterility of the early shopping center gradually became
recognized by the shopping center builders themselves, and
they began to add other facilities: theaters, sometimes clinics
and office buildings, beginning to re-create a downtown of
sorts, providing for diverse linkages within the center, and not
just for a one-purpose trip to and from.

As *Business Week* recently put it:

> No longer are shopping centers simply the small retail
> hubs they used to be . . . now, more and more, they are
> becoming miniature downtowns with three, four, five de-
> partment stores, scores of smaller stores and services, plus
> hotels, apartment houses, office buildings, cultural cen-
> ters, churches and theaters. Along the way, shopping cen-
> ters are developing the same kind of ambiance and per-
> sonality that was previously found only in downtown
> business districts. In fact, many developers are taking
> their centers back into downtown districts and trying to
> revitalize some of the very core areas that are hit hardest
> by competition from suburban centers.

The latter, of course, is made possible by downtown expressways which can bring customers fast from remote suburban
areas that were formerly better served by an outlying center.
The trip to downtown on an expressway may take slightly
longer than that to a closer-by suburban one-purpose shopping
center, but it may be more worthwhile, because more is happening in the bigger, diversified center. Such large, integrated
centers are still very few but, to continue the quote: "they
heavily outdraw small- and medium-sized centers and can pull
shoppers from much longer distances. The more facilities you
have going for you . . . the more traffic you create for the
retailer." The two major multipurpose centers actually built in
cities include Broadway Plaza in Los Angeles, and one in
Worcester, Massachusetts. Why put a huge new center into
downtown Worcester, seemingly a decaying city? The devel-

oper answered: "An interstate highway leads right here and connects with all central New England. We're not talking about Worcester. We're talking about a regional shopping center for central New England that happens to be in Worcester where the roads lead."

On a smaller scale, similar developments have been put into downtown New Haven and downtown Bridgeport, restoring the downtowns as retail hubs to a sub-region, fed by new expressways. Trenton and Stamford are embarking upon new, multipurpose mall projects. And other downtowns, such as Paterson, are located at an intersection of expressways, which could be a far superior place for a strong, multipurpose center than the intersections of expressways amid open fields, which is where shopping centers have tended to locate up to now. Think if Willowbrook were in Paterson, rather than in Wayne. Or doesn't this matter? Or is it nicer in Wayne?

If only half the projected 20 million square feet of department store floor space in the Region were put into our 15 downtowns, each would have, on the average, two new above-average size department stores of 300,000 square feet each. Or, all 66 stores could be strung out along highways, in the manner of Routes 4, 17, and 46 in New Jersey, Sunrise Highway on Long Island, or Central Avenue in Westchester.

CHOICE FIVE: Where should new department stores predominantly be located?

	MOST	SOME	NONE
A. In old city downtowns			
B. In new downtowns on vacant land			
C. In single-purpose shopping centers			
D. No opinion			

Housing Related to Centers

In traditional cities, the pull of access to economic activities in the center attracted housing, like a magnet attracts iron filings. Housing density was highest near the center, and declined toward the periphery. A mix of different housing densities and life-styles was pretty automatically insured by the workings of the market mechanism and transportation access.

Today, with fairly ubiquitous access by auto and the checkerboard pattern of zoning maps, higher-density housing breaks through the zoning envelope rather haphazardly, with apartment developments too often in the middle of nowhere. We have touched upon this issue in connection with the location of low-cost housing in the first town meeting, and in connection with public transportation service in the second town meeting. In this discussion, we have seen that the opportunities to build whole new cities in the Region from scratch, re-creating traditional density patterns all in one piece, are fairly limited. Does that mean that we have to live with a haphazard location of higher-density housing?

Building large, compact clusters of nonresidential activities could go far beyond just clustering stores and offices and colleges and hospitals and museums and social services, and become a way of organizing the residential fabric of a region into a pattern that provides diversity, urban excitement, and greater equality of opportunity. For example, anthropologist Margaret Mead said: "If women are to live and play a role in the world like men, they can't live in the suburbs as they do now. You can't live in a suburb with children and run a house and still have any occupation . . . women spend too much time chauffeuring people around." For another example, the use of the museums and other cultural events in Manhattan by suburbanites is much lower than the educational and income level of the suburbanites would suggest. They seem to be simply missing out on cultural opportunities in the absence of strong urban centers in their own area.

We have seen from population projections that the market for more compact housing types and neighborhoods will grow, because of a greater number of young people without children, a greater number of small families, a greater number of older people, many of whom are likely to want to live without the physical strain of maintaining a suburban house and relying on the auto. Finally, lower-income people, whose housing locations we have discussed in the first town meeting, need easy access to supporting facilities that only a higher-density place can provide, and can be spared the expense of owning an auto in an area where transit is naturally available.

There are two ways of encouraging the clustering of more compact and varied housing within easy reach of both new and rebuilt urban centers. One is by large-scale zoning, cutting across municipal lines where necessary, assisted by public taxation policies, which we will mention shortly, and with public acquisition of undeveloped land tracts in the vicinity of the centers. We have missed the opportunity to build large new metropolitan centers from scratch in such places as central Bergen, or central Nassau County after World War II. But we can fill in a new pattern piecemeal, as opportunities arise, and we can accelerate the residential renewal of existing old cities, if sufficient relocation housing for lower-income families is available, and if that relocation housing does not have to be confined within existing municipal lines.

On the periphery of the Region, we can still build entire new communities from scratch. They would not be the metropolitan communities that a large urban center could create, nor would they be new towns. They would be local communities, components that together make a metropolitan community. They would provide a full range of services that are needed locally—local schools, local shopping, local services—tied for their regional needs to existing centers—be they Poughkeepsie or Trenton, and supporting, rather than draining away, the central, regional activities of the cities.

Such predominantly residential communities, of perhaps 10,000 to 50,000 people, inserted into vacant tracts near existing developments, related to downtown urban centers outside, and offering a variety of housing types for a variety of income groups, are likely to be our version of new towns. The concept is similar to the concept of "growth units" advanced by the American Institute of Architects, where new development is conceived "not as individual buildings or projects, but as human communities with the full range of physical facilities and [local] services that ensure an urban life of quality."

CHOICE SIX: Should housing be tied to centers of urban activity by:

	YES	NO	NO OPINION
A. Higher density zoning around old and new downtowns?			
B. Building complete residential communities with mixed housing types and price ranges on vacant land, in lieu of traditional subdivisions?			

Part C: Some Notes on Implementation

The Federal Role

Obviously, in order to be able to accept and handle new development, the older cities will have to be relieved of the nationwide burden of poverty they are bearing, at first purely financially. At present, they cannot provide adequate municipal services—garbage collection, park maintenance, library service, police protection—because their budgets are drained by costs imposed on them by poverty.

Setting National Priorities: the 1973 Budget, a study of the Brookings Institution, put it this way:

> Public expenditures per capita in big cities are generally higher than in the suburbs and are rising at least as rapidly. Revenues per capita, however, are growing much faster in the suburbs, where property values, sales, and income are all climbing more rapidly than in the city. The cities are caught in a fiscal squeeze, and many of the actions they might take to extricate themselves, such as raising taxes or cutting services, are self-defeating because they would hasten the flight to the suburbs . . .

Apart from the burden of poverty-related services, since 1966, the greatest single cause of rising central city budgets, nationwide, has been the steeply rising wages of municipal employees who had been underpaid and who, through increased unionization and militancy (strikes by municipal employees have expanded dramatically since 1966), have forced an income redistribution of their own. This has been a national phenomenon not confined to New York City.

Federal and state aid to local governments also increased dramatically, from $8.8 billion in 1963 to $43.5 billion in the 1973 budget, but has not been sufficiently concentrated in large cities. The federal aid programs aimed specifically at large cities amount to about $4 billion in 1973, and go mostly for capital construction (public housing, urban renewal, parks, mass transit) or for new programs, such as Model Cities and community action. They do not aim at day-to-day operations.

As *Setting National Priorities* puts it, revenue-sharing as now conceived "is an inefficient means of dealing with the special plight of large cities because much of the money will be distributed among suburban governments that are not facing critical fiscal problems." Thus, in 1970, New York suburbs spent $459 per capita for municipal services from their own local sources, whereas New York City spent $509; New Jersey suburbs spent $339 per capita, whereas Newark scratched up $459 from its own meager sources.

In essence, the poor and those who stayed with them are asked to pay for the costs of poverty, while those who escaped get off free.

In its 1968 report, *Public Services in Older Cities,* Regional Plan Association urged that "all anti-poverty services should be paid for by the federal government. Poverty is a national problem; many of the poverty-stricken began life far from the cities in which they now reside. The financial sacrifice being made by the older cities of the Region to support poverty-related services is draining their ability to carry out strictly municipal programs."

Clearly, a strong case can be made for a large-scale federal program of financial aid to large cities, which would compensate them fully for the extra costs that poverty imposes on them: the extra costs of police and fire protection, of health care and anti-narcotics programs, of social services and compensatory education.

Of course, it will take more than federal takeover of poverty costs to attract more private investment into the old cities. Their image, their amenities, and their crime rates will have to change. Federal funds are not a panacea, but rather a prerequisite.

Business will be attracted when other business agrees to come into a center, along with related public facilities. Each awaits the other; so a consortium of several large corporations might have to get together to "adopt a city" and agree to put their investment there. The corporations not only would locate some of their increase in office personnel in the center, they also could assure critical investment and use their influence to channel state and federal policies into support for such centers. They could work with the city school system to relate its courses to their job needs; management assistance might be made available to city government. The possibilities are endless; a broad enough recognition of the need is lacking.

CHOICE SEVEN: Should the federal government take over all poverty-related costs of municipalities and counties?

APPROVE   DISAPPROVE   NO OPINION

The State Role

While the bulk of outside financing to compensate urban areas for the costs of poverty and for the other extra public costs of cities should plausibly be federal, guiding the development pattern either away from or toward the scattered highwayside and into or out of urban centers would logically be a responsibility of the state, perhaps implemented in some part by counties (or planning regions in Connecticut).

To quote Peter A. Morrison of the RAND Corporation:

A number of federal and state programs have broadly influenced the population's spatial arrangement with unintended but important effects. . . . The contention that government has no business influencing the spatial arrangement of population flies in the face of past experience. Failure to adopt deliberate policies merely invites hidden ones, whose social consequences are passively accepted as everyone's doing but no one's responsibility.

For example, the state could guide the zoning of land for large facilities—office buildings above a certain size, department stores, colleges, hospitals, high-density housing. These could only be put into the spots earmarked for urban clusters by the state plan.

To implement the plan the state would set guidelines for its own capital investments in all region-shaping elements such as expressway interchanges, transit stations, hospitals, colleges, subsidized housing, and open space. It would also set guidelines for municipal, county, or sub-regional land-use controls, affecting the more important people-gathering facilities as well as critical natural areas that should stay open for ecological reasons: flood plains, wetlands, aquifers, streambanks, and mountain slopes.

Effective land-use guidelines, set by whatever level of government, are directly related to taxation because the value of the land is a measure of the property tax which is the main support of municipal investments and services. Broader-based state (income and sales) taxes are, however, increasingly being called upon to equalize the quality of services and facilities among the residents of all of the state's municipalities. In keeping with this trend and in order to avoid windfall profits to property owners, in areas affected by state land-use guidelines a related move could be a high capital gains tax on the sale of land.

After all, the value of land—in contrast to the value of the buildings on it—is created by society as a whole through its transportation facilities, its zoning decisions, and not by the owner. As Paul H. Douglas stated in a publication of the National Commission on Urban Problems: "We are becoming rapidly aware of the need for land reform in the countryside of Asia and Latin America. There is an even greater need for land reform in the cities and suburbs . . . to be obtained . . . by society asserting the right to the differential rents and values which the forces of . . . productivity create."

CHOICE EIGHT: Should the state, through its own investments in buildings and transportation, through land-use control guidance and taxation, encourage:
A. Spread urban development?
B. Compact urban development?
C. No opinion.

AFTERWORD

We can boil our discussion of the New York Region down to two choices:

To build an Urban Region spread rather homogeneously over several thousand square miles, except for one center in Manhattan, dependent on private spaces, on more mechanical locomotion in private vehicles, with sharp divisions between rich and poor and limited opportunities for many, consuming progressively more natural resources. This is our present course.

or

To build an Urban Region focused on Manhattan plus a relatively few city-scale centers in the Region's other counties with more walking in public spaces and more public transportation, more opportunities for everyone, less social contrast, less penetration of nature with the activities of man, and consequently more conservation of land and other natural resources.

A planner can do two things: he can tell people what would happen if the future were like the past, and he can tell people what he might want.

There is one thing he cannot do: he cannot foretell what people will want.

But it is the latter that has been decisive in history.

As Alvin Toffler says in *Future Shock,* "We need to initiate . . . a continuing plebiscite on the future . . . On the edge of a new millennium, on the brink of a new stage in human development, we are racing blindly into the future. But where do we *want* to go?"

Hopefully, CHOICES FOR '76 will show some directions.

SIGNET and MENTOR Books You'll Want to Read

☐ **MARIHUANA: A Signal of Misunderstanding; The Official Report of the National Commission on Marihuana and Drug Abuse.** With a special foreword by Raymond P. Shafer, Chairman. The most comprehensive study of marihuana ever made in the United States. Who smokes it? And why? Does it trigger crime? Harmful or innocuous? A psychic euphoriant? A sexual stimulant? The future of its medical and legal status? (#Y5218—$1.25)

☐ **THE LIVELY COMMERCE: Prostitution in the United States by Charles Winick and Paul M. Kinsie.** The shocking exposé of America's billion-dollar industry—prostitution. "Comes at a good time . . . when Americans seem almost obsessed with frankness and plain speaking about sex."—The New York Times (#Y5205—$1.25)

☐ **UP AGAINST THE LAW: THE LEGAL RIGHTS OF PEOPLE UNDER 21 by Jean Strouse.** A legal primer for the under-21 set which presents all the regulations concerning minors and talks about them in layman's rather than lawyer's language. His rights as son or daughter, student, draftee are covered as well as the laws governing him in relation to marriage, drugs, cars, employment, contracts and arrest. (#Q4315—95¢)

☐ **POPULATION: A Clash of Prophets edited by Edward Pohlman.** Is increasing population the source of a nation's health, or a disease that must be checked? Are the world's resources about to run out or are there virtually limitless possibilities of expansion? Overpopulation —myth or menace? Here's what the leading authorities think. (#MJ1183—$1.95)

THE NEW AMERICAN LIBRARY, INC.,
P.O. Box 999, Bergenfield, New Jersey 07621

Please send me the SIGNET and MENTOR BOOKS I have checked above. I am enclosing $_____(check or money order—no currency or C.O.D.'s). Please include the list price plus 25¢ a copy to cover handling and mailing costs. (Prices and numbers are subject to change without notice.)

Name_____

Address_____

City_____State_____Zip Code_____
Allow at least 3 weeks for delivery

SIGNET and MENTOR Books of Special Interest

☐ **THE SEA AROUND US by Rachel L. Carson.** An outstanding bestseller and National Book Award winner, an enthralling account of the ocean, its geography and its inhabitants. (#Y5342—$1.25)

☐ **UNDER THE SEA WIND by Rachel L. Carson.** The story of life among birds and fish on the shore, open sea, and on the sea bottom, by the prize-winning author of **Silent Spring.** Illustrated. (#Y5374—$1.25)

☐ **BEWARE OF THE FOOD YOU EAT; The Updated and Revised Edition of POISONS IN YOUR FOOD by Ruth Winter.** A book that should be read by anyone concerned about his health, BEWARE OF THE FOOD YOU EAT shows what has and what has not been done to correct the abuses in food processing. (#Y5061—$1.25)

☐ **THE FUTURE OF INDUSTRIAL MAN: A CONSERVATIVE APPROACH by Peter F. Drucker.** Outlines the shift from an agrarian to an industrial economy illustrating the structures and dynamics of this new order and indicating the abuses inherent in the system. (#MW1114—$1.50)

☐ **AUTOMATION: ITS IMPACT ON BUSINESS AND PEOPLE by Walter Buckingham.** An economist at the Georgia Institute of Technology analyzes the impact of the "technological explosion" on business and people. Index. (#MY1061—$1.25)

More SIGNET and MENTOR Books of Special Interest

☐ **THE NEW AMERICAN MEDICAL DICTIONARY AND HEALTH MANUAL by Robert Rothenberg, M.D.** Over 8,500 definitions of medical terms, disorders and diseases, with more than 300 illustrations, make this the most complete and easy-to-understand book of its kind. Also includes a comprehensive first-aid section and guides to better health. (#W5513—$1.50)

☐ **LET'S EAT RIGHT TO KEEP FIT by Adelle Davis.** Sensible, practical advice from America's foremost nutrition authority as to what vitamins, minerals and food balances you require and the warning signs of diet deficiencies. (#E5379—$1.75)

☐ **LET'S GET WELL by Adelle Davis.** America's most celebrated nutritionist shows how the proper selection of foods and supplements can hasten recovery from illness. (#J5347—$1.95)

☐ **THE LIVING CLOCKS by Ritchie R. Ward.** In this pioneering and fascinating book, Ritchie Ward unfolds the dramatic researches that have made the living clocks, the "biological clocks" that govern the behavior of all life, a central concern of those seeking to understand our total environment. (#MJ1158—$1.95)

☐ **NOT SO RICH AS YOU THINK by George R. Stewart.** The author presents the challenge posed by environmental pollution for the general reader and in an easy-going style gives a history of the pollution problem. Despite the horrors he is concerned with, Stewart doesn't only sound the alarm but also offers advice—suggesting where we can start looking for the remedies. (#Q4310—95¢)